2030: Your Children's Future in Islamic Britain

By David Vincent

Copyright© 2015 by David Vincent

CONTENTS

Chapter One **Inside the Gates** 6

Chapter Two **Days like These** 13

Chapter Three **Jihad on the Dole** 24

Chapter Four **An Inconvenient Census** 55

Chapter Five **One School of Thought** 80

Chapter Six **Not in Our Name?** 98

Chapter Seven **Strong Horse Tactics** 131

Chapter Eight **The BBC** 152

Chapter Nine **Black Flag Over Europe** 177

Chapter Ten **Just a Shot Away** 205

Chapter Eleven **Just Shut Up!** 216

Chapter Twelve **Separation** 245

Bibliography

On 15 September, 1940 The Battle of Britain reached its climax. At that point in time RAF Fighter Command had only 367 operational Hurricanes and Spitfires to face down the might of the German Luftwaffe's 2,250 combat ready aircraft.

Great Britain, and possibly the whole world, may owe its freedom to around 500 trained RAF pilots who stopped Hitler in his tracks and saved Britain from invasion.

It's too late now for Roger Morewood, Gordon Sinclair, "Skeets" Ogilvie and the rest of the legends of 1940 no longer with us to be honoured by their country, but why have the handful of Battle of Britain heroes who are still alive not been given a knighthood?

One of them should have been Spitfire pilot Kenneth Tyrer, kicked to death on an NHS hospital ward, aged 90, in 2015.

There will never, ever, be more deserving recipients and it is an omission that shames a nation. This book is dedicated to the last of the few, we owe them everything.

CHAPTER ONE

INSIDE THE GATES

A Labour MP I know was telling me the other day about a constituent of his who had been in a minority part of East London. She walked for 20 minutes without seeing another white person. Then when she did see one she said they smiled in recognition, like you do when you see a British person on holiday. That is quite a nice way of putting it.

David Goodhart founder of the British magazine Prospect, currently director of the London-based think tank Demos

On July 7, 2011 the Muslims Against Crusades (MAC) website released this statement:

"In the last 50 years, the United Kingdom has transformed beyond recognition. What was once a predominantly Christian country has now been overwhelmed by a rising Muslim population, which seeks to preserve its Islamic identity, and protect itself from the satanic values of the tyrannical British government. There are now over 2.8 million Muslims living in the United Kingdom – which is a staggering 5% of the population – but in truth, it is more than just numbers, indeed the entire infrastructure of Britain is changing; Mosques, Islamic Schools, Shari'ah Courts and Muslim owned businesses have now become an integral part of the British landscape. In light of this glaring fact, Muslims Against Crusades have decided to launch 'The Islamic Emirates Project,' that will see high profile campaigns launch in Muslim enclaves all over Britain, with the objective to gradually transform Muslim communities into Islamic Emirates operating under Shari'ah law. With several Islamic emirates already well established across Asia, Africa and the Middle East, including Iraq and Afghanistan, we see this as a radical, but very realistic step in the heart of Western Europe, that will inshaa'allah (God willing), pave the way for the worldwide domination of Islam." (1)

In 2050, when we look back in time from the ruins of our rubble strewn, smoking cities, trying to pinpoint how we could possibly have allowed ourselves to be deceived and then ruined by a religious death cult, we will know where the blame lies.

It will be with the New Labour government of 1997 to 2010, aided and abetted by our taxpayer funded national broadcaster, the BBC.

By 2030 we will be well on the way to the balkanisation of Britain into Muslim and non-Muslim controlled areas. This will be in the context of a dogged economic recession and massive government borrowing needed to fund expanding welfare payments. The indigenous British taxpayer, burdened with an oversupply of unskilled migrant workers, consuming more than 60% of all welfare spending, will be held to ransom by continuous disorder across the nation's major cities. Demands for the transfer of political power will eventually be agreed by fearful and submissive Left/liberal politicians, smoothing the transition from what remains of democratic Britain to the establishment of sharia zones, Muslim states within the British state, that will in time join together to create an Islamic republic in Britain.

In Great Britain today those who would have regarded themselves as being left of centre pre-1997, or in any way mildly patriotic, have found themselves marginalised by a massive shift of Britain's political polarity; a direct result of the Labour Party's open door immigration policy of 1997-2010 allied with the imposed dogma of multiculturalism, which has transformed Britain in a way no other nation has been transformed since Stalin forced collectivisation on the Soviet Union after the Second World War.

In 1951 there were less than 20,000 non-white citizens in Britain. If it had been suggested to the average man in the street just 15 years ago that what used to be reasonably described as the white Christian majority population of Britain would become a *minority* in many major English cities by 2030 the reaction would surely have been astonishment followed by hilarity. If, just ten years ago, any politician or political commentator had dared to predict that by 2011, in 23 out of the 33 London boroughs, white Britons would have become a minority, they would have been met with looks of disbelief and the collective dropping of jaws. If they had gone on to say that in London, the cultural and historical capital of Britain, white Britons would have become a rapidly *shrinking* minority, they would have been politely advised to seek medical advice.

Yet, as the 2011 census revealed, that is precisely the situation we have in London and in Britain today.

In 2008, it was a brave man who was willing to go against the grain and risk the ire of the New Labour/BBC "cry racist" lynch mob to make comment on these fundamental social upheavals. One man who did dare was Pakistani-born Bishop Michael Nazir-Ali. He warned then that parts of Britain had become no-go areas for non-Muslims. He said there had been attempts to "impose an Islamic character on certain areas", for example, by amplifying the call to prayer from mosques. (2)

At the time, Nick Clegg, leader of the Liberal Democrats, condemned Bishop Nazir-Ali's comments as: "a gross caricature of reality". The response from the Muslim Council of Britain (MCB) was that the mosque's loudspeaker call to prayer was "no different from church bells ringing" and accused Nazir-Ali of "frantic scaremongering".

Like the canary in a coalmine Nazir-Ali's comments were advance warning that the fabric of Britain's traditional culture was being torn apart. Then, there were only small signs that indicated the upheavals that were to come, but they were there for all to see who wanted to look.

That same year an article by Mary Jackson appeared in a prominent literary magazine, reporting that: "In February this year, Christian evangelists Arthur Cunningham and Joseph Abraham were doing what Christian evangelists do: handing out Bible extracts. They were stopped by a representative of the law, threatened with arrest if they carried on preaching in 'a Muslim area' and warned that they might get beaten up if they came back. Where did this incident take place? Saudi Arabia, Iran or Pakistan, where Christian preaching is forbidden and apostates sentenced? No, this 'Muslim area' was in Alum Rock, Birmingham, England. That's right - England, cradle of free speech; England, a country with an established - if enfeebled - Church, and where seventy-five per cent of citizens (at the 2001 census) described themselves as Christian. The man who stopped the evangelists, calling their preaching a 'hate crime', was Naeem Naguthney, a Police Community Support Officer (PCSO), and a Muslim. Granted, a PCSO is not a full Police Officer, and has only limited powers of law enforcement. But which law was he enforcing? It looks suspiciously like Sharia." (3)

Events often move quicker than the limited imaginations of Westminster politicians and by 2011 there was a concerted move by "Muslim Patrols" to make Tower Hamlets (London's old East End) a non-Muslim no-go area ruled by sharia law. The Islamic

Emirates Project, launched by the Muslims Against Crusades group, had a longer term goal. A target list of 10 British cities and two London boroughs they wanted to take over in order to achieve what they called "the end of man-made law, and the start of sharia law".

On the hit list were the already heavily Muslim-populated cities of Birmingham, Bradford, Derby, Dewsbury, Leeds, Leicester, Liverpool, Luton, Manchester and Sheffield, as well as Tower Hamlets in east London and Waltham Forest in northeast London. They may have been ambitious but they knew that the demographic changes mass immigration was bringing to Britain would mean that time was on their side. The 2011 census proved they were correct.

Based on official statistics from the Office of National Statistics (ONS), up until 2001 there were less than 1.5 million Muslims living in Britain. The 2011 census showed that the Muslim population in the UK had nearly doubled between 2001 and 2011 from 1.5 million to more than 2.8 million. That's a rate of increase 10 times faster than the rest of society. The Pew Research Centre in 2014 showed that there were now more Muslims living in London than there were in the whole of Spain. In 2014, *The Times* ran a front page story revealing that one in ten of *all* children under the age five in England and Wales were Muslim, with huge implications for future school provision, healthcare, housing and welfare costs. (4)

The story did not feature in any of that day's BBC news bulletins. Should the Muslim birth rate be of any greater importance than that of any other ethnic grouping? Why should we focus on Muslims? Isn't this just proof of what our national broadcaster would call bigotry, Islamophobia, or the catch-all….racism?

The reason we need to look at the Muslim birth rate is that it has profound implications for the way our children and their descendents will be forced to live in the future and because we are not being told the truth about Islamic immigration.

If 5% of the population are producing 10% of all of its children and that 5% are Muslims where do our political leaders think all this is heading within the next 25 years? As that Muslim 5% becomes 10% and the 10% becomes 20% the basics of what we have been proud to call our Judeo-Christian culture begins to change into something else entirely. Something Islamic, and those who point this out will have to face the new accusation of the Left, "Islamophobia".

"Islamophobia" is a phrase created by revolutionary Islamist group The Muslim Brotherhood to demonize anyone who attempts to make legitimate criticism of Islam. It has been taken up by the Left as a tool of censorship in the same way as accusations of racism were used to silence objections to mass immigration in the last decade, but how phobaic is it to fear murder and terrorism perpetrated in the name of Islam?

Those who cry "Islamophobia" need only look at the FBI's most wanted list of terrorists. The list was compiled in the immediate aftermath of 9/11 and contains the names of persons who have been *formally charged* in US district courts with terrorist crimes. Muslims make up 30 out of the 31 names on the list (which is about 97%) and ethnic Arabs account for 25 of the 30 terrorists. The one non-Muslim terrorist on the list is an animal rights activist.

There are many other ethnicities who have been welcomed en masse into Britain since the Labour Party's open door immigration experiment began in 1997 but the rapid expansion of the Muslim birth rate should give us the most cause for concern because significant numbers of other ethnicities or religions don't desire to fundamentally change the nature of the society they have settled in by the imposition of sharia law on the wider population. The gamble our multicultural politicians took, that a reasonable proportion of these new Muslim immigrants would assimilate and take up employment, has catastrophically failed. The vast majority remain dependent on welfare benefits and unwilling to assimilate, almost 20 years after permanently settling in Britain.

What we are not allowed to ask is why our politicians are *still* importing immigrants from Islamic nations in vast numbers, resulting in exponentially increasing welfare payments, when it is clear that what new immigrant Muslims desire is not Western democracy but sharia law. Most worrying of all, a large percentage of these new Muslim immigrants are *Islamists*. What percentage is debatable (most experts say between 15-25%) but Islamists are the people who flew the planes into the Twin Towers in New York City, bombed London Transport on 7/7, cut off drummer Lee Rigby's head in broad daylight on a London street and tortured and killed children at the Westgate Kenyan Mall. That's the same people now running Islamic State (IS) who pluck out your eyes then burn you alive for refusing to convert to Islam, who massacred the journalists at Charlie Hebdo in

France for daring to poke fun at their prophet. All of these terrorist acts are linked and bound by a fanatical belief that sharia law must be the law of every nation on earth. Islamism, like fascism and communism, is a 20th century totalitarian plague. It began with the overthrow of Iran by the Ayatollah Khomeini in 1979. It's the same kind of scourge that killed 55 million people during the Second World War, 20 million in the Soviet Union under Stalin soon after and 67 million under the rule of chairman Mao in China. (5) Like Nazism and Communism, Islamism has no time for democracy, free speech or human rights. As with Nazism it is fuelled by hatred of Jews but also of Christians, atheists, homosexuals, liberated women and ethnic minorities in the Islamic world. Only those who have experienced Islamist rule in tooth and claw can know of its full horrors. Freedom is the first victim of Islamism and all those in the West who want their children to live free must become aware of the urgent need to identify and destroy this horrific ideology. Yet in this titanic struggle the freedom loving people of the West will be opposed by many institutions within our society staffed by those more sympathetic to the forces of Islamism than they are to freedom.

The next stage of Britain's ongoing transformation by mass immigration will be to a quasi-Islamic state. The groundwork was laid by the Labour Party with the consistent support of their handmaiden, the BBC. Part one was the campaign to make the British public accept mass immigration without mass dissent, part two will see the epithet "islamophobic" applied to anyone who voices opposition to the destruction of traditional British culture by the Left's dogma of enforced multiculturalism.

How that scenario will work out in practice is the focus of this book. The demographic explosion that brings this new Dark Age ever closer to our children and their children not yet born is still grinding inexorably on.

A new analysis of the 2011 census figures by the Office for National Statistics focusing on the four biggest built-up areas in Britain: surrounding London, Manchester, the West Midlands and West Yorkshire shows that a quarter of people living in Britain's biggest cities are immigrants with one in three big-city residents now a member of a non-white ethnic minority and that in these areas one in ten homes now has no-one who speaks English as their main language.

There are no official statistics available showing how much extra welfare spending has been allocated to new migrants since the door to Third World mass migration was opened wide by Labour in 1997, but we do know that in 1997 *total* government welfare spending was £111 billion. By 2011 that figure had rocketed up to £227 billion, more than double, and that figure of £227 billion *did not* include government expenditure on the NHS or Education. Britain's 30 million taxpayers now pay at least £4,000 a year more than they did in 1997. What could have caused this historic, bankrupting change, what major social upheaval occurred within this time frame? Why did our welfare bill more than double if mass immigration was a net economic benefit to Britain, as our leaders told us it was. Ever get the feeling you've been lied to?

CHAPTER TWO

DAYS LIKE THESE

If the Muslim population of the UK were to continue growing at an annual rate of 6.7% (as it did between 2004 and 2008,) its share of the total UK population would rise from just under 4% in 2008 to 8% in 2020, to 15% in 2030 and to 28% in 2040, finally passing 50% in 2050.

Historian Niall Ferguson, from his bestselling book, *Civilisation*

There were many decisive events in recorded history that tore up the fabric of what had gone before, uprooting empires and great nations and taking history in a completely new direction. Moments like the victory of Muwatallis over Ramses at the Battle of Qadesh in 1285 BC, the defeat of the Persian army by the Greeks at Marathon in 490BC, Alexander's victory over the Persians at The Battle of Issus in 333BC, Valerian's defeat at the Battle of Edessa in 260, the assassination of Archduke Franz-Ferdinand in 1914 or the atomic bombs dropped on Hiroshima and Nagasaki in 1945.

It is no exaggeration to say that such a moment will soon arrive in Britain but such is the palpable fear of discussing that breaking fault line from our politicians and taxpayer funded broadcaster that one must suspect they believe that the game is already up and the towel thrown in.

This astounding fact needs to be repeated: between 1997 and 2010 the Labour governments of Tony Blair and Gordon Brown allowed open door immigration into Britain. During that period more than 5.5 million foreigners were allowed permanent residence in a nation that was already the second most overcrowded in Europe.

More than 80% of those new immigrants came from *outside* the EU. In 1997, just before Labour was elected, net migration to the UK was just *47,000*. The first wave of these new immigrants came not from Europe but from the Muslim nations of Pakistan, Bangladesh, Somalia, Iraq, Iran and Afghanistan as well as India and Nigeria, which have large Muslim populations. In 2002 alone, asylum seekers made 84,000 applications to stay in

Britain. The Labour government even recruited a special tier of immigration officials devoted to help speed up the process, for *unskilled* Muslim migrants to Britain. Most of these new permanent residents spoke little or no English, many were illiterate even in their own language. In the most deranged policy in the history of the Anglosphere Britain's borders were thrown open to allow in millions of the Third World's most illiterate and unemployable at a time when our need for unskilled labour was coming to an abrupt end.

Government statistics (2011) tell us that 4.8% of the UK population is now Muslim. We have no idea how many illegal immigrants there are in Britain but unofficial estimates say there may well be more than one million living in London alone. Before Labour came to power in 1997 there were 1.1million Muslims in Britain, representing less than 2% of the population. By 2010 that figure had more than doubled to 2.8million, or 4% of the population as a whole. The 2011 census saw the number of Muslims in Britain increase to 4.8% of the total population and the highly respected Pew Research Centre say that by 2030 that number will double again to 5.5million, more than 8% of an estimated 68 million population.

As it stands today one in every three primary school pupils in Britain now come from an ethnic minority, a staggering increase of more than 25.5% on figures released by the Department for Education (DfE) just five years ago in 2010, and this figure has yet to include the 614,000 extra immigrants who came to live in Britain in 2014.

At the sharp end of another Labour government, post 2015, any criticism of Islam will become increasingly rare and probably illegal as the strong horse of Muslim demographics, given supine assistance from an increasingly fearful Left/liberal elite of Westminster politicians, hacked-off celebrities and public sector Marxists, demand that those who speak out against Islamic immigration are brought to trial with beefed up hate crime legislation. This army of the appeased will then bear down on an already intimidated free press, arm in arm with legal aid activists, to stifle the last gasp of debate on the issue. The Pew Research Centre's study *The Future of the Global Muslim Population* (January 2011) was published before the results of the 2011 census but still concluded that due to mass immigration and high Muslim birth rates one in ten Britons will be Muslim by 2030. A forecast that means that by 2030 Britain will be home to more

Muslims than Kuwait. Even if the Muslim birth rate became the same as the indigenous British average birth rate overnight, that figure would not change. The changes taking place in our society are now unstoppable. As of 2011 the most popular name for boys in Britain is Mohammad (22 different spellings) with a total of 8,146 boys born that year being named after the Muslim prophet compared to Harry, in second place with 7,523. So what will the attitude be of this burgeoning Muslim majority to the secular, Christian and democratic people of Britain after 2030? On the evidence it doesn't look good. The number of Muslim children in England and Wales has doubled in a decade, according to the most detailed study of its kind. An analysis of 2011 Census data for The Muslim Council of Britain (MCB) concluded that one in 20 of the population was now Muslim and that Muslims now made up one in 12 children attending school. They concurred with the official census that the Muslim population of Britain had increased by more than a million in ten years. The politicians and broadcasters who assured the electorate that there would eventually be a "demographic transition", where Muslim birth rates would level out to indigenous British/European norms have been proved comprehensively wrong.

At the moment there is no sign of British Muslim birth rates significantly falling. According to the ONS, Pakistan-born women in Britain each have an average of 4.7 children, while Bangladeshi women in Britain have 3.9, both above the average British birth rate of 1.6 children. As the MCB figures show, after more than 60 years, Britain's Pakistani and Bangladeshi Muslim communities continue to have birth rates way beyond the national average because the large number of poor Third World immigrants Labour allowed to come to Britain have retained their historic cultural patterns of having large families, a pattern encouraged by Britain's welfare state which rewards larger families with larger benefit payments.

Without any discussion of the underlying motives of the MCB or the wider implications of Muslim demographics, the BBC broadcasted, without contradiction, (6) MCB conclusions that: "Muslims face a double penalty in entering the labour market - of racial discrimination as well as Islamophobia." So now we know the reason why, according to their own statistics, only one in five Muslims are in full-time employment in an expanding British labour market, it's all to do with "Islamophobia".

What the BBC didn't point to was the implication of a growing replacement population in our schools, doubling in size every decade. The MCB survey produced a graph showing that in the age group that counts most of all, the 0-4 age group, Muslims are already 10% of Britain's total population. Even some critics of Islam have been fooled into believing that the Muslim birth rate will eventually decline but what is being hidden is that even in decline (if and when that ever happens) Muslim birth rates will *still* outstrip indigenous British birthrates while *still more* Muslim immigrants pour into Britain.

In February 2015 the government announced that immigration had reached record levels with 624,000 more foreigners coming to live in Britain in the 12 months up to last September while 327,000 of the brightest and the most able left for Australia, America, Canada and New Zealand. That left 298,000 more immigrants to cope with, *two thirds of whom were from non-EU countries* and had no automatic right to work in Britain. This continued immigration influx was clearly supported by left-leaning senior civil servants in the Treasury and Business Department who, ignoring the clear evidence presented by the House of Lords in 2008, quietly believe mass immigration is an economic benefit to Britain.

It was left to Labour MP Frank Field to voice his concern at what is happening at a rapidly increasing rate. He said: "Every set of immigration data reinforces the need to control our borders. How can one expect a country to maintain its common identity and memories when in one year the population change alone was almost one million people - 327,000 leaving and 624,000 arriving. That's over a one-seventieth change in the entire population. At this rate in the next parliament it'll be the equivalent to the whole of inner London's population being changed."

By 2050 the Muslim birth rate will be huge and Britain will be a majority Muslim nation. That is an inescapable fact and the MCB know it, while the majority of the British public does not. Nor does the average Briton have *any* idea about the effect this unasked for transformation will have on the lives of their children and grandchildren.

The MCB report, always keen to stress the British values of immigrant Muslims, claimed that despite more than half of all Muslims in the UK being born outside of the country: "73 per cent of those practicing the religion said their national identity was British".

Of course, it all depends on how you phrase the question, but contrast that with a survey by the respected Pew Research Centre (2006) who found that: "a crushing majority of British Muslims (81 percent) considered themselves Muslims first, identifying with their respective European nations only to a secondary extent." One can only marvel either at the massive change of allegiance by British Muslims over such a short period or the gullibility of our national broadcaster which transmitted this nugget of Islamist propaganda without analysis.

If we wanted a snapshot of our children's future in Islamic Britain it was there for all to see in central London on February 8, 2015 when more than a 1,000 Islamic demonstrators presented a petition to Number 10 Downing Street, signed by 100,000 Muslims, in a protest *against* free speech. Clambering over the statues of Britain's wartime heroes, Field Marshall Montgomery and Viscount Alanbrooke, men who had bravely led a nation into war to defend freedom, these inheritors of the land that stood alone against the Nazis demanded that Britain submit to Islamic blasphemy laws following the jihad murder of the Charlie Hebdo cartoonists. On display was the perfect example of why mass Islamic immigration is the biggest threat Britain has ever faced and why Muslims are the biggest victims of their own religion.

While the overall numbers of Muslim immigrants remains low the fraction supporting the literal application of Islamic texts remains insignificant and can be ignored by established British Muslims who want no truck with a violent ideology. However, as the number of Muslims increase so do the number of Islamists.

A 2015 survey, conducted by ComRes for BBC Radio 4, revealed that more than one in four Muslims (27%) sympathised with the Charlie Hebdo killers, that's nearly three quarters of a million Muslims in Britain, with 11% saying those who drew such pictures of the prophet "deserve to be attacked". Over 80% of British Muslims said they found images of their prophet were deeply offensive when published with 10% of British Muslims surveyed saying they "knew" of British Muslims who agreed with the actions of Islamic State (beheading, murdering Christian children, burning captives alive).

Then the real scary stuff, what "British" Muslims really think about the rest of us. The poll found that 11% of British Muslims sympathise with jihadists fighting against the West (that's more than 100,000 Muslims in London alone) and one in five believe that

Islam can *never* be compatible with our Western liberal society. Longer term and scarier still, almost half of British Muslims believe that Muslim clerics who preach murder and violence against the West are preaching the correct version of Islam and not the "perverted ideology" Barack Obama would have us believe. Based on the evidence, there are now between 100,000 and 800,000 Jihadi activists or sympathizers living in London alone, including almost every single Muslim under the age of 25. Surveys in Holland have produced similar results with 80% of Turkish youth saying they do not believe that there is anything wrong with IS violence so long as it is committed against non-Muslims. Best-selling Canadian author Mark Steyn spells out what's in store for Britain: "The free world's Muslim populations are growing more radical with each generation, so within the ever larger Muslim population is an ever larger Western Muslim population and within that ever larger Western Muslim population is an ever more radicalized Western Muslim population." (7) Clearly, there has been very little integration of Muslim immigrants who have arrived in Britain since 1997, hardly any adoption of what used to be known as traditional British values and very little absorption of what were once known as "civilised norms". What seems to be occurring among Muslims is the mainstreaming of Dark Age savagery from Islamic State in tandem with a wholesale rejection of Western values. Existing British Muslims are not to blame for this but what the authorities continue to refer to as "moderate Islam" must be.

Unfortunately, with unceasing Islamic immigration from radicalised and war-torn Arab nations the peaceful Muslim well of tolerance has become poisoned by Islamist intolerance. What the Left call "diversity" cannot be applied to an ideology that forbids diversity as its central tenet and gives non-Muslims only three options; be conquered; convert or die.

Is this the "diversity" that indigenous British citizens will be forced to submit to when Muslims become the majority? Those who say we have nothing to fear from Muslim demographics need to ask themselves where were the Muslims in London protesting *in favour* of free speech and against the Charlie Hebdo murderers in France or the beheading of Lee Rigby or the continuing atrocities of Islamic State? They also need to ask why this significant demonstration of Islamic focal concern appeared nowhere on BBC television news? There can be no other conclusion drawn than while there are many who identify themselves as Muslims and who are not interested in waging all out war (jihad) against non-Muslims there is no form of sharia law that *does not teach* that the Islamic community has a responsibility to *wage war against and subjugate unbelievers.* Look up "jihad" in the dictionary and you will find its meaning.

Jihad [struggle, contest, spec. one for the propagation of Islam.] A religious war of Mohammedans against unbelievers in Islam, inculcated as a duty by the Koran and traditions. *The Oxford English Dictionary*

All four schools of Islamic jurisprudence: Maliki, Shafii, Hanafi and Hanbali agree on this basic aim. We won't hear any discussion of that basic Islamic fact from the BBC or the Labour Party or the police or the social services or our schools, who must ignore the jihadist teachings of Islam and stress its allegedly peaceful aspects. Islam may be the world's most violent religion but sharia law needs our special attention.

Many casual readers of the popular press have heard of it and not taken it seriously. Someone gets one of their hands and one of their feet chopped off for stealing in a far off land, a woman dressed all in black gets stoned to death for having an affair, a child who insults the prophet is arrested and then killed for blasphemy. But sharia law will be applied to everyone unfortunate enough to fall under Islamic rule, even in England. Here is an example. Gillian Gibbons, a middle aged primary school teacher from Liverpool, found out about sharia law the hard way. In 2007 she was working at the Khartoum Unity School in Sudan, teaching six-year-olds, both Christian and Muslim. After innocently allowing one of the children to name a teddy bear "Mohammad" she was hauled out of her classroom for insulting the prophet. Sudan's legal system is governed by sharia law which forbids any depictions of Mohammad and other prophets. On 25 November, 2007 Gillian was arrested by Sudan's religious police, interrogated, then put in a cell before being charged under the Sudanese Criminal Act for: "insulting religion, inciting hatred, sexual harassment, racism, prostitution and showing contempt for religious beliefs". That charge should have led to imprisonment or a public flogging consisting of 40 lashes. On 29 November, 2007 Gillian Gibbons was found guilty of "insulting religion" and was sentenced to 15 days' imprisonment and deportation. The next day more than 10,000 Muslim protesters took to the streets outside her prison waving their swords and machete's demanding that she be *executed* rather than deported... for naming a teddy bear Mohammad. The demo took place after she had been denounced by imams at the local mosque during Friday prayers. A terrified Gibbons had to be moved to a secret location because of fears for her safety; she was eventually released after protests by the British government allowed sanity to prevail. Those who think that this is a joke, that it may happen in some godforsaken hellhole but never in Britain, need to think again. Who in their right mind could bear to live under such laws? The Left's denial of reality will not hold in the face of the Islamic threat we face but are unable to discuss because of race hate laws and media self-censorship, underpinned by political correctness.

Daniel Greenfield, a Shillman Journalism Fellow, is a New York writer focusing on radical Islam. Quoting a 2014 Populus poll, Greenfield comments that the Muslim population in London is 12.4% (1.03 million) of London's 8.308 million people (2013 survey). Of those surveyed *the vast majority*, as high as 80% said they *support* Islamic State to some extent. That's the organisation responsible for burning alive a Jordanian pilot and posting it online. That's more than 800,000 Muslims living in London, and Greenfield concluded: "These numbers suggest that most or virtually all young Muslim settlers in the UK support ISIS." For those multiculturalists who have trouble taking this all in these statistics coincide with a Pew survey of "British" Muslim attitudes (2006) that found 1 in 4 Muslims believed the killing of innocent civilians by suicide bombing was justified. That figure was higher (35%) among 18-35 year olds, a figure *higher* than for Muslims living in Pakistan! What we have now in London is a terrorist powderkeg about to go off. To give you an idea of the potential threat from radical Islam in London we need to look at the 30-year armed struggle Britain had with the IRA. At the height of its campaign in the early 1970s the Provisional IRA, which then controlled large parts of Belfast, Londonderry and the Irish countryside, had "several hundred" members.

The IRA army council ran the whole organisation with only *seven* members.

To be sure there were thousands, possibly hundreds of thousands of sympathisers and fellow travellers of various types, but those within the Roman Catholic community in Northern Ireland who did not support the IRA's goals were simply intimidated into silence by gangs of toughs who patrolled the streets of their communities enforcing discipline as they saw it. If the IRA could bring Britain to its knees with several hundred members what can radical Islam do in London with a million supporters?

As the thread of this Islamic immigration nightmare unravels the Labour Party elite who brought it on; the Blair/Brown/Miliband axis may well be glimpsed looking out of the windows of their chauffeur driven limo's as they sweep past the mess they left behind for the people who once voted for them, en route to their high tech security mansions.

The most toxic legacy of Labour's great immigration experiment is not just that the vast majority of our two million plus new Muslim citizens have never worked and *will* never work but that a large and growing minority of this new Muslim community are Islamists, *whose aim is the total destruction of our way of life.*

Here's a fact supported by intelligence services around the world. Once the percentage of Muslims grows beyond 2%, as a total of the population, they cease to become the cultural enrichers so beloved of the multiculturalists and begin to morph into something else entirely, as an Islamist groupthink takes over. The tipping point into widespread Islamic unrest within society comes when Muslims form 10% of the population as a whole, as is the case now in France.

Dr Peter Hammond is the director of Frontline Fellowship and the founder and chairman of Africa Christian Action. Dr Hammond looked at the way Muslims first establish themselves in liberal Western society then, as their numbers increase, begin to agitate for change using threats of violence and the manipulation of the tolerant and politically correct. Hammond's study is a stark warning to those who regard increasing Muslim numbers as a benefit.

He found that: "As the percentage of Muslims grow in each country so do their demands. As long as the Muslim population remains around or under 2% in any given country, they will be for the most part regarded as a peace loving minority, and not as a threat to other citizens. At 2% to 5% they begin to proselytize from other ethnic minorities and disaffected groups, often with major recruiting from the jails and among street gangs. From 5% on they exercise an inordinate influence in proportion to their percentage of the population. For example, they will push for the introduction of halal (clean by Islamic standards) food, thereby securing food preparation jobs for Muslims. They will increase pressure on supermarket chains to feature halal on their shelves – along with threats for failure to comply. At this point they will work to get the ruling government to allow them to rule themselves (within their ghettos) under sharia, the Islamic law. The ultimate goal of Islamists is to establish sharia law over the entire world. When Muslims approach 10% of the population they tend to increase lawlessness as a means of complaint about their conditions. In Paris, we are already seeing car burnings. Any non-Muslim action offends Islam, and results in uprisings and threats, such as in Amsterdam, with opposition to Mohammed cartoons and films about Islam. Such tensions are seen daily, particularly in Muslim sections. At 40% nations experience widespread massacres, chronic terror attacks, and ongoing militia warfare. From 60% nations experience unfettered persecution of non-believers of all other religions (including non-conforming Muslims), sporadic ethnic cleansing (genocide), use of sharia law as a weapon, and jizyah, the tax placed on infidels." (8)

That 10% threshold will be reached in Britain, officially by 2030, but it may well be sooner given that we have only a general idea of the total Muslim population, circa 2015. As the Muslim population becomes 10% of the total British population and more ominously, becomes more than 50% of the population of some boroughs and cities, the attitudes and values of this rapidly expanding minority come into play and it will be the Islamists among the wider Muslim community who will be calling the shots in cities across Britain, urging Muslims to rise up and demand sharia law, backed by jihadi violence. This evidence, as well as the facts produced by the government's own statistical service (ONS), the national census of 2011 and even the Muslim Council of Britain, are being ignored by politicians of all persuasions, in chains to multicultural dogma.

If Muslims are willing to adapt to Britain's traditional way of life with its historical values of individual freedom; freedom of speech, secularism, democracy and rule of law then we don't need to worry but what if this growing population are not so inclined to adapt or even co-exist?

What we *do* know about the attitudes of the official 4.8% of Muslims currently living in Britain (5.2% in England) is disturbing to say the least because extensive polling suggests that nearly half want sharia law and there's little evidence of any of our traditional values gaining any acceptance at all in Muslim communities over time. Another survey in 2009 (WikiLeaks) revealed that of 600 Muslim students polled at 30 British universities 32% of respondents believed killing in the name of religion to be justified. That same year a poll by the Centre for Social Cohesion confirmed that 40% of Muslims living in the UK wanted sharia law and more than half (54%) wanted a Muslim party to represent their world view in Parliament.

The time has now come to define our Western culture and its values in law and establish that as the majority culture these values are dominant and must remain dominant over time. New Muslim citizens may be loyal to Islam in private with the same rights to religious freedom as any other citizen but must be asked to pledge their civic loyalty to their country of citizenship.

If they feel they cannot do this then they should not be granted citizenship, as happens in America. Those new citizens who violate their pledge by engaging in or promoting jihad activity should be deported. If this vital change is not secured soon there is trouble just around the corner. Can we be sure that, as the size of the Muslim population increases relative to the size of the British population as a whole, demands for the expansion of sharia law and its medieval punishments will not drown out the voices of reason? In 2030, after a British Charlie Hebdo, who will be brave enough to argue for our freedoms or be willing to defend them? Not anyone on the Left, who remain lockstepped to continued Islamic immigration.

On every issue that counts, in every poll taken we see that there is little difference between so-called "moderate" Islam on free speech, the role of women, blasphemy, the Jews and what our political class calls "radical islam". These "moderates" want to be governed by sharia law, they still agree with stoning adulterers and killing those who blaspheme against their prophet and they don't want democracy. That makes Islam incompatible with modern Western civilisation, the place where you and I live, and where the Left have invited Islam to come and stay for good.

As the feminist polemic Julie Birchill wrote of the Left's relationship to Islam: "Good luck apologising for them, all you gutless Western lefties — but you can put your fingers in your ears and sell out other sections of humanity all you like, and squeeze your eyes shut like a child in a storm, determined to see no evil, hear no evil, speak no evil — and still that evil storm may come at you with hands like knives one day. Look what they did to an Islamic convert on a humanitarian mission to help Muslims. You think they wouldn't do it to you?" (9)

CHAPTER THREE

JIHAD ON THE DOLE

It's almost impossible to say anything against Islam in this country, because you are accused of being racist or Islamophobic.

Richard Dawkins, British evolutionary biologist and popular science author

During a House of Lords debate on welfare reform Baroness Flather warned that

Pakistani and Bangladeshi communities were failing to adopt the values of British society and said they should have their benefits slashed. (10)

Cue rapid mobilisation of outraged liberal and social media lynch mob to condemn this shocking racism. Then, more horror as the outraged Left realise that Baroness Flather was... noooo! Britain's first, female, Asian peer.

In a speech the House of Lords during the second reading of the Welfare Reform Bill in September 2011, she said: "The minority communities in this country, particularly the Pakistanis and the Bangladeshis, have a very large number of children and the attraction is the large number of benefits that follow the child. Nobody likes to accept that, nobody likes to talk about it because it is supposed to be very politically incorrect."

No shock whatsoever that the Labour Party subsequently accused Baroness Flather of racism. Clearly, no white politician would have dared to raise the issue and doubtless it was only because Baroness Flather was of Asian origin that she dared to speak of Muslim welfare benefits, illustrating the strangulation political correctness now exerts over our democratic institutions. This is a fact we need to live by. Britain is sitting under a debt mountain that must come crashing down at some point, impelling Britain's economy towards a massive correction. This was not initially caused by Islamic immigration; it was the result of the deranged economic policies of the man now widely regarded as the worst prime minister in British history, Gordon Brown. The governments own statistics agency, the Office for Budget Responsibility (OBR), looked at how public money was spent by the Labour Party during their time in office. They found that in a single decade

Britain's fiscal future and the prospects of generations of those not yet born had been recklessly transformed by the madcap taxpayer-funded largesse of Gordon Brown. In the fiscal year 1999-2000 overall government expenditure was £488.5 billion. By 2009-10, a mere decade of Labour economic mismanagement later, and that figure had almost doubled to £737.3 billion.

The largest, most sustained public spending splurge in British history. Where did all this public money go to and why was it needed?

Anything to do with the influx of more than 5.5 million foreign nationals allowed into Britain, thanks to Labour's open-door immigration policy? Of course not, say the Westminster elite, and if you ask for the figures detailing how much of this massive increase in spending went on extra school places, extra doctors and nurses and translators and primary and secondary health care through the NHS, extra prison places, more social housing for new migrants you will be told that the government doesn't supply those sort of statistics, based on race or religious groupings.

Just requesting that sort of information will leave you open to accusations of racism, as Baroness Flather found out to her cost. Yet it is beyond question that without an honest look and reappraisal of the massive amounts of welfare spending being consumed by the most recent wave of Islamic immigrants (and yet to be consumed by their dependents), we cannot begin to understand why Britain still needs to borrow more than £100billion each year, despite a now "booming" economy.

The budget speech given by the Coalition chancellor George Osborne on March 19, 2013 was a glimpse into the future of bankrupt Britain as horrific as any frightener produced during the heyday of Universal Pictures. In effect, Osborne flew the white flag and gave up on the (admittedly gargantuan) task of even trying to get to grips with the mountain of debt bequeathed to him by Gordon Brown. As the BBC news presented its traditional "cuts" mantra Osborne's accounting showed that the £800bn national debt inherited from Labour would morph into £1.5 trillion by 2015.

As for spending cuts; watching the news I was gripped with the certainty that either the Coalition were ignoring just how deep into the danger zone we now were or worse, they knew but realised that there is no long term solution, and were just hoping for the best in the short to medium term. Over the previous decade public spending, said Osborne, *had risen by 53%.* The government's independent Office for Budget Responsibility (OBR) figures show that between 2010 and 2018, the effect of the draconian "cuts" the BBC so vigorously derides will be a reduction in public spending of just 3.4%, taking total government spending all the way back to…. where it was in 2005, when Labour was in power. So here's an update for those who have just read the last chapter and thought maybe I was exaggerating the fear factor baked in the pie of Osborne's budget speech. In October 2014, official government economic statistics came in and were enough to send shivers down the spine of all but the fantasists advising the Labour Party. The economy is growing at 0.7pc per quarter, we learn, far faster than last year. Yet public sector net borrowing over the first half of 2014-15 was *10% higher* than for the same period in 2013-14. Borrowing in September alone was £12 billion, a staggering 15% *up* on the same month the year before. While tax receipts were up 3.1%, revenue growth was outstripped by even higher spending. For all the talk of "austerity", central government expenditure in September was 5.4% *above* that spent the same month one year ago, as welfare payments spiralled.

The Government, having already borrowed £58bn between April and September, is now certain to miss its £96bn annual borrowing target by a country mile and that means a *sixth straight year of £100bn plus borrowing* to bail out our largely unproductive non-EU immigrants, a sixth successive year of triple-digit, billion-pound deficits, five of them under the Tories.

There have been no spending cuts of any note to deal with the economic emergency the Tories inherited from Labour. At one time, up until 1997, British governments used to run a surplus but as immigration went up so did our borrowing and deficits; from £19bn in 2002 to more than £156bn in 2009. In 2009 that meant we borrowed £156bn more each year than we collected in tax revenue. Where is this money going to? What possible reason could we have for an increase of 53% in public spending over the last decade? The answer is, in one word, immigration.

As Nobel prize-winning economist Milton Friedman famously said: "You can have open borders or a welfare state but you can't have both". Friedman was an economist, not a politician and his point was that mass immigration was the quickest way to bankrupt a modern economy.

Thanks to the last Labour government we don't collect statistics on where welfare spending goes based on race or religion, we're not even allowed to know how much of our schools, prison, social work or NHS resources are being used up by recent immigrants or even how much they are contributing in tax in return for those services. We can't collate this vital information for the same reason the police and social services in Rotherham couldn't respond to the mass rape of non-Muslim children; because of Labour's race hate legislation and the fear of being labelled a racist or Islamophobic. Those of us who are interested in such politically incorrect matters are thus forced to look elsewhere for the information. *And what we find is both staggering and frightening.* According to (modest) numerical calculations based on government statistics from wikileaks and a leak from Ritt Bjerregaard, the Danish Socialist spokeswoman for immigration and integration (1999), the following conclusion was arrived at. Muslims, who in 1999 made up 5% of the Danish population, were receiving 35% of *all* welfare payments. As a minimum, the British government currently spends £14 billion a year from tax revenues to pay Muslims registered and claiming for Jobseekers Allowance. In Britain our current situation, regarding the number of Muslims claiming benefit among the wider population, closely mirrors Denmark where, by 2014, more than 40% of their total welfare budget was spent on supporting the unproductive Muslim population. In the absence of official data all that can be done is to estimate, based on what is available from non-governmental sources. These are Danish statistics.

A leading European periodical reported in 2005 that: "According to Claus Hjort Frederiksen, the Minister for Employment, immigrants from countries such as Somalia, Iran, Iraq and Lebanon are a huge burden on Danish welfare. We are simply forced to adopt a new policy on immigration. The calculations of the welfare committee are terrifying and show how unsuccessful the integration of immigrants has been up to now," said Frederiksen. The committee calculated, among other things, what it would mean if immigration to Denmark from third-world countries could be blocked completely. The conclusion was that 75% of the cuts needed in the welfare system in the next decades would disappear. One look at the Islamic books and a reality check was swiftly rushed in by Frederiksen so that immigrants allowed into the country now had to have a job waiting for them. (11) It should be noted that after 10 years attendance in Danish state schools

67% of Muslim students still could not adequately speak the Danish language. Not only Denmark has noted the excessive burden that Islamic immigration placed on its finances. In 2013 Finansavisen a Norwegian financial newspaper went through the official figures released by SSB, the Norwegian Bureau of Statistics, revealing that each non-western immigrant, on average, costs Norway NoK 4.1 million (£416,000). These sums are worrying, especially when considering how few (15,400) non-western immigrants arrived in Norway in 2012, compared to the 269,000 non-western immigrants who arrived in Britain that same year.

The signs were all there in 2004, and New Labour did nothing about it. Leaked statistics showed then that a third of working-age Muslims in Britain had no qualifications at all, the highest rate of any religious group. At that time, one third said they were self employed and of all those who said they were working, one in ten, said they drove a taxi or a private hire cab. (12)

Since 2004, and mostly during the time when Gordon Brown was prime minister, there was a remarkable change in public expenditure figures. With the arrival of new waves of non-EU immigrants Britain's welfare bill, like Norway's, ballooned out of sight. *The Daily Telegraph* reported in 2012 that 75% of all Muslim women were unemployed while 50% of all Muslim men are unemployed (67.5% of all Muslims in Britain).

The massive rise in welfare expenditure over the previous decade mirrors the huge influx of Pakistani, Bangladeshi/Somali/ Iraqi and other Muslim immigrants into Britain over the same period of time. A jump from 13% men and 18% women claiming benefits in 2004 to 50% men and 75% women in 2012. Take just one group of the recently arrived, the Somalis. The Government still has no reliable statistics on how many Somalis now live in Britain. One official reckoned that there were 150,000 legal Somalis and three times as many illegal ones. They live mostly in London but there are sizeable numbers living in Liverpool, Sheffield, Bristol, Cardiff and other English cities.

This is the biggest Somali community living anywhere outside of Somalia in the world. Of all the Somalis who have entered Britain since 1997 what we do know is that around 81% are unemployed and most have extremely low levels of education, many of them are illiterate even in their own language. A 2008 report by the Institute for Public Policy Research said that 46% of all Somalis living in Britain had arrived since 2000 and that

48% had no qualifications and barely a quarter of those of working age were employed — those who were had mostly menial jobs.

In 1997 Haringey Council found that 50.6% of its Somali adults were illiterate in any language. The Somali community in Britain is fractured, has failed to integrate and has lost its traditional social structures but what it has retained is a strong connection with Islam and a rejection of the civic structures of the country it chose to adopt when arriving in Britain with open hands begging for help, which they were given, with incredible generosity. How can gratitude be measured in any meaningful way?

Britain has had only one Somali mayor, in Tower Hamlets, East London. Young Somalis are found everywhere in London gangs, like the Tottenham Somalis, the Woolwich Boys or Thug Farm. Two Somali brothers, Mustaf and Yusuf Jama, murdered PC Sharon Beshenivsky during a robbery in Bradford in 2005. Many others have become radicalised by Islam, through the mosques. Two of the four men who tried to bomb the London Underground on July 21, 2005, were Somali asylum-seekers. What possible benefit has there been to British society from the influx of Somali migrants and asylum seekers who must have crossed multiple safe borders to get to Britain and can therefore only be described as bogus asylum seekers? If we take MigrationWatch's estimate of the lifetime costs of an unemployed immigrant just this one ethnic group are using up vast amounts of taxpayer resources; 80% of Somalis live in social housing compared with just 17% of indigenous UK residents. Huge sums are going to be needed to pay for social housing for this one ethnic group over the next 15 years, but how much?

Even if each Somali worked for 40 years on minimum wage they would still be eligible for pension credits on retirement as well as council tax benefit and housing benefit on the way, at a cost to the taxpayer of more than £310,000 for each Somali, a mammoth bill that is already starting to break Britain financially.

Tower Hamlets has become a magnet for new Muslim immigration where, in six months following April 2013, 17,584 new patients registered with GP surgeries there– an average of 463 per practice. Doctors in Tower Hamlets say their in-trays are overflowing, which means they can't keep on top of blood test and scan results. How many of these people are here illegally or working and paying taxes? We don't know and are not allowed to know, but we do know that the cost of servicing this new diversity must be met by the taxpayer either way, and that cost is skyrocketing along with the immigration figures. Yet the Labour government flung the door wide open to all-comers based on their assumption that immigration was good for the economy, and still the Left/liberal elite cling to the greatest lie ever told, that mass immigration is good for the economy.

This was the underlying theme of the BBC's *Don't Cap my Benefits*; an hour-long prime time current affairs programme pouring shame on the heartless Coalition government cutting the benefits of London's deserving immigrant poor. There was no mention of the fact that this year (2014) the government will spend more than £167 billion on benefits, that's £27 billion a year *more* that was spent 10 years ago.

There was no mention of the possible connection between mass immigration and an increase in the benefits bill or any mention of Britain now having to borrow more than £100 billion plus each fiscal year. In the BBC film we saw, among the families besieging Brent council's housing offices, the family of Khaled Kassem, a Palestinian refugee with his wife and seven children. Their efforts to harangue the staff and use their children as pawns almost got them evicted from the waiting area for what the housing staff referred to as "emotional blackmail". Mr Kassem was incensed at being asked to move from his subsidised residence in London to another subsidised residence in Buckinghamshire, 30 miles away. As the lachrymose BBC background music blared on like the soundtrack from a holocaust drama the Kassem family wailed and threatened then, after a brief resentful stay in High Wycombe, were allowed to remain in their subsidised council house in London after repeated complaints about the "dangerous" stairs in their rejected Buckinghamshire abode. The clincher was, apparently, that Mr Kassem would have been unable to travel to his part time grocer's job in London. This job paid him £150 a week, the hook which enabled him to claim £800 a week in working tax/child tax benefits. The logic of this economic madness clearly escaped those who were making the programme. Instead of another "poor immigrants" sob story from the BBC what we really needed to learn was just how much money this one family will be costing the British taxpayer in comparison to what they have contributed. Most of the Kassem's seven children appeared to be under 10-years-old; so if we assume Kassem will continue pocketing his current level of benefit for only another 10 years the taxpayer hit is already racked up to over £338,000. To subsidise his job as a part-time grocer! That's not counting their free access to the NHS, council tax benefits or pension credits and ignoring the likelihood most of their children will never work full-time either. There was not a microgram of gratitude in evidence from the Kassem family at the news that they'd hit the council house jackpot. Shouldn't the BBC have questioned the justification of allocating council houses in London on the basis of "need" rather than on the basis of time spent on the waiting list or of having local roots?

On display from the Kassem family there was only dull resentment and a broader sense of entitlement from a family with no cultural, historical or blood ties to Britain. A family who will be a net drain on the public purse for the rest of their lives, who should never have been allowed to settle in Britain in the first place and who should have been fast-tracked back to where they came from on to the next available plane. (13)

The sad parade of multiculturalist politicians/celebrities/race activists and legal aid parasites will be long gone by the time cultural diversity has drunk its last free round from the taxpayers' watering hole but until that day here's a small slice of life in New Britain, reported by a London newspaper in 2014: "Rudi Ion struggles to count up the children from his huge Romanian clan who now call Britain home. It could be 100, he tells me. 'I've got 25 cousins all living around Nottingham, each with three or four kids,' he adds with a loud laugh. Rudi is speaking from his rented three-bedroom terrace house in Bridlington Street, a shabby part of the Midlands city where he's settled with his wife Anda and their two sons, nine-year-old Ionut and Constantin, six. His mother Elena, 53, and sister Ana, who is 32, live there, too. Rudi is an ebullient 28-year-old who speaks English well. He doesn't seem surprised when I tell him that a recent controversial report from the Office for National Statistics (ONS) shows that more than 25 per cent of children born in England and Wales in 2011 were to foreign mothers — up 16 per cent on the decade before. What is particularly striking, according to the ONS, is that Romanians who come to Britain are actually having more than twice as many children as they would at home, where the average is 1.25 children born to each family.

'Your benefits system is crazy — I would actually say it was sick,' he says, as he makes a gesture involving sticking his two fingers down his throat. Of course Romanians will settle in Britain if they get this kind of money. It is like walking down the road and seeing a sack full of cash that has been dropped, picking it up and no one saying anything. If my people bring more children in, or have more children here, there are more benefits. So, of course, they have babies.' His family came here from District Two, a multicultural area of the Romanian capital, Bucharest, after Rudi had first tried his luck in eight other countries dotted around the European Union. He admits: 'I made my way by pick-pocketing, thieving and other small crimes. But I don't do bad things anymore because I am not poor and live on your benefits,' he told me. 'I arrived in the UK on January 7, three years ago, and went to the Nottingham job centre to get a National Insurance number a few weeks after. I came to Nottingham to stay with a cousin and found a good private accountant who told me how to claim the benefits. I soon brought over my family, too. I have never been told to look for work by the job centre. I have never called back there after I got the National Insurance number. Why would I want a real boss when I get £300 put into my bank account each week for nothing? There is the child benefit of £170 a month for Ionut and Constantin, too. In Romania, we were only given £17 a month for them. Now I sing "God praise your Queen Elizabeth" every day, because we have arrived in heaven.' He adds: 'It is political strategy to say there are few Romanians arriving in the UK. If the authorities tell the British public that we are claiming benefits there will be a row. They do not count the numbers because they dare not. They need the matter to remain a secret.' He introduces me to six other adult members of his family who, he says, all claim benefits of some kind. In the living room, two of the extended Ion clan's many children — Antonio, three, and Andrea, six — are bouncing on a bed, which serves as a sofa. 'Of course, we want to be here. I will only run away when your country starts sinking under the weight of people, which will happen one day.' (14)

In 2012, before the newest influx of Romanian and Bulgarian immigrants, Scotland Yard announced it was arresting almost 200 foreign criminals a day in London. That's every single day of the year amounting to almost 73,000 ...each year. This includes murderers, rapists, shoplifters and armed robbers, just in London. This crime wave was happening elsewhere on a smaller but increasing scale. In the West Midlands police reported the arrest of 11,801 foreign nationals between April 2011 and March 2012. That means more than 100,000 more foreign criminals active in Britain that weren't active before 1997, because they weren't living here. The number of actual crimes the additional 100,000 foreign criminals actually commit will run into millions. Information provided in 2001 found that Muslims also make up 40% of Britain's prison population for the most serious criminals (category A and B)

Who were the experts in Labour's ranks who formulated this Third World immigration policy of permanent dependency and national bankruptcy? Certainly not Nobel prize-winning economists like Milton Friedman who had previously advised Conservative administrations on matters economic, nor heavyweights still active in the Labour Party like Peter Shore or former chancellor Denis Healy. No, these new architects of our future prosperity were David Blunkett the Labour Home Secretary who, speaking on BBC2's Newsnight programme (November 2003) said there were "no obvious limits" to the numbers of immigrants who would be allowed to settle in the UK. Blunkett boasted that immigrants brought economic benefits and the (then) current inflow of more than 170,000 migrants a year was "permanently sustainable". He went further and warned that without legal migration, "growth would stall, economic flexibility and productivity would reduce". This was the same David Blunkett who, fast forward to 2013 and with cumulative immigration into Britain since 1997 exceeding 7.5 million, gave an interview to BBC Radio Sheffield where he warned that tensions between local people in his Page Hall constituency and Roma migrants "could escalate into rioting".

The irony is enough to send you looking for a straight-jacket. Blunkett held high office during Labour's 13 years in power dealing with billions of pounds worth of taxpayers' money, despite having no formal knowledge of economics. Blunkett had studied politics at Sheffield University. He was typical of so many New Labour cabinet ministers with degrees in politics but with little understanding of much else, least of all the practical realities of working in a wealth creating industry rather than occupying state funded posts in local government or the NHS. Many on the Left who grasped the reins of power under Tony Blair's pro-business umbrella were fellow travellers boning up on Gramsci.

None of them had a clue about how money was created in the real world, only how easy it was to spend it in the bubblewrap land of Westminster.

It was the old white working-class communities that were being asked to cope with the influx of foreigners with no homes, jobs, money or the ability to speak English while Labour's new metropolitan elite were quaffing their chardonnay in west London wine bars. Other Labour ministers/politics graduates included Ruth Kelly, Jacqui Smith and Ed

Miliband. Chancellor Gordon Brown didn't fall into this category, he was a history graduate.

Thus it was possible for Labour health minister Patricia Hewitt to preside over a £12.7 billion loss on a centralising NHS computer system that failed to work and had to be scrapped at a loss of £12.7 billion! That works out at £600 for every household in the country, enough to pay the wages of 60,000 nurses for 10 years. There was no apology from Hewitt, after all it was only the taxpayers' money and, as far as Labour's fiscal incompetents were concerned, tax money flowed like water from household appliances. No wonder even Lib-Dem leader Nick Clegg later remarked that Labour should never again be trusted with the nation's economy. The word "scandal" is often overused. This was, however, a true scandal but so casual was the attitude to other peoples' money by ministers that auditors found Labour government officials paying ten times the market rate even for bog standard laptops. This lack of responsibility is a key difference between public and private sectors. "If I had people spending £3,500 on laptops, I'd haul them in and discipline them," said the head of one leading technology company. "There's not enough outrage over these things in government." Instead of being drummed out of government in shame and disgrace former minister Hewitt now enjoys a highly-paid directorship at BT. Do we laugh or cry?

Luke Johnson, an entrepreneur who writes a regular business column summed Labour's *current* economic incompetence thus: "I have read the biographies of Labour's parliamentary candidates on the website. The vast majority work in the public sector for unions, charities and think tanks. A tiny proportion works in the private sector. Yet the private sector provides 82% of jobs in Britain. No wonder Labour fails to relate to business. Its philosophy centres on redistribution. It has no experience or understanding of how firms are started, jobs created, innovation funded and exports generated or indeed where the money to pay taxes actually comes from." (15)

What it was all about for Gordon Brown was the redistribution of wealth, not its creation. Gathered around Brown in the Treasury was the current Labour leadership of Ed Balls and Ed Miliband, who also saw Labour's support coming from the ranks of those on benefits, hence the massive borrowing splurge that characterised Brown's tenure at Number 10 and the transfer of taxpayer cash to the incoming idle. Those lapping up this avalanche of new welfare benefits were mostly the new Muslims, arriving en mass after 1997, and who will now hold the balance of power in every inner city Labour constituency come the election of 2020. Under normal circumstances the leadership of a political party that had near bankrupted the nation one parliament ago would have been out of power for a generation in the same way that the Wilson/Callaghan governments of the 1970s were punished for their economic incompetence with 18 years of Tory rule. Yet these are no longer normal times in Britain and as I write Ed Miliband, a clownish misfit almost beyond caricature and the most unlikely Labour leader in their history, stands as bookies favourite to become the next prime minister. The reason, of course, is the change of demographics brought about by mass immigration. If Labour wins the 2015 general election it is likely they will be there for a good while thanks to their new immigrant constituents. Should the Conservatives pull off an unlikely election victory it will be against the demographic trend and be entirely due to Labour being wiped out in Scotland due to the rise of the Scottish nationalists. This set of circumstances will never be repeated and so the 2015 election will be the last ever chance for the Conservatives to gain a majority as the clock of Muslim demographics begins to tick ever faster.

A survey by the MCB in 2015 revealed that 21.3% of British Muslims have *never* worked, a figure that excludes full-time students, whereas for the UK as a whole, the figure is just 4.3%. Naturally this swathe of the population who will remain on benefits will hope that the Labour Party of welfare will return to power, for ever.

Just before the last election, at the height of Blair/Brown's unpopularity over Iraq 35% of Muslims said they still intended to vote Labour and *40%* actually did. In 2015 an Ashcroft poll showed that a massive 62.9% of Muslims intended to vote Labour at the coming general election in 2015.

So what was the intellectual calibre of the people who decided, without a vote or a manifesto commitment, that mass immigration would be good for the economy? Here's a humorous anecdote indicative of a wider truth.

In December 2008 the minister for higher education, David Lammy, appeared on Celebrity Mastermind. Lammy's specialist subject was Muhammad Ali and he scored a paltry eight points, considering it was his speciality. One of his first general knowledge answers revealed that he didn't know what English cheese was traditionally drunk with port...not terribly important I grant you but the rest of his replies were astounding. With Lammy's answers in bold, this was the bravura performance of the man running Britain's universities at that time.

Q) What was the married name of the scientists Marie and Pierre who won the Nobel Prize for Physics in 1903 for their research into radiation? A) **Antoinette**. Q) Which fortress was built in the 1370s to defend one of the gates of Paris, and was later used as a state prison by Cardinal Richelieu? A) **Versailles**. Q) Who succeeded to the English throne aged nine on the death of his father Henry VIII in 1547? A) **Henry VII**. Q) Which country's Rose Revolution of 2003 led to the resignation of President Edward Shevardnadze? A) **Yugoslavia**.

So, the scientist who pioneered research into radiation was, according to Lammy, "let them eat cake" Queen Marie Antoinette, whose palace of Versailles was, he believed, used as a state prison! Next, on a basic level of cognitive reasoning how many primary school children could not have improved on Lammy's historical howler naming Henry (the seventh!) as succeeding to the throne *following* the death of Henry (the eighth!), a space time anomaly that would have baffled Dr Who. Lammy's rapid rise up Labour's ministerial pole, of course, owed nothing to the fact he was black, and even suggesting such a thing would bring accusations of racism. Perhaps foreign secretary would have been his next merited appointment had he been aware that (see question three) Yugoslavia no longer existed as a country in 2008. That small matter of the Balkans war he managed to overlook...you know the one...deadliest conflict since the Second World War, fought from 1992-1996, just one year before Lammy's party took power. When it came to general knowledge his final score was five points, placing him last. Lammy's score on the general knowledge section was not an all-time low, however. That dubious honour was held by the man who scored just two points in the 2003 edition of Celebrity Mastermind ... David Blunkett, Labour's education secretary.

This might sound very trivial and meaningless but these are the people who formulated the policy of mass immigration for Britain, the Labour ministers who bankrupted Britain with their fiscal incompetence and changed the traditional culture of our historic nation forever. It matters. These are the ministers whose corruption of government departments with politically correct appointments now means that no one can research or reveal the mess Britain is in without being accused of racism. Today, there are no official figures to work on detailing the demand Britain's expanding south Asian population is making on general taxation.

A 2013 report by the Public Administration Select Committee said that migration figures now being used by government ministers couldn't be trusted and were little better than guesswork. In the year to June 2012, immigration was *estimated* at 515,000 while emigration was *estimated* at 352,000. Committee chairman Bernard Jenkin said: "Most people would be utterly astonished to learn that there is no attempt to count people as they enter or leave the UK. They are amazed when they are told that government merely estimates that there are 500,000 immigrants coming into the UK each year." Migration estimates, it said, were based on random interviews of around 800,000 people passing through ports and airports, only about 5,000 of whom were actually immigrants. This was research intended to monitor the behaviour of tourists not provide a measure of the government's progress in stopping our slide towards fiscal disaster.

You have to be over 30 now to remember a time when travelling by plane from England was as easy as getting on a bus and, at one stage, almost as cheap. In the 1990s low cost airlines offered walk-on flights to cities across Europe for less than a fiver.

Thanks to Islamic terrorism the cost of flying has soared since 9/11. In America the "September 11th Security Fee" of $2.50 per plane came into force. With 1.5 million passenger flights per day in America that works out at $3.75 million *per day*, totalling approximately $1.4 billion per year. The same fee is levied on the passengers leaving from more than 200 other countries, including Britain, and now that fee has risen to $5.60 per flight. Go figure that increase yourself and work out how much cheaper your flight would have been without the cost of massive airport security needed to deter mainly Muslim males aged between 16 and 35. We know this yet we must still spend billions each year to make sure every granny, auntie and uncle or baby gets thoroughly searched. As *Daily Mail* columnist Richard Littlejohn noted: "Not even judges are exempt. I've heard from a circuit judge (I've agreed not to identify her) who was passing through Manchester Airport last week. At security, the box containing her official, full-bottomed horse-hair wig, labelled 'Her Honour Judge So-and-So' was taken from her. The ceremonial syrup was then led away to a special machine to be swabbed for explosives.

The judge's 84-year-old mother, travelling with her, was frisked and forced to remove her shoes. While all this was going on, the judge tells me, a woman (man?) in a burka was waved through without even being asked to remove her full-face, pillar-box veil." (16) The airport authorities will not profile those most likely to fall into the category of terrorists because they fear they may be accused of racism, possibly by their own security staff, many of whom have a Islamic backgrounds.

Now back to the hidden cost of mass immigration. There is no nationally accepted data on the fiscal cost of immigration, so to base projections on a nation with comparable ratios of immigrants to population (Denmark) and with similar spending on welfare is entirely justified. Based on Denmark's comparable 40% figure we find that in the fiscal year ending 2010, the year that Labour were finally booted out of office, Britain's total welfare spend was £110.7 billion with £44.28 billion being paid annually to unproductive Muslims and their dependents, more than the entire defence budget that year. (17) With no curbs in welfare benefits for larger families in sight this figure will be seen as a benchmark as the Muslim birth rate increases.

If mass immigration is good for the British economy, as the Labour Party claims, why did welfare spending increase from £64.4 billion in 1997, (their first year in office) when the population of Britain was 58.4 million to a whopping £110.7 billion in 2010 (their last year in office) with the population by then at 62.3 million. Could there be any connection between the arrival of 3.9 million more people in Britain under Labour's open door immigration experiment and the near doubling of the welfare bill? Why is our suicidal welfare state spending allowing multiple Muslim wives to each claim income support benefit and child support for each baby produced as well as one-off maternity benefit payments for each child? Why can a Muslim male claim housing benefit for each wife even if she is abroad, for up to 52 weeks, as long as the absence is temporary? Do we know how many women living in Karachi or Islamabad are being subsidised by the British taxpayer? This is your money they are spending!

The fear that Westminster politicians and their willing partners, the broadcast media, have of mentioning Islamic immigration means that to listen to the debates on immigration (including those from UKIP), the impression given is that EU immigration is the whole picture. Then some official statistics temporarily interrupt this fantasy. In 2014 official figures from the Department for Education (DfE) showed that the number of pupils from ethnic minorities had massively increased in the past 10 years in England, while the population of indigenous white children had fallen dramatically. The number of ethnic minority pupils in primary and secondary schools rose by over 61% in the decade to January 2014, while the proportion of white British children fell by almost 12% in the same period.

If this trend continues white British pupils aged 5 to 18 will be in a minority in England in a mere 23 years. They are already outnumbered by other ethnic groups in many schools in London, Birmingham and Manchester as well as other inner cities. Thanks to Labour Party immigration policy, the decade from 2004 to 2014 has seen white English culture effectively removed from English inner cities in a way no English family ever voted for. The DfE's annual school census found that children of Asian origin (Muslims) were now the biggest ethnic minority group in English schools. This means that white British children will be a minority in English state schools by 2037, eclipsed by Asian-origin children. That this policy was a heinous act of treason on behalf of foreign nationals at the expense of an indigenous population surely cannot now be denied.

On November 27, 2014 the ONS released figures to show that while 228,000 EU citizens came to the UK in the year to June 2014, the number of people coming in from *outside* the EU rose to 272,000. More than a quarter of a million more Muslim immigrants have come to live in Britain in just this last year, and that figure will go on rising.

How many of these non-EU immigrants have skills, can speak English, will claim immediate welfare benefits, will qualify for a full state pension and crucially, will go on to become radicalised Islamic terrorists? The more immigration we allow from Islamic nations the more we risk reaching a critical mass of Islamic terrorism that the security services will be unable to contain. At that point all of our freedoms will be sacrificed to the needs of state security and for what? To guarantee the continued influx of a culture whose religion rejects everything the host culture offers? At the very least all our politicians should be implementing *now, a brake on migration from Islamic countries.* Before we look at why that course of action is an urgent necessity for our physical preservation we need also to look at why it is a necessity for our future economic continuation. The Muslim population of Britain topped 3.3 million by the end of 2013 to become around 5% of the overall population of 63 million, according to figures extrapolated from the 2011 census (This figure does not include those here illegally and some unofficial estimates have the Muslim population of Great Britain (2014) at closer to 10% of total population). In Britain's second city, Birmingham, there are more Islamic children than Christian children. In Tower Hamlets, London's old East End, 62% of children are Islamic.

To the last free man in Britain I will point out what should be carved in stone. The vast majority of Muslims living in Britain today are supported by welfare benefits and contribute nothing in taxes. In this inactivity they are no different from their co-religionists in Europe. As stated, leaked statistics from official government sources in Europe point to at least 40% of total welfare expenditure being directed to Muslim immigrants resident in Britain since 1997. If I am wrong then the DWP needs to clarify the exact figures without resort to the stock response that it does not collate statistics based on ethnicity or religious grouping. This is a financial crisis that is impacting on every aspect of British society and British taxpayers have the *right* to know where their money is going. During 13 years of Labour rule a huge race equality industry was put in place then expanded and filled out with consultants and advisers whose main purpose was to record every interaction with public services on the basis of ethnic status. You know, those boxes you have to tick every time you fill in a form at the council asking you about your race or ethnicity. So the data must be there, but not even a Freedom of Information (FOI) request can get it released. There is the most urgent need for fiscal clarity on this matter but you won't see *The Guardian* or *Newsnight* looking into it. What they will focus on is the £74.22bn (2011-12) paid out for the state pension while omitting that those British pensioners who get it have already paid for it, from their NI contributions after long years of work. That's work, rather than on the basis of "need", as do immigrant claimants, thanks to Gordon Brown's closing down sale welfare giveaway.

Since current statistics fail to clarify how many actually collect benefits and whether unemployment figures include those on disability or in jail, only crude estimates can be made but this one errs on the side of caution. Assuming that Muslims are consuming roughly 40% of welfare spending as they are in Denmark where the proportion of Muslims are 5% of the general population, as it is officially in Britain (2011 census), we can also assume that **unproductive Muslims are costing the British taxpayer at least £43.92 billion each year.** I say that this estimate errs on the side of caution because what that figure of £43.92 does *not* include are the other substantial costs of Muslim immigration; access to free NHS treatment, social housing, free state education, prison places etc and completely ignores illegal Muslim immigrants who also have access to state benefits.

Just one example of unrecorded expenditure is unproductive Muslim use of the NHS. As reported in the national press: "Muslims, both male and female, had the highest rates of reported ill health in 2001 when age-standardized rates of "not good" health were attributed to 13% of Muslim males and 16% of Muslim females. Muslims had the highest rates of claims for disability benefit with 24% of females and 21% of males claiming a disability in 2001, when there were at least 2 million less Muslims living in Britain than there are now. We know that the Muslim custom of first cousin marriage has placed a tremendous strain on other European health services. Other data does exist. An EU report published by a national newspaper found that more than 600,000 unemployed European Union migrants living in Britain were costing the NHS £1.5 billion annually." (18) If we use this figure to get a conservative estimate of unproductive Muslims and their cost to the NHS what would that figure be? A rough estimate would be upwards of £6 billion annually but the NHS does not keep these kinds of records anymore, because of political correct guidelines that forbid the collation of statistics based on race or religion. In 2013 the BBC reported on a long term study of 13,500 children, born at Bradford Royal Infirmary between March 2007 and December 2010. The Born in Bradford Study found that the number of babies born with congenital defects was twice the national average because of the prevalence of first cousin marriages. While British Pakistanis accounted for 3.4% of all births in Britain, they produced 30% of all British children with genetic disorders such as deafness, blindness and Mucolipidosis, which prevents the body from expelling waste. So how much is a lifetimes spoon feeding and dressing, attendance at special schools followed by lifelong palliative care going to cost for Pakistani Muslim children? £1billion, £5 billion, £10 billion? At what point is the question going to be asked? Will it be when all our NHS Trusts are bankrupt and all those over the age of 70 face the rationing of the healthcare they paid for with 50 years of tax contributions, as has been suggested. It's a medical fact that the closer the blood relative is when conception happens the bigger the risk that the child will be mentally or physically retarded or suffer from schizophrenic illness. Research shows that the risk of having an IQ of less than 70, the equivalent of being retarded, goes up by 400% for the offspring of cousin marriages. When do we ask about the cost to the NHS of the average Pakistani Muslim family of five? The answer is obvious, we must ban intermarriage among first cousins, but with the Left/activist lobby bellowing "racist" or "Islamophobe" at anyone who suggests this course of action how can common sense prevail?

Family and religion are the bedrocks of Muslim culture and by intermarrying Muslims insulate their family from their host nation and prevent its members from integrating. By not banning first cousin marriage not only is the NHS rapidly abolishing itself, it is also actively encouraging more Muslims with large families, who insist on continuing this cultural practice, to come to Britain in ever greater numbers. So, far from responding to the consequences of this disastrous practice the numbers of first cousin marriages in Britain are actually increasing with 75% of British Pakistanis in Bradford now married to their first cousins and almost 60% nationwide. We keep hearing that we should be grateful to the 26% of doctors and 40% of nurses from over 200 foreign nations who keep our NHS alive, but who is the NHS for anymore? We know that as immigration has increased so has the overall cost of the NHS, with consultants now being paid up to £3,000 per shift. The truth is that the NHS has been bloated out of all recognition to become an arm of overseas aid serving an international immigrant base, paid for by mostly English taxpayers.

Before the immigration door was wedged open in 1997 the NHS was mainly staffed by indigenous British doctors and nurses, trained in Britain at a total cost of less than £40 billion a year. In 2011 this figure had shot up to more than £106 billion a year and then to £110 billion in 2013. If we still had the same population as we did when the NHS was first launched in 1948, in today's terms the NHS would cost UK taxpayers £9 billion per year. The NHS is funded by the taxpayer, it is not a wealth creator. Since 2000 the Labour government have recruited 50,000 more doctors, 10,000 more GPs and 100,000 more nurses and midwives. Official NHS statistics showing the number of registered doctors in 2012 found that because of an NHS quota system some of the best students from Britain were being turned away from medical courses at home universities while the NHS was hiring more than a third of its doctors from 143 foreign nations. This included nearly 10,000 doctors from Pakistan, 4,000 from Nigeria, more than 3,000 from Egypt and thousands of others from countries as far flung as the Sudan, Libya, Liberia and Syria. How many of these new doctors had jihadist sympathies, how many had forged qualifications, how many of them had been trained to the standard of native English doctors? Nobody knows and we aren't allowed to ask.

They were needed in these numbers not for the existing British population pre-1997 but increasingly to service the needs of waves of new immigrants who are in turn being treated by a new army of immigrant doctors and nurses who *we didn't need before 1997*. As immigration from non-EU nations continues to accelerate the bill to the NHS continues to balloon out of sight, almost in tandem. We need only look at the huge sums now being spent on agency nurses by NHS Trusts. A report by the Royal College of Nursing (RCN) reported on BBC news showed that of 168 Trusts who responded by providing figures showing how much they were now spending, £327 million went on agency nurses in 2012-13 and that figure *rose* to £485 million the following year.

In 2014 Maidstone and Tunbridge Wells NHS Trust in Kent revealed it had paid *one nurse* £1,800 for *one single* 11-hour shift at its Accident and Emergency unit.

Based on figures for the first two quarters of 2014-15, the respondent trusts will spend *£714 million* on agency nurses - estimated to work out at £980 million (when including those Trusts who failed to respond). Therefore by the end of 2015 the NHS will face a bill for £1billion a year, just for agency nurses, a bill that will escalate as the number of foreigners who use the NHS, and don't pay for it, continues to escalate.

In an address at the Chartered Institute of Environmental Health conference in October, 2011 Professor Peter Davies, a consultant chest physician at the Liverpool Heart and Chest Hospital recommend that people from the Indian subcontinent and sub-Saharan Africa should be given a blood test when registering with a GP. Speaking about the test he said: "It's a no-brainer. If we screen for latent TB we would eliminate the majority of cases of people coming into this country. Now we've got the blood tests, for goodness' sake let's use them." His advice was ignored because of political correctness within the NHS. The Left leaning Institute of Public Policy Research declared that health tests on all immigrants would be "morally wrong". In 2014 Duncan Selbie, chief executive of Public Health England, said that tuberculosis was showing a dangerous resurgence, fuelled by immigration. He stated: "Tuberculosis has begun again to be a big problem for us as a nation. This time next year, and maybe sooner, we will generate more new cases of tuberculosis in England than the whole of the US." More than seven out of ten cases involve people born outside the UK and though normally treated by a six month course of antibiotics concerns have risen that antibiotics are now increasingly ineffective after being over prescribed. (19)

The main risk area is still London with 3,588 cases reported in 2011, accounting for 40% of the UK total. And nearly three quarters of those suffering from the disease were those not born in the UK. Certain high-risk groups such as those with HIV, those from Eastern bloc countries and Asia, and those living in crowded living conditions were found to be particularly susceptible to TB and senior health consultants have long advocated testing immigrants from these areas. The cost of treating immigrants with communicable diseases is subsumed within the general NHS budget because it would be "racist" to identify how much of the NHS budget is now being used up by foreigners. Meanwhile old people who have paid for their NHS treatment with a lifetime of National Insurance contributions are singled out by Labour policy wonks as "bed-blockers".

The arguments for internationalising the NHS trotted out by Labour, blaming an ageing population requiring more NHS resources are absurd: did they think that the 5.5 million immigrants who arrived here under their watch and their dependents were going to pack up and go back to Pakistan or Bangladesh or Somalia when they got old themselves? Would they be immune from needing the NHS or other welfare services? In 2012 more than 84% of births in the London borough of Newham were to at least one foreign born parent. More than 81.9% of babies born in Brent had foreign-born parents. Only 18% of Brent's residents now describe themselves as white British. This can be described in no other terms than the ethnic cleansing of the white working-class from large parts of London. Of the 63 wards in Brent, Labour now hold 56, and the leader of the council is Mohammad Butt. Remind me, when did we get a vote on all of this?

If the Left think immigration is a righteous punishment for Britain's colonial past just how far can they go with the punishment before Britain ceases to be anything other than a globalised transit camp for the world's dispossessed?

The author and columnist Douglas Murray worries that the influx of foreigners is nowhere near its end, commenting: "The Ottoman Turks ran one of the longest, largest and bloodiest empires in history. Ought we to treat modern Turkey as a country which deserves to be altered completely? Where should we encourage the waves of immigration to come from? Should the Turks also be expected to take this lying down? When, if ever, would a halt be called? Since all countries, peoples, religions and races have done something terrible in their time, and since most races and cultures are not punished in this way, is it wrong to see anti-Western racism as the motive behind all recent justifications? Motivations aside, this of course throws up the ultimate question which our politicians remain too paralysed to address: how much longer must all this go on? Are we approaching the end of this transformation? Is change at this pace the new norm? Or only the beginning? The census provided a wonderful opportunity to address this, and it was, like everything else in this supremely dishonest discussion, wretchedly missed. Perhaps one could put the pertinent question like this: is the fact that 'white Britons' are now a minority in their capital city a demonstration of 'diversity' as the man from the ONS said? If so, when does it cease to be so? There are London boroughs already lacking in 'diversity' because there aren't enough white people around to make them diverse. But what levels, after all's said and done, do the celebrants of diversity want to get to? What is their ideal target figure? Is a ceiling of 25 per cent white Britons in London — or the country at large — optimal? Or would it be 10 per cent? Or none at all? A final, and perhaps harder, question: how — given the concatenation of claims against them — might 'white Britons' ever acceptably argue, let alone complain, about such unspecified or unspecifiable odds? The answer remains for now that nobody can tell us, and nobody can address this. Here is [Will] Self again, speaking to wild applause from his *Question Time* studio audience: 'The people who line up on the opposition to the immigration line of the argument are usually racists [audience applause] . . . [with an] antipathy to people, particularly with black and brown skins.' We long ago reached the point where the only thing white Britons can do is to remain silent about the change in their country. Ignored for a generation, they are expected to get on, silently but happily, with abolishing themselves, accepting the knocks and respecting the loss of their country. 'Get over it. It's nothing new. You're terrible. You're nothing." (20)

Yet it's whitey who goes on paying for his/her own extinction. With the highest earning 1% of the population already contributing just under 30% of *all* annual tax receipts who will Labour's economic experts identify as ripe for an additional squeeze in 2030? You don't need to answer that, but my guess is that "the rich" will, by then, be long gone from Labour's septic isle. Current projections based on the foreign baby boom that has seen a quarter of all births to foreign mothers means the NHS will need £230 billion a year to keep it running by 2030, more than twice its current budget. Labour's team of crack economists may have also forgotten that the children of this massive new public sector workforce as well as the armies of migrant no-skilled no-English speaking unemployed will also need to go to school. Migrationwatch's analysis of ONS figures show that over the next decade Britain will need one million extra school places at a cost of £100billion. If we factor in just the current Muslim birth rate that means that roughly £1bn more per year (above and beyond the sums already being spent) is earmarked for the offspring of Muslim children (of parents who are 67% unemployed). So let's just add up the cost of unproductive Muslim benefits and try, temporarily, to sidestep the inevitable cries of Islamophobia or racism by disregarding NHS access and free education. It means that every British family paying taxes is currently having to fork out approximately £2,000 each year just to support new Muslim families on benefits in Britain, a figure about to go north thanks to the Muslim birth rate. If Joseph Heller had been alive today the absurdity of this situation would surely have inspired a novel greater then his masterpiece, *Catch-22*. To show just how inadequate are our official statistics and just how out out of touch our political managers of catastrophe are we need to look at what happens when a small dose of reality interferes with their world.

In February 2013, an NHS surgeon, Professor J. Meirion Thomas, blew the whistle on health tourism. At that time the Department of Health's official position was that health tourism was costing the country just £12 *million* annually, hardly worth bothering about comrade. Had Labour still been in power Merion Thomas's claim that *billions* not millions of pounds was being sucked out of the system by health tourism would have been ignored, with Thomas himself probably accused of racism. As it happened, Meirion Thomas *had* been under investigation by the doctors union, the GMC, for refusing to treat ineligible health tourists. However Jeremy Hunt, the new Health Secretary, wanted the facts and went and commissioned an independent report which found that non-British residents are each year scamming more than *£1.9 billion* of free treatment from the NHS. (21) Without any official figures about how much Muslim immigration is taking out of the system the Left and its useful friends in the BBC can feel comfortable talking about European immigration because European immigration is *not* the real problem.

Many European immigrants without dependent children are skilled, hard working, able to speak the English language and therefore able to make a contribution, but the BBC's willingness to only talk about EU immigration provides a convenient smokescreen for the one issue no-one will talk about or produce any statistics for, and that's non-EU immigration.

Those who have stepped in to fill this void are inevitably the Left's pro-immigration academics, funded by the EU. A report published in November 2013 by the Centre for Research and Analysis of Migration (CReAM) at University College London attempted to show that between 2001 and 2011 European immigrants made a contribution of £25 billion to the public purse while completely ignoring the question of non-EU (Muslim) immigration. The authors of the report found that since 1995: "The positive contribution is particularly evident for UK immigrants from the European Economic Area (EEA – the European Union plus three small neighbours): they contributed about 34% more in taxes than they received in benefits over the period." (22) The BBC lapped this up and made the report headline news trumpeting the assertion that yes, yes! migrants had made a net contribution to Britain's finances. Ignored was the fact that the report assumed migrants were not claiming any more means tested or housing benefits than the rest of the population. Why? We need to take a closer look at who wrote it.

In 2003, ahead of Poland and seven other ex-Eastern Bloc countries joining the EU, Professor Dustmann was one of the authors of the now notorious Labour Home Office study predicting that there would be between 5,000 and 13,000 migrants a year coming to the UK. In the end, more than one million arrived, one of the biggest blunders in the history of public policymaking. Professor Christian Dustman runs (CReAM) which is a pressure group for immigration. Dustman's co author, Dr Tommaso Frattini, has a PhD in economics from University College where he was taught by... Professor Christian Dustmann. Yet the coincidences don't end there. Charles Clarke, (NUS president in his student radical days) was Labour Home Secretary during Britain's most frenetic open door immigration period of 2004-6 and Clarke also just so happens to be visiting professor in Economics and Migration at... University College London, and a fellow at CReAM since 2012. As Home Secretary from 2004-06 Clarke had direct responsibility for Migration, including the February 2005 White Paper, *Controlling our Borders: Making Migration Work for Britain* which allowed huge numbers of unskilled and Third World migrants to flood, unchecked, into Britain. In 2013 Dustman organised *Migration: Global Development, New Frontiers*, a conference on migration where one of the speakers was the BBC home affairs editor Mark Easton who had previously been accused of bias by taking the side of the European Union over benefits paid to migrants. Two years later on BBC News at Ten Easton incomprehensively compared the Islamist hate preacher Anjem Choudary to Mahatma Gandhi and Nelson Mandela, stating: "History tells us that extreme views are sometimes needed to challenge very established values that people at the time hold so dear." Choudary wants democracy to be abolished in Britain and replaced by sharia law and Easton was roundly condemned, not only by Choudaray himself who later said that Ghandi was a "kuffar" but even by Labour's Keith Vaz. This is indicative of where the sympathies of many senior BBC reporters lie in respect of radical Islam and the urgent need for their opinions to be disconnected from taxpayer subsidy.

Summary: A pro-immigration Professor funded by the EU who has worked hand in glove with the Labour Party to promote the big lie about the benefits of mass immigration and whose organisation has among its ranks the Labour home secretary who opened the doors to mass immigration and lest we forget, the unwavering support of the BBC. So no in-depth look at the real costs of immigration from the BBC, ever, and you can see why. It took the independent think-tank MigrationWatch to point out that figures in a table at the back of the initial report showed that the net cost of non-EU migrants between 1995 and 2011, rather than the 2001 to 2011 period the authors focus on, actually left Britain £104 billion out of pocket.

Academics ignored by the BBC's headline news included Mervyn Stone, Emeritus Professor of Statistics at UCL, who had immediately cast doubt on the study's impartiality saying it was "obviously driven to make the case it claims to have made". Also buried in the small print of the report (page 41, should you wish to plough through it) was hard fiscal evidence ignored by the conclusions. There was statistical evidence that over the same period non-EU immigrants received public services and benefits worth £104 billion *more* than they paid in taxes. Their statistics showed that even when taking account of any tax contribution from the relatively small number of non-EU migrants who were paying into the system, that between 1995 and 2001 non-EU immigrants received £104 billion more in benefits and public services than they paid in taxes and that massive sum *didn't include* other big ticket benefits like health and education.

Bear in mind that this study was no right wing "racist" think-tank, it was funded by the EU using a staff of mostly immigrant researchers whose notional starting point was that immigration was good for Britain... but even they could not conceal the plain fact that non-EU immigrants were bankrupting Britain at a rate of knots and that the allocation of these massive sums of taxpayers' money had been deliberately hidden from the British public. On November 5, 2014 the UCL report was updated to reveal that non-EU Immigrants, those who came to live in Britain from outside Europe had *cost* the British taxpayer £118 billion over 17 years. The study also found that recent immigration from mostly Eastern Europe gave the economy a £4.4 billion boost over the same period. More pro-immigration glee, commented on by Ed West: "That figure of £118 billion is not entirely fair, of course, because the low labour participation of Bangladeshis and Pakistanis reflects the fact many of them are doing a job Brits don't do: having families. And the benefits of eastern European immigration will in the long term have to take into account that these mostly young migrants will get old and need their pensions paid, and will have children who will be a net drain on the economy (working households without children pay the exchequer twice what they receive back so it is of little surprise that Poles are a benefit). At that point if we want to continue to benefit financially we must continue to import more young workers, who in turn will grow old and have kids etc. I don't know about you but I can see one tiny, weenie little glitch with this economic model." (23) So, even the pro-immigration UCL report admits that non-EU immigrants coming mainly from Commonwealth countries like Pakistan, Somalia and Middle East nations like Iran, Iraq, Afghanistan and Syria took out £118 billion more than they contributed over 17 years, that's nearly £7 billion a year. Sorry to be pedantic about this but what we need to add to that figure is the additional costs incurred by this non-EU influx on housing, welfare, health care provision, extra school places, prison places, legal aid, in work and out-of-work benefits and translation services. If we were allowed to know this additional figure we would find the £7billion a year annual cost of non-EU immigration dwarfed by an additional sum of at least £25 billion per year. The figures from 1995 to 2011 covering Labour's open door immigration policies during which period Labour "sent out search parties" looking for immigrants (according to Labour's Lord Mandelson) found that migrants from outside the European Economic Area (EEA) made a *negative* contribution to the public purse of £117.9 billion. A different report, published in the *Economic Journal*, said that this non-EEA group, made up of immigration from countries such as India, Pakistan, Bangladesh and African Commonwealth countries, contributed less because they did not work and had larger families with more children. "Immigrants from non-EEA countries ... contribute less than they receive," the 50-page report concluded.

Commenting on the first UCL report, Sir Andrew Green, of MigrationWatch UK, said: "It is very interesting that this report finds that non-EU migrants since 1995 have made a negative contribution to the national budget, yet they have accounted for two thirds of foreign immigration over the past 15 years." Commenting on the second report he reaffirmed his concern over the cost of EU immigration, saying: "As for recent European migrants, even on the authors' own figures - which we dispute - their contribution to the Exchequer amounts to less than £1 a week per head of population." Again, because the report makes no mention of the additional costs to taxpayers of providing the new immigrants and children of new immigrants with a job subsidy in the form of child tax credits (more than £150 per child per week), access to state education, the NHS, social housing and the rest. This money, it is assumed, grows on trees or is conjured into existence by a good fairy hiding in a money tree.

In November 2014 official ONS statistics showed that in a single year to June 583,000 immigrants came to live in Britain, driven by immigration from outside of the EU.

A net increase over the whole year of 260,000. Almost in tandem with this bombshell, in December 2014, home office inspectors criticised the Home Office itself for dishing out British passports to any Tom, Dick or, most likely, Mohammad who asked for one, including murderers and rapists and those who used false documentation in order to acquire, what is in effect, a lifelong entitlement to welfare benefits worth hundreds of thousands of pounds. Wouldn't it have been more sensible to grant passports only to those with a proven link to Britain, a grandparent at least, or a close relative who had been a member of Britain's armed forces? That British citizenship should be so indiscriminately handed out is outrageous. Inspectors found that out of 235,000 applications for British passports in *one year (2013) alone*, the refusal rate was just three per cent! That's a three times *lower* refusal rate than when Labour was in power in 2007. More than *two million* British passports have been dished out in this way, like so much confetti, over the last 10 years.

The knowledge that this sort of unstoppable change was being delivered to our doors thanks to our Westminster elite has produced another significant change among those who pay more than their fair share of tax to finance welfare payments for foreigners with large families. Once again that night's news bulletins masked a significantly greater and more alarming trend than just huge increases in net immigration; they also ignored the start of a white flight out of Britain. The highly taxed, highly educated, highly successful British, (323,000 of them in 2014) were starting to get the hell out of the country! A country they suspected was doomed to become bankrupt in the very near future.

As Rod Liddle commented in *The Spectator*: "The gross figure of people coming to live here from abroad was 583,000; it is that yearly influx which is irrevocably changing the nature of the country. Because we have to be honest about this — the people who are leaving this country to work abroad and the people who come into this country to work, or not to work, are not quite the same people, are they? It is not a like-for-like swap, as the headlines sort of imply. For a start, those who are leaving tend to speak English as a first language, which is not true of the overwhelming majority of those who are coming in. And those leaving here tend to be higher paid, better skilled and better educated than the people who arrive." (24)

In 2008/09, UK gross income tax receipts were £152.5 billion and in that same year UK welfare benefits cost the taxpayer £150.1 billion, so in theory we had £2.4 billion left for everything else; defence, the justice system, the NHS, the roads and railways, Europe, old peoples' homes, winter fuel payments etc. Then in 2009/10 *calamity!* the Treasury took in only £140.5 billion in gross income tax receipts against social security benefit costs of £164.7 billion. For the first time in our history we had spent more on social security benefits than we collected in taxes. In his autumn statement of 2013 chancellor George Osborne admitted that welfare payments accounted for £120 billion of the £720 billion the Government spends each year. In 2009 an independent think-tank reported that: "An immigrant couple living on the minimum wage, who then retire on Pension Credit, will receive Housing Benefit and Council Tax Benefit throughout their working life and throughout their retirement. The total Housing Benefit they receive will be £291,000 plus a further £19,000 in Council Tax Benefit." (25)

Welfare spending, not the banks, will bankrupt Britain. What are we going to do with all these people who will never find work?

Globally, the talk is now about about improving productivity, with robotics replacing unskilled workers. Foxconn, one of China's biggest electronics manufacturers, recently announced plans to replace its human workforce with an army of more than one million robots. Yet our multicultural state will continue to pay the crippling cost of an unemployable foreign workforce until the country reaches a point of economic anarchy. The great fear is that as the immigrant population accelerates, not only are we unable to pay this huge welfare ransom but we also become unable to speak about it because corrupt and cowardly politicians, with interests vested in ever growing immigrant constituents, will fear losing votes.

The Left has never really understood or been interested in the struggle needed to create wealth, its only interest is in the control and redistribution of wealth and because only the state can do the redistributing so the state will grow under Labour in order to impose Labour's values on society. It was this basic equation Labour had to square to ensure the spread of Marxist/anti-racist pro-equality law throughout society. As the state sucks dry the productive sections of the economy only more borrowing and more taxation can supply the needs of the ever growing welfare state. What happens when the higher rate of income tax tops 75%, as it could well do at the end of another Labour administration?

It won't matter because the global market will regard Britain as the proverbial dead parrot and the politicians who led us to disaster will shrug their shoulders and head for the hills. Anyone seen Tony Blair in England lately? As Milton Friedman didn't say but surely would have: In an overpopulated, energy depleted world you can have freedom and prosperity or you can have multiculturalism and mass immigration, but you can't have both. If the Muslim population continues to grow at its current rate, by 2030 Britain will have a 40% Muslim population. At that point not only is there nowhere for the British economy to go but off a fiscal cliff, while a huge built-in Labour/Islamic majority will have effectively handed the country over to sharia law. In 2010 just paying the interest alone on our national debt cost the nation £42.9 billion, that's more than the entire defence budget and is predicted to rise to £58 billion by 2015.

If we add up all the money collected in tax from all the working people in Britain for one year it would not be enough to pay for what we now spend on the welfare state. To make up the shortfall Britain needs to borrow more than £100 billion each year, and has done for the last six years. That vast amount would be more than enough to pay the tuition fees of all British students who wanted to go to university and restore the maintenance grant; clear the national deficit, give free travel and subsidised heating for all pensioners, stop all library closures, double the state pension and allow old peoples' homes to stay open, finance new high speed rail investment as far as the north east of England and build a series of new nuclear power stations that would put Britain in the best possible position to meet the coming energy crisis. That is only part of the price we have paid for Islamic immigration.

With only slight growth in the economy we put back the day of reckoning to the day after the next election, but no further. . the doctrine of multiculturalism means that the people who paid for the welfare state in the first place, the white working-class, can only stand by and watch as their safety net is pulled from under their feet.

The ones who have most to fear from our PC overlords are those we should be most thankful to, the wartime generation whose hard work and sacrifice earned them every last penny of the state pension they draw. Yet it is this very group that cowardly politicians will target when the welfare spending crisis comes home to roost. The £79 billion the government pays out for pensioners is already being eyed up by Ed Balls, Labour's shadow chancellor, who has indicated that he would be prepared to cap the state pension if his party wins another general election.

Mr Balls was quoted warning that "the clear large bulk" of social security spending went to those over 60. It is this group, the wartime generation and the elderly, who are most despised by the British Left because of their traditional views on Christianity, the family, marriage, homosexuality and what used to be referred to as common decency. They are the last barrier to the full implementation of Labour's hard left ideology, the last link to that common sense, courageous, honest nation that will no longer exist in 2030.

If one were to believe in conspiracy theories then this would be the biggest since Roswell, but it's not. The deafening silence about the real cost of immigration is the sound of fear. Fear of Labour's race hate legislation that has now cowed every British institution; police, social workers, the education sector and the broadcast media.

It is mainly the fear of disclosing how much of the welfare cake is being consumed by non-productive Muslims in case there is a backlash from taxpayers. Fear of provoking the same Muslim rage that was stoked by the Danish and French cartoons.

What kind of a madhouse are we living in that the governing Coalition and the opposition parties are either so restricted by their own hate law legislation or so fearful of Britain's new Islamic nation within a nation that they will not produce accurate statistics telling us where this reservoir of borrowing is being directed? We don't need to look far to see that the disaster that is Islamic immigration is not just a British phenomenon, because the house of welfare is coming down all over Europe.

CHAPTER FOUR

AN INCONVENIENT CENSUS

...it is the duty of those who have accepted them [Allah's word and message] to strive unceasingly to convert or at least to subjugate those who have not. This obligation is without limit of time or space. It must continue until the whole world has either accepted the Islamic faith or submitted to the power of the Islamic state.
Professor Bernard Lewis, British-American scholar in Oriental studies

I remember the 1960s fairly well. I was born at the very beginning of 1961 when Churchill was still alive, JFK was the new president over the water and The Beatles were still in Hamburg. As a child rapidly accumulating the jigsaw pieces of memory I recall just how much fun it all was. I lived near the countryside and we played all day in the hay and the sunshine without much of a care. My family were from the working-class but even so there were no recessions and living standards rose every year, along with spending power. The great toys from that era of childhood innocence were a Beatles guitar; Avengers cane, James Bond Aston Martin dinky... all quintessentially English and quirky, signposting a new era of irreverence and fun after the privations of war. We went to the cinema with our parents and friends to see *The Sound of Music*, *Chitty Chitty Bang Bang* and Disney's *The Jungle Book* and sang the songs in the playground the next day. Our heroes were the cool understated working class, Sean Connery, Michael Caine, John Lennon. On TV we watched *Blue Peter* with John Noakes and *Crackerjack*, with Peter Glaze. Schoolboys still wore caps on *Top of the Form* and played cricket and football while the girls played netball and hockey. On TV during the school holidays there was *The Flashing Blade*, *The Banana Splits* and *The Avengers* and during term *Joe 90*, *Thunderbirds* and *Captain Scarlet*. The space race was as exciting as the music and as children we knew the names of all the Apollo astronauts and even the difference between a Lunar Module and a Lunar Excursion Module in just the same way as the wartime generation of kids knew the names of the aircraft fighting in The Battle of Britain.

Only this time the future was brighter and there was a definite warmish optimism knowing that exploration and science, jets and cars, music, fashion and sport were leading the way towards an ever improving future for a country that had saved the world from Hitler just a generation earlier, and just won the World Cup.

Then, an Englishman regarded it as his right to express any opinion he liked and that right was backed up by English common law, the gold standard of free societies across the globe. Our welfare state was paid for by the people who had worked for it, as were their old age pensions, earned mostly by backbreaking labour. Real sweat and blood shed in factories and shipyards and trenches and fields across two world wars that had cemented Britain as a bulwark of tradition in a world of chaos. At the heart of our stability was family life; not just mum and dad but grandparents and uncles who had been overseas and had returned home safe. We were then the nation that had remained an extended homogenous family, speaking the same language, with the same history and blood ties. None of this was challenged by either of the two main political parties who shared government and a broad consensus, until the Labour Party gained power in 1997. If we count up all of the immigrant groups who had ever reached our shores before 1997, including the Normans, Irish, Jamaicans and the myriad other nationalities who we welcomed and assimilated, they would never have amounted to more than one per cent of the total UK population at any given time, before 1997.

In 2011 the last ever census showed that 7.5million residents were now foreign-born, making up 13% of the UK population. That's one in eight, a huge increase, up from 4.6 million foreign born in 2001. However, just because our census has been prematurely retired it doesn't mean that other countries aren't still collating their own statistics. Move on to 2014 and figures released by Italy's national statistics service, Istat, show that immigrants now make up 8% of their country's total population. This is compared to Germany with 9%, France with 12% and now way out ahead in first place, the UK, with 15%.

Evidence that Britain's immigrant population is accelerating away at a ferocious rate. The census of 2011 recorded a total population of 63,182,000 which, according to Istat statistics, means that almost a million more immigrants have entered Britain in just three years.

The biggest headline from the census of 2011 was that London, for the first time in its 2000 year history, now had a minority white population. According to the census, the city of Leicester and towns like Luton and Slough had already become places where the majority of people were either foreign or ethnic minority members. Britain's second city, Birmingham, where already more children are Islamic than Christian, is certain to become the next English city with a majority of foreign or ethnic "minority" members by 2020. Britain's pro-immigration newspaper, *The Guardian*, remarked: "You don't have to be a senior wrangler to work out that if a population grows at 4% a year, it will double its size in about 17 years. Say that population currently is about 6% of a bigger whole. Other things being equal, it will form a majority of the bigger whole inside 60 years. Cue the headline: 'UK whites overtaken by ethnic minorities by 2060'." (26)

In 1961 there were less than 50,000 Muslims living in Britain, about 0.01% of the population and they attended just seven mosques nationwide. Now Muslims, officially, account for more than 5% of England's population and there are more than 1700 mosques nationwide as their number doubles every decade. To put this figure in context we need to know that there were just *one* million Muslims living in the whole of the USA in 2001 and within 10 years that had increased to 2.6 million, according to Pew statistics. Over roughly the same time scale (2001-2011) Britain, a tiny island off the coast of Europe, has seen its Muslim population increase to such an extent that it now has more Muslims living within its borders than in the *whole* of the United States of America. According to the Pew research team the Muslim population of Britain reached 3.4 million in 2014 to become around 5.3% of the overall population of 64 million.

There is a possibility that the number of Muslims now living in England is actually much higher than the 5.3% of the total population stated, because the 2011 census confirms that fully seven per cent of the population refused to reveal their religious belief. Many commentators speculated that the census of 2021 would see the Muslim population of Britain rise to well over 10%. That was before the news that the census was to be cancelled and that the survey of 2011 was to be the last.

In 2013 there was a new analysis of the 2011 census results by Professor David Coleman of Oxford University, an expert in demography, for the Migration Observatory think-tank. In it, Professor Coleman confirmed the prediction he made in 2011, that at current rates of migration white British people will be a minority of the population by 2066. An analysis of his study shows that between 2004 and 2008, the Muslim population of the UK grew at an annual rate of 6.7%. Based on the current Muslim birth-rate this means that the Muslim population of Britain will rise to over 15% by 2030 and by 2050 would exceed 50% of the total British population. At that stage Britain officially becomes an Islamic nation, and there is no majority Muslim nation in the world not governed by sharia law.

A survey of 60 Islamic countries in 2012 showed seven where death by public beheading is the punishment for either blasphemy or apostasy (renouncing belief in Islam or switching belief to another religion). By 2013 a more comprehensive study showed six more nations joining the beheaders club which now boasted: Afghanistan, Iran, Malaysia, Maldives, Mauritania, Nigeria, Pakistan, Qatar, Saudi Arabia, Somalia, Sudan, United Arab Emirates and Yemen. All of them Islamic societies, all governed by sharia law. And just to reiterate, Qatar will be hosting the 2022 FIFA World Cup. Could Britain be a member of the beheaders club in 2066? Don't bet against it given current Muslim birth rates. As Professor Coleman gloomily predicts: "The moment that the white British become a minority will symbolize a huge transfer of power. It will underline a changed national identity - cultural, political, economic and religious."

This was spelled out by Nonie Darwish, a former Muslim, born in Egypt. She is a human rights activist and the author of *Cruel and Usual Punishment: The Terrifying Global Implications of Islamic Law*. Darwish helpfully supplies us with sharia's top 10 (actually 34 but I've cut it down slightly) laws. These are not laws from the pages of some brutal, medieval, now reformed past but laws fully functioning across the Islamic world today. Laws ready to be applied to any democracy willing to submit to the demands of sharia law. Darwish spells out the application of sharia law as follows:

1. Jihad, defined as "to war against non-Muslims to establish the religion," is the duty of every Muslim and Muslim head of state (Caliph). Muslim Caliphs who refuse jihad are in violation of Sharia and unfit to rule.

2. Apostasy, a Muslim who leaves Islam must be killed immediately.

3. A Muslim will not get the death penalty if he kills a non-Muslim, but will get it for killing a Muslim.

4. Sharia dictates death by stoning, beheading, amputation of limbs, flogging even for crimes of sin such as adultery.

5. Non-Muslims are not equal to Muslims under the law. They must comply with Islamic law if they are to remain safe. They are forbidden to marry Muslim women, publicly display wine or pork, recite their scriptures or openly celebrate their religious holidays or funerals. They are forbidden from building new churches or building them higher than mosques. They may not enter a mosque without permission. A non-Muslim is no longer protected if he leads a Muslim away from Islam.

6. Non-Muslims cannot curse a Muslim, say anything derogatory about Allah, the Prophet, or Islam, or expose the weak points of Muslims. But Muslims can curse non-Muslims.

7. It is obligatory for a Muslim to lie. If the purpose is for the sake of abiding with Islam's commandments, such as jihad, a Muslim is obliged to lie (taqiyya) and should not have any feelings of guilt or shame associated with this kind of lying.

8. Banks must be sharia compliant and interest is not allowed.

9. Homosexuality is punishable by death.

10. There is no age limit for marriage of girls. The marriage contract can take place anytime after birth and can be consummated at age 8 or 9. (27)

Just to emphasise that these are not laws from the ancient past but laws being implemented in the here and now. In January 2013, a London newspaper published a photograph released by the Iranian news agency. It showed a man about to have his hand chopped off by a crude looking circular saw after being found guilty of theft and adultery by a sharia court in the city of Shirwaz. Two hooded men, looking like grim reapers, hold the man's hand in a vice while the grisly machinery does its work before a baying crowd of onlookers. After the deed is done the man's bloody stump is held up before the jeering crowd, before being dipped in iodine. All in accordance with sharia law, the law of the land in Iran. (28)

Today, in Iran, Article 1041 of the Civil Code of the Islamic Republic of Iran states that girls can be engaged before the age of nine, and married at nine: "Marriage before puberty (nine full lunar years for girls) is prohibited. Marriage contracted before reaching puberty with the permission of the guardian is valid provided that the interests of the ward are duly observed. This is what is happening in Iran now, this is Islamic law in action in the 21st century.

This is what is happening in Iraq now. In 2013, just 10 years after thousands of allied troops died deposing their dictator Saddam Hussein, Iraq's Justice Ministry introduced a new draft measure to their Cabinet. Under the proposed measure, known as the Jaafari Personal Status Law, girls as young as eight would be allowed to marry and a related law would allow a man to have sex with his wife without her consent, commonly known as rape in civilised societies. The bill would also prevent women from leaving the marital home without their husband's permission and make it easier for men to have multiple wives. Under current Iraqi law the legal age for marriage is 15 with a guardian's approval but there is no *minimum* age for marriage although there are rules regarding *divorce* for girls aged eight. The Jaafari Law was approved in February 2014 and now needs only to be ratified in the Iraqi parliament. Despite opposition from human rights campaigners the new law is believed to be a priority for Prime Minister Nouri al-Maliki, whose own Government statistics show that in 2011 more than a quarter of marriages in Iraq involved someone under the age of 18, a ten per cent *increase* since 1997.

If the demographers are correct and Britain becomes a Muslim majority nation in 2050 do we really think that this kind of law won't become the new norm? If we don't then we're kidding ourselves, but by then who will be able to stand up and say that this is not the kind of "diversity culture" that belongs in a civilised nation?: Labour's Harriet Harman MP and her husband Jack Dromey MP or perhaps Labour's Patricia Hewitt MP? What the war in Iraq taught us, if nothing else, was that what Muslims want and what we think they want are two entirely different things. All the evidence shows that what they don't want is democracy and what they do want is sharia law.

Today, in Britain, the *establishment* of sharia law is proceeding at a rapidly accelerating pace, in our schools, in our courts, on our streets and in our shops and supermarkets. What is being sold to us by our politically correct elites is not only multiculturalism but a seemingly unstoppable eradication of Britain's traditional values.

Although Muslims may fight among themselves, when push comes to shove the dividing line will be between Muslims and the infidel (non-Muslims). Of course, Britain's traditional laws, tolerance and culture will cease to exist long before the Muslim population reaches 50%. With Muslims at 20% of the total population Britain will cease to be recognisable as we used to know it, a free society, and that will happen around 2030 when the Muslim birth-rate eclipses that of the non-Muslim birth-rate.

The killer of Lee Rigby was a British-born convert and that conversion made him a member of the Ummah, the worldwide community of believers in Islam. When surveys show an overwhelming majority of Muslims saying they are proud to be British what they are really saying is that they are proud to be British *Muslims*, a totally different thing altogether. The greater allegiance to the Ummah, the worldwide community of Muslims, is unquestioned.

In 1940 *Time* magazine ran a front page cover about *The Legacy of Britain*, a valedictory end of an era story about the demise of a civilisation that had changed the world for the better. Their ambassador, Joseph Kennedy, had already told his government that Britain was finished and would soon be overrun by the Nazi's. In 2030 will *Time* be running a similar cover? It might, because instead of encouraging Muslim immigrants to integrate and become part of society, the Labour governments of Blair/Brown allowed them to gather into segregated parallel societies run according to sharia law. The absence of contact with and assimilation of Britain's traditional values gave radical Islam free reign to flourish as a welfare subsidised mob of Muslim clerics, allowed unfettered entry into Britain, were then allowed to preach the literal texts of jihad in British mosques.

The radical Islamists we see gathering strength in Britain today or "extremists", (so called by Obama, Cameron, Clegg and Hollande), learned jihad during Friday prayers, dictated to them by Labour's immigrant imams preaching from British mosques, supplemented with more hate from the social media during the rest of the week.

Being on the dole gives unemployed Muslims the ideal start to their careers as jihadists. What they learn in the mosques then on the internet is also reinforced should they manage to get to university where jihad is preached openly by officially invited speakers. Mohammed Emwazi, now known to the world as "Jihadi John" is an extreme example, but an example nevertheless, that there are no "root causes" other than those being broadcast from the pulpits of Britain's mosques, for the radicalisation of Muslim youth. No matter how generous, how welcoming, how forgiving we are of this particular culture, there is nothing we can do to change it fundamentally. We must separate from it or be consumed by it, as reported by the national press: "The mother of Mohammed Emwazi knew instantly he was Jihadi John when he first appeared in front of the cameras in the murder of American journalist James Foley after recognising his voice, Kuwaiti investigators have been told. Ghania Emwazi screamed 'that's my son' as she viewed last August's footage of the knife-wielding executioner making a speech in English while standing behind Mr Foley moments before beheading him. But she did not tell the authorities." (29) Emwazi went on to hack off at least five more heads on IS videos (with more to come?). Islamist groups like CAGE, funded by the deceived British taxpayer or by gullible charities will say the violence is all because Muslims are victims of racism or Islamophobia while the Left blame inequality, lack of opportunity or the security services. Let's look at Emwazi, for a moment. How badly treated was he and his family by the British state?

Emwazi's father Jasem, 51, with his wife Ghaneya and family including Mohammed, 6, fled to Britain from Kuwait in 1994, claimed asylum and were immediately given British passports by Tony Blair's Labour government in 2001. Since their arrival neither of the Emwazi parents have ever worked, yet they were still able to settle into a plush Little Venice apartment in London before resettling into an even plusher £1million terraced home in Westminster, with the £1,950-a-month rent paid by Westminster City Council. Despite claiming welfare benefits Emwazi senior made the landlord a £300,000 cash offer for the house, which was declined, so the whole family upped sticks again to a £600,000 apartment near Lord's Cricket Ground, in North London, then to a £1.4million apartment in Maida Vale, finally settling in a £600,000 flat in upmarket Queen's Park, their last address before their son's unmasking as a psychotic serial killer. Mr Emwazi claimed £23,400 each year in housing benefit, £678 in council tax support and £5,929 jobseeker's allowance before he skipped off back to Kuwait, but the rest of the family continues to receive state benefits for their London home in Queens Park.

Other family members being "victimised" by the British state included the Emwazi's 12-year-old daughter, Hana, for whom the Emwazi's are still claiming £7,821 a year in child benefits and child tax credits and daughter Shayma, 23, who is studying at Brunel University London, and entitled to free upfront tuition and a grant of £3,387 each year. Mohammed Emwazi's younger brother Omar Emwazi, 21, voiced support for the radical

Islamic cleric who inspired one of Lee Rigby's killers on his Facebook profile, then deleted it just after his brother was identified as "Jihadi John". His inspiration is Sheikh Khalid Yasin Yasin, a notorious preacher named by Woolwich terrorist Michael Adebowale as *his* inspiration for converting to Islam and once featured in a famously "unbiased" BBC documentary *The Most Dangerous Man in Europe*, which portrayed the Dutch politician Geert Wilders as a threat to peace in Europe and guilty of hate speech (along with the courageous feminist Ayan Hirsi Ali) while Sheikh Khalid Yasin was presented by the BBC as a moderate, describing him as "an American Muslim teacher...on a mission to de-radicalise them (young Muslims)".

Mohammed Emwazi himself was part of an "Islamic mafia" while at school and a regular attender of the Regents Park mosque in London. He also benefitted from free up front tuition, at University of Westminster.

So, refuge for a whole family in the land of free speech, rule of law and freedom of religion, free accommodation in an expensive part of London and generous welfare handouts for the whole family as well as free access to higher education. All from the British state, all without being asked to contribute a penny and what is the net benefit for Britain? At least one psychotic killer, supporters of a psychotic preacher and parents who refuse to turn in their psychotic offspring to prevent the further butchery of innocents. A family that is fundamentally opposed to the society and culture that took them in. If such generosity produces this level of animosity then is it not about time we looked closer at this "culture" we naively assume is compatible with ours?

Another victory for New Labour's cultural diversity is a university system now riddled with the cancer of Islamic fundamentalism on every campus. Islamic youth, with little interest in anything other than Jihad, can join any number of proliferating "degrees" in Cultural Studies, Islamic Studies or Middle East studies which are barely disguised courses in Islamist ideology. These courses are priced the same as subjects like Engineering or Technology or Science degrees, so does anyone ever ask why the taxpayer should be subsidising their own cultural extinction? Why not double the course fees for Jihad B.A and half them for Science B.Sc? How many foreign imams are supported by the halal supper circuit of university hate preaching?

Jihadi John's alma mater, the University of Westminster, was forced to cancel a speaking engagement the day after his identity had been revealed. The preacher scheduled was Haitham al-Haddad, a senior judge at the Islamic Sharia Council in east London. This is one of his recorded pearls of wisdom: "I will tell you the truth about the fight between us and Jews who are the enemies of God and the descendants of apes and pigs."

All of the above mentioned courses have a common (Marxist) ideological thread that blames the West in general for all the problems of the Middle East and the Third World and white males in particular for every colonial and imperial crime ever committed while the dark-skinned innocent victims of this imperialism are idealized and encouraged to revolutionary violence. The foundation of this claptrap is the work of literary critic Edward Said whose discredited study *Orientalism,* described as a work of "malignant charlatanry" by one critic, has established the paradigm in British and American universities that allows white scholars to be labelled "racist" and "imperialist".

Said's postcolonial diversity bible has become the go-to theory for interpreting almost any subject as a tool of "white imperial racists" and the stranglehold that Said's dogma now has over university liberal arts and humanities departments (especially History and English) means that each generation of teachers heading for our state schools come out of higher education and teacher training more radicalised than the last, eager to impart their "Western crimes and white imperialist guilt" agenda on successive generations of schoolchildren.

We have now entered into what is the next stage of the Islamic transformation of Britain where the majority indigenous population is forced to obey sharia law by the multiculturalist state. This is now happening everywhere in our towns and cities. When our speech is rigorously policed for signs of "Islamophobia" because of race hate legislation, where our children have no choice other than to eat halal food in our state schools, where our legal system is crippled by the craven fear of offending medieval values that demand Muslim defendants be concealed under a burka. All of this is just a prelude to the final transaction that will occur as the Muslim population of Britain steadily grows to become a majority soon after 2030.

It seems that what now marks out Islam in Britain is not its claim to be a religion of peace but rather its readiness to threaten violence against those who are deemed to have insulted it…and to get away with threatening violence without coming into contact with the law of the land. The guiding motivation is the desire for sharia law, the religious law of Islam, to be the law of the land in Britain.

After the Danish cartoon cave-in and the media's craven response to the Charlie Hebdo killings and the lack of any meaningful response from the Muslim community to the IS beheadings and the burning alive of a Jordanian pilot, Islamists in Britain realise that under the guise of multiculturalism they can get away with just about anything on their way to transforming secular Britain into Islamic Britain. At every staging post it has been the Left/Labour that have opened the door, allowing Islam to gain another foothold in its aim of sharia law for Britain and our eventual submission to Islamic totalitarianism.

From Magna Carta in 1215 there was gradual progress towards equality under the law, and this was achieved, in almost perfect balance, just before 1998. Then the clock started to move backwards when New Labour brought in their aggravated crimes act, imposing much heavier sentences for assaulting a member of a specified minority than for the assault of the ordinary man or woman on the street.

It was section 82 of the Crime and Disorder Act 1998 that first allowed massively increased sentences for crimes "aggravated" by a racial motive. In 2001 religion was added to race in the category of aggravated offences that specifically favoured Muslims. The new guidelines laid down up to a 70% "enhancement" of a sentence where a racial motive was involved. Judges were to determine the normal sentence first then up it, so a five-year sentence could be increased to seven years and a six months conviction could be boosted to two years. It didn't take long for the New Labour thought police to follow the law.

A national newspaper reported that: "a village primary school with just 13 pupils was put into special measures after an Ofsted inspection found too many incidents of 'racist or homophobic bullying and serious acts of violence'. But the chairman of governors at Ravenstonedale Endowed School in rural Cumbria has fought back, claiming the report was based on a single incident of one child using the word 'gay' as a throwaway comment and not knowing what it meant. Liz Morgan said it had been 'blown out of proportion' and also denied there had been any racism at the remote school, where all of the children are white. She said she believed Ofsted had an agenda against small schools and suspected they'd been unfairly labelled racist because racism and homophobia were treated as one category by Ofsted. Parents of pupils said the report was 'ludicrous'. Ravenstonedale Endowed School, near Kirkby Stephen, was labelled 'inadequate' – the lowest rating out of four grades. Ofsted Inspectors visited the school in April, where pupils range from ages five to 11 and travel in from nearby hamlets and farms. Their report condemned the behaviour of pupils and highlighted 'too many incidents of racist or homophobic bullying', and 'serious instances of violence'.

Staff were warned they urgently needed to improve pupils' behaviour as parents had already pulled out 12 children, out of just 25, in a six-week period this year. Ofsted claimed this was because parents were 'concerned' about behaviour. However the chairman of governors insisted that pupils had been taken out of the school mainly because of parents being anxious about the need for them to engage with larger numbers of children. She said: 'Parents have taken children out for a variety of reasons – racism and homophobic bullying have never been a reason. As the school is getting below a certain size, parents have been worried about the social side of education they think their children need.' She said she believed Ofsted's criticisms had been based on a single report in the school's own discipline record about children using the word 'gay'. She said the school did not tolerate it and spoke to the child and their parents – and had since challenged the report with Ofsted but received no response. Helen Buckler, 43, who has three children at the school, said: 'It is all absolute rubbish and upsettingly inaccurate. It is totally ludicrous. I've never heard of any racism, homophobia or serious violence. There aren't even any ethnic minorities at the school – every kid is white.' A statement from the school said: 'We were particularly upset by the allegations of racist and homophobic bullying as we do not believe there have been any such incidents in the school.' Ofsted stood by its report, insisting that both racist and homophobic comments had been made by pupils." (30)

For the record, almost every other episode of The Simpsons cartoon series, the most popular animated series in history and shown daily on both Channel Four and Sky One, features the use of the word "gay" in some sort of comedic context. There is unlikely to be a school age child in the British Isles who has not watched an episode of this series or not heard the word "gay" in this context. This is true for other many pre-watershed cartoons from America. If logic were to be applied this show should be banned from the airwaves in Britain before Ofsted are allowed to stigmatise innocent children too young to know its meaning, as received from their TV sets. Should Labour return to power the criminalisation of language will proceed apace. Tristram Hunt, Labour's shadow education secretary, has publically stated that children will be expelled from school if they call each other "gay" and that Labour would enforce "zero tolerance" of homophobic bullying in "every classroom, dinner hall and playground". All teachers would be trained to deal with bullying and "age-appropriate sex", relationship education would be made compulsory in all schools beginning when pupils are aged five.

"The use of homophobic language and other forms of homophobic bullying is damaging the life chances of so many young people," said Mr Hunt, on a visit to Little Ilford School in London. Will Labour be as keen to tackle the homophobia routinely taught in the nation's mosques? Or will it be the white working class who are held up to their new crucible of PC tyranny? How long after this measure will children be labelled and expelled for "Islamophobia" "transgendaphobia" or any criticism of mass immigration?

In October 2006 Codie Stott, a 14-year-old schoolgirl from Salford, England, was arrested for racism and spent three-and-a-half hours in police custody because she had refused to study with a group of five Asian pupils who did not speak English. When the Asians began talking in Urdu, Codie went to speak to the teacher. "I said 'I'm not being funny, but can I change groups because I can't understand them?' But the teacher started shouting and screaming, saying 'It's racist, you're going to get done by the police'."

A complaint was made to the police and Codie was placed under arrest. She was not prosecuted as she was too young, but the experience was traumatic. Jamie Bauld from Cumbernauld, Scotland, is an 18-year-boy with Down's syndrome and the mental age of a five-year-old. In September 2007 he was charged with "racial assault" after he had pushed an Asian girl on the playground. On the road to where we are now these are just a few of the transformational changes that have led to the Islamisation of Britain by degrees, reported in the press.

Example A

A CHURCH of England school where 75% of pupils are Muslim is conducting its assemblies without Christian hymns and has allocated separate prayer rooms to boys and girls. "The secondary school, which does not take account of church attendance in its admission criteria, treats the Bible on a similar footing to other religious texts in its communal worship. This weekend Paul McAteer, headmaster of Slough and Eton Church of England Business and Enterprise College, said Anglican schools still have a purpose even when the majority of their pupils are Muslim. Christian families are such a rarity in some inner-city communities that in a number of Church of England schools every pupil is a Muslim." The article also mentioned that, in accordance with sharia law, the school had allocated separate prayer rooms for boys and girls. (31) This is submission to sharia law and of course there should be no separate prayer rooms for Muslims in any of our schools, airports, civic buildings or workplaces if we are to survive as a Christian nation.

Example B

Another national daily newspaper reported on November 22, 2013 that parents had complained about Lynn Small, the headmistress of Littleton Green Community School, in Huntington, Staffordshire. The complaint was that she had tried to blackmail their pupils into attending an Islamic workshop. The following letter had been sent by her school to parents warning them of the consequences of non-attendance on a school trip they were expected to pay £5/head for:

Dear Parent/Carer,

As part of the National Religious Education Curriculum together with the multicultural community in which we live, it is a statutory requirement for Primary School aged children to experience and learn about different cultures. The workshop is at Staffordshire University and will give your child the opportunity to explore other religions. Children will be looking at religious artefacts similar to those that would be on display in a museum. they will not be partaking in any religious practices.

Refusal to allow your child to attend this trip will result in a Racial Discrimination note being attached to your child's education record, which will remain on this file throughout their school career. As such our expectations are that all children in years 4 and 6 attend school on Wednesday 27th November to take part in this trip. All absences on this day will be investigated for their credibility and will only be sanctioned with a GP sick note. If you would like to discuss this further please contact our RE Coordinator, Mrs Edmonds.

The threat is explicit; take part in an Islamic workshop or be labelled as racist and have your future prospects destroyed by the attachment of a 'racial discrimination note' to your child's file. The paper later reported that: "Mother Gillian Claridge, 55, said: 'How dare they threaten to brand the children racist at such a young age? It's going to make them feel like little criminals. 'The very nature of religion is all about choice - on this occasion they were not being given any choice at all. It was draconian move and it has left a lot of parents fuming.' Mother-of-four Tracy Ward said: 'I was shocked by the letter. To be told my kids have got to attend this workshop is disgusting. Everyone should have a choice, but that's my opinion and I don't want a stain on my kids' record as a result. They are not old enough to be called racist.' Her sister Donna, whose daughter also attends the school, said: 'It's not our religion. We should have a right to stop our children going.' (32)

Example C

"A DEFENDANT was allowed to enter a plea in court while wearing a burka. The 21-year-old defendant had previously been told by Judge Peter Murphy that her case could not go ahead with her face covered. The woman – who cannot be named for legal reasons – was allowed to enter a plea with only her eyes visible behind a face covering known as a niqab. She was allowed to confirm her identity by lifting her veil in front of a female police officer in a side room of Blackfriars Crown Court in London. Judge Murphy feared an imposter could take her place or a jury might not be able to decide her innocence or guilt with her features shrouded. But he reluctantly gave his permission, so the court could "move on". Last night Philip Hollobone, Tory MP for Kettering, said: "The public would be staggered that anybody should be allowed to appear in court with their face covered." Mr Hollobone, who is trying to ban face coverings in public, added: "For justice to be seen to be done, you have to be able to see who a person is."

The defendant, an East London woman *accused* of intimidating a witness in a different case, was ordered last month to remove the veil. When she refused, Judge Murphy adjourned the case for three weeks." (33) This meant that the defendant, a Muslim woman *on trial* for the intimidation of a witness had the privilege of being shielded from the public and the media. Only the judge, jury and trial lawyers would be able to see her face. One could ask… what of the age-old concept of everyone being equal before the law? It's the basis of English common law and the 1000-year-old bedrock of all our freedoms as well as being the legal gold standard, the model of justice. Again and again we see Islam; mono-cultural and implacably opposed to Western cultural norms being appeased by our judges, police and politicians.

The burka isn't even required to be worn under Islamic law! Again, this woman was the *accused*, so why did her status as a Muslim mean she could be given special treatment? Why? Because a craven legal establishment, in its desire to appease Islamic totalitarian practices, are willing to give away our only real protection, the law. "We'll do anything you like, just don't hurt us" is the ethos that allows Islamists to gain absolute victory over our liberal institutions without even the pretence of a fight being offered. How many *Islamic* states allow the wearing of the burqa or the niqab by the way, or go as far as our appeasing judges in caving in to the demands of those who would destroy us?

Malaysia: Malaysia does not, where Islam is followed by 61.3% of the population. Head scarves are permitted in government institutions but public servants are forbidden from wearing either the burqa or the niqab. A judgment from the then-Supreme Court of Malaysia cites that the niqab, or purdah, "has nothing to do with (a woman's) constitutional right to profess and practise her Muslim religion" because Islam does not make it obligatory to cover the face.

Tunisia: Tunisia does not and Islam is the religion of 98% of the population, with the majority being Sunnis. In 1981 Tunisia banned women from wearing Islamic dress, including headscarves, in schools and offices of the state (courts). The ban was largely ignored until 2006 when the government cracked down on those wearing the hijab in an attempt to deter extremism.

Turkey: In Turkey 98% of the population is Muslim, restrictions on wearing the headscarf in state institutions have been in place for decades but as Turkey is rapidly morphing into a full Islamist entity under its president Erdogan Turkish women are now encouraged to wear the hijab (the headscarf covering the head and hair, but not the face) for civil service jobs.

Morocco: Morocco does not and 98% of the population is Muslim (mostly Sunni). In Morocco the hijab is seen as a sign of political Islam or against the secular government.

Reminder: And so it goes... another of the bedrocks of Western civilisation chipped away by our craven judges in order to accommodate anti-equality sharia law. That's the same law that kills those who leave Islam, chops off hands and feet, stones adulterers, insists that women who have been raped have four independent male witnesses, allows barely post-pubescent girls to marry old men…and regards free speech and democracy as man-made law and therefore not permissible under Islam.

Example D

"A DINNER lady has been sacked from multi-faith Moseley School in Birmingham, for unintentionally serving non-halal meat. All 1,400 students at Moseley school are served halal meat, regardless of their religion. (*tough luck if you're a Christian then*) It has not been specified what type of meat was served, but the person responsible for serving the food was dismissed following a disciplinary hearing last Monday. Parents were informed of the mistake this month, and reacted with outrage, forcing headteacher Carl Jansen to apologise for the 'unintentional error'. However, Muslim parents are demanding others be held accountable for the mistake, which they call 'an insult to our faith'.

'The school have failed the children,' one parent said yesterday. 'How did this meal get into the school system to be fed to the children? It's just shocking that dietary requirements haven't been met. It is a disgrace that this could be allowed to happen and we demand more action is taken,' a father of a sixth form student said yesterday. 'It could not just be the error of one lady, there must be people at the top responsible too who also need to be sacked. It is an insult to our faith.' (34)

What makes this craven attitude displayed by our school system even more ludicrous is the fact that the Koran specifically says that Muslims are allowed to eat non-halal food if none other is available. As with the veil in court scenario our institutions must prostrate themselves to appease sharia law. The council apologised, the headmaster apologised, the poor dinner lady was sacked but that wasn't enough for the Muslim parents who wanted more sackings, more retribution. The non-Muslim (Christian) children who were being fed halal meat as a matter of course had no option but to shut up and eat up. As the Muslim population increases so will the demands for sharia compliance, life lived according to the norms of 7th century desert nomads.

Public service announcement

At the heart of our passive acceptance is ignorance of what is really going on under our noses. Has there ever been a BBC documentary critical of the halal meat industry in the UK? The gist of it is that halal meat is food prepared according to sharia law as described by the Muslim's holy book the Koran. A live animal has its throat cut without being stunned then dies slowly as it bleeds out. As the animal is killed the Muslim slaughterer faces Mecca and chants the Bismallah, which means "Bless this food Allah". Laws of Western countries require that animals are stunned to an unconscious state before being slaughtered, but allow exceptions for Muslim ritual slaughter. Government advisory bodies, like the Farm Animal Welfare Council and the British Veterinary Association in the UK, have produced reports and made declarations saying that ritual slaughter causes terrible suffering to the animals and have demanded that the practice be banned. British Sikhs have an anti-halal petition because they consider the utterance of Allah's name at the moment of slaughter as idolatry. These demands are ignored. By ignoring we condone and this is what we are condoning.

The Halal Food Authority (HFA) estimates that more than 25% of the entire UK meat market now consists entirely of halal meat. By default nearly all halal meat must be certificated by the HFA. All of our supermarket chains: Morrisons, Tesco, Asda, Sainsbury's etc submit themselves to endorsement by the HFA, despite Muslims numbers being officially 4.8% of the UK population.

This also means that there is five times more halal meat in the UK than there are Muslims to eat it. Where does the rest of this huge residual amount of halal meat go? It goes to feed the rest of us…the non-Muslim infidel majority and we have no say in the matter because there is no legal requirement to properly label meat as halal in any supermarket or store.

All over Britain our schools, hospitals, restaurants and pubs are blindly participating in this food certification scam. At one end is taxpayer funded support of Islamic food practices in our schools and hospitals sanctioned by local councils and the NHS and at the other end thousands of small fast-food retailers are being 'persuaded' to pay an illegal tax on their food with demands and threats. Fast food chains are rapidly falling into line with Muslim demands for halal meat. The sandwich chain Subway is reported to have removed ham and bacon and replaced them with turkey in 200 of its outlets in order to placate Muslim customers. Subway explained its decision on its website saying it had to

balance animal welfare concerns with 'the views of religious communities'. (35)
So this is multiculturalism in action. From where I sit it appears that the only culture being catered for here is that of Islam and sharia law. This is what happens now in multicultural Britain as a matter of course, if Islamic law comes into conflict with traditional non-Muslim culture and practice then it is the non-Muslim who must give way. And behind that is fear, the fear of Muslim violence and the threats of Islamists who know that all they have to do is wait and let the liberal left do its work for them.
To rub this point home just a week after the Subway report it was revealed by another national newspaper that Pizza Express is serving up ritually-slaughtered halal chicken in every chicken dish on its menu but customers weren't allowed to know because it was not stated on its menus that the meat had been slaughtered in accordance with sharia law. (36) Again, what about those who might object to eating halal chicken? Couldn't Pizza Express have offered Muslims the option of halal chicken in certain dishes rather than serving up halal meant in *every* dish on the menu?
This is the kind of alternate reality the novels of Phil K Dick would struggle to describe and yet in Britain it goes on apace. As the burka and the niqab become the face of the English high street in tandem goes the spread of Islam's gastronomic fifth column.

Example E

"THREE-QUARTERS of schools under Waltham Forest Council control serve only Halal meat, The Guardian can reveal. A total of 46 schools and academies supported by the local authority order only Halal meat from Waltham Forest Catering, their supplier. Just one school serves both Halal and non-Halal meat and 15 serve meat from animals slaughtered using 'standard' methods. The news comes after a row erupted at Larkswood Primary School in New Road, Chingford, last month when parents were informed meat served there would be replaced by food prepared according to the rituals of Islam from mid-April. Parents said they had no issue with Muslim children practicing their faith and eating Halal meat but did not want these religious beliefs imposed on their own sons and daughters. A council spokesman said: "All meat provided to local schools is certified by the Halal Food Authority. HFA certified meat is from animals that are stunned prior to slaughter." (37) With halal, the ship has only just begun to sail and as it gathers pace we will experience the rapid Islamization of a nation in tandem with the rapid increase of

Muslims as a percentage of the population as a whole.

Halal meat is not labelled because our sharia-compliant local authorities and national politicians are afraid of how indigenous British people will react when they see up close and for the first time just how far the Islamization of Britain has advanced under their noses. How they have been forced to live by sharia law without their consent and bow and surrender to Islamic supremacism without being able to utter a word of protest.

It's not only meat that Halal products include, there's a long and expanding list of goods containing the slaughterhouse by-products of ritually slaughtered meat like gelatin and collagen, which are ingredients in various foodstuffs ranging from cosmetics, toiletries and pharmaceuticals to cat food and chocolate.

Allied Bakeries, the makers of four of our biggest brands of bread (Kingsmill, Sunblest, Allinson and Burgen) have now submitted to regular auditing by the HFA with regular payments now made to the HFA. There's more than a whiff of *The Sopranos* in all this and no doubt Allied were "persuaded" of the benefits of paying zakat to a new and growing Muslim market. As a result all ingredients used by Allied Bakeries at its Walthamstow plant will now have to meet the HFA halal standard even extending down to cleaning products, which must also be halal and not contain alcohol.

Most of the halal certification agencies springing up are registered religious charities claiming non-profit making status and thereby able to take advantage of UK tax and VAT exemptions. Why are we allowing this? Allied Bakeries is one part of a huge conglomeration, one of three divisions of Allied Milling and Baking, part of Associated British Foods (ABF) plc. ABF has an annual turnover in excess of £11.1bn employing more than 102,000 people in 46 different countries. They also supply the bread to our schools, which is halal. The HFA also licenses the giant food conglomerate Tate and Lyle as well as KFC chicken restaurants. They are raking in astronomical payments from large and growing areas of British industry without having to pay any tax, so we must surely be aware of where all this money goes…aren't we?

The principle of "zakat" in Islamic law makes it obligatory for all Muslims to give 2.5% of their income to charity – but only in aid of their Muslim co-religionists, of course. Zakat has to be distributed among eight categories of recipients, *one of which is the jihadists fighting for the cause of sharia law at home and abroad*. The "charities" that dish out this zakat should have their charitable tax-free status removed. France, much further down the line than Britain in terms of its Muslim population, has more than 60% of its halal food under the control of organizations belonging to the Muslim Brotherhood, the organisation dedicated to making sharia law the law of every nation on earth, whether we like it or not.

Example F

PAUL GRIFFITH, a 75-year-old retired hair salon owner was stopped at Stansted airport on his way to Malaga and asked to take his shoes off after setting off the security scanner. "I'm not Muslim, am I," he joked, then boarded his plane. Unknown to him a Muslim security guard employed by the airport had reported him for the use of "racist" language and he was arrested the moment his plane touched back down in the UK after his holiday in Spain. He found himself charged with causing "racially or religiously aggravated harassment, alarm or distress".

He was photographed, had his finger prints and a DNA swab taken and told to report to Colchester police station. There he was told he had been charged with an offence under the Crime and Disorder Act but could accept a caution instead. Mr Griffith recalls: "I refused to do that - I had done nothing wrong and I wasn't going to admit to a criminal charge if I wasn't guilty of any crime." Months later he appeared at Chelmsford Magistrates' Court where he pleaded not guilty to the offence, but 24 hours before appearing at Crown Court the Crown Prosecution Service dropped the charge due to lack of evidence. The retired hairdressing salon owner, from Colchester, Essex, yesterday criticised the police for their heavy-handedness. Deputy Chief Crown Prosecutor for CPS East of England, Frank Ferguson said: 'Following receipt of the evidential file a full review of the evidence took place'. (38)

Example G

"JOHN LEWIS is offering the hijab in its school uniform department for the first time. The headdress is to be sold in the company's stores in London and Liverpool after it signed contracts with two schools – one which was set up to educate Muslim girls and a second that welcomes pupils from all religious communities. There has been controversy over whether it is right for girls attending state schools to wear religious dress rather than the standard uniform. But the fact that a mainstream retailer is starting to stock the hijab alongside blazers and blouses is likely to be welcomed as a breakthrough by Muslim parents who have so far had to rely on specialist shops.

Last year, former Lib Dem Home Office minister, Jeremy Browne, triggered controversy by calling for a debate on whether women should be banned from wearing the veil in public places such as schools. He suggested Muslim girls were being pressurized into wearing the religious dress, saying: 'We should be very cautious about imposing religious conformity on a society which has always valued freedom of expression.' His comments were rejected by Mohammed Shafiq of the Ramadhan Foundation who said he was 'disgusted' by them, adding: 'Whatever one's religion they should be free to practise it according to their own choices.'" (39)

Example H

"One of Britain's biggest hotel chains has removed Bibles from its rooms to avoid upsetting non-Christians. The decision by Travelodge has been condemned as 'tragic and bizarre' by the Church of England, which says Bibles in hotel rooms are important to provide hope, comfort and inspiration to travellers. But the chain, which runs 500 hotels, said the country was becoming increasingly multicultural and it had taken the action for 'diversity reasons'. It said the policy was implemented 'in order not to discriminate against any religion' – despite having had no complaints from guests. Bibles were taken away at the same time as a refurbishment of its rooms, removing drawers where they were kept. The Bibles, which were provided free by the Gideon Society, have been retained and are stored behind reception for guests to borrow on request, the company says. A Church of England spokesman said: 'It seems both tragic and bizarre that hotels would remove the word of God for the sake of ergonomic design, economic incentive or a spurious definition of the word 'diversity'.'The practice of placing Bibles in British hotel rooms originated with the Commercial Travellers' Christian Association late in the Victorian era." (40)

ELLIOT

ON FEBRUARY 20, 2012 *The Yorkshire Post* reported that seven-year-old Elliott Dearlove had asked a five-year-old boy at Griffin Primary School in Hull if he was "brown because he was from Africa". The younger boy's mother complained to the school which launched an investigation then phoned Elliott's mother, Hayley White, telling her that her son had been at the centre of a "racist incident". She was summoned to the school by her son's teacher where she was read the school's zero-tolerance policy on racism and asked to sign a form saying her son had made a racist remark. Miss White, an NHS healthcare worker, refused to sign saying: "Elliott does not even know the meaning of the word racist." Since the incident she has attempted to move Elliot to a different school, without success. Not just for the sake of Elliot Dearlove but for the sake of all our children, there is now an urgent need to repeal all of Labour's race hate legislation.

Voting with their feet

We need to be sure just what we are talking about when we refer to sharia law. The first thing is to be crystal clear that in sharia law there is no separation of religion and state, no recognition of man-made laws. The very idea of man-made law; democracy, freedom of the press, free speech, equality under the law, is entirely at odds with sharia law. While it is true that not every Muslim majority state implements full sharia law it is the case that in every majority Muslim nation; Iran, Iraq, Afghanistan, Saudi Arabia, Yemen, Qatar (host of, incredibly, the 2022 World Cup), UAE, Gaza (slightly modified in order to keep huge amounts of EU aid flowing in) sharia is the law of the land, where floggings, religious courts and marrying off barely pubescent girls is regarded as the norm.

The reluctance of Islamic communities to assimilate in Britain is the start of a trend that will eventually see our cities abandoned as white flight gathers pace…firstly to the countryside but then where? Between 2002 and 2012, according to the Office for National Statistics, more than 600,000 white Britons left London.

The latest census data shows the breakdown in telling detail: some London boroughs have lost a quarter of their white, British residents. The number in Redbridge, north London, for example, has fallen by 40,844 (to 96,253) in this period, while the total population has risen by more than 40,335 to 278,970. It isn't only London boroughs. The market town of Wokingham in Berkshire has lost nearly 5% of its white British population. Areas in London like Newham have seen the white population fall from 58% in 1991 to 41% in 2001. If the government not only won't stand up to the Islamization of its towns and cities but actively conspires with the process in the name of multiculturalism then is it any wonder the indigenous population are voting with their feet. The only trouble is that Britain is a very small island and before very long there will be nowhere left to go. Even the BBC and the Labour Party will find that such deception cannot fool the masses forever. How much longer can feminists continue to twist themselves in knots defending the indefensible; female genital mutilation, wife-beating, honour-killing and polygamy? Gender separation of public meetings? What the Left are doing for Islam is a mirror image of what the Left did in their defence of Stalin's purge trials and terror famines, how much longer can this doublethink continue?

Look at any 7th century map of the world and you will see that there are no Islamic nations anywhere in the Middle East, which was then ruled by the largely Christian Byzantine empire. All of the Islamic nations that exist today have gained power by force. Nowhere on earth has Islam been willingly adopted by its native population, but once conquered by Islam there is no return (with the notable exception of Spain) from that particular abyss. As recently as 1918 Jews made up a third of the inhabitants of Baghdad, now there is not a single Jewish family left. It's 2014, and two days after IS captured the Iraq city of Mosul the whole of the surrounding area was under sharia law. That's how fast it happens, accompanied by mass murder and crucifixion of those not deemed sufficiently Islamic. In the 21st Century, a four hour flight from London.

The speed of the transition to sharia law was noted by *The Washington Post*: "Now, as a de-facto government, they (ISIS) have released a document aimed at civilians in Nineveh, a province in the country's northeast that contains the major city Mosul. Branded a 'Contract of the City,' the document contains 16 notes for residents. There is a mass exodus of Christians from the Iraqi city of Mosul, the second largest city in Iraq. The Muslim fanatics who have taken over the city, calling themselves the Islamic State, issued an ultimatum to the city's Christians earlier this month, saying that if they didn't leave by Saturday, July 19, 2014 they 'must convert to Islam, pay a fine, or face 'death by the sword.'" As of Tuesday, most of the city's estimated 3,000 Christians had fled. Further, the Islamic State, formerly known as ISIS, had marked homes and businesses owned by Christians with a red, painted ن (pronounced "noon"), the 14th letter of the Arabic alphabet and the equivalent to the Roman letter N. The ن stands for Nasara or Nazarenes, a pejorative Arabic word for Christians. Mosul has played a role in Christian history since the first and second centuries, when the Assyrians in the city converted to Christianity. It is the home to many churches, as well as mosques and synagogues. Al

Jazeera described, via an Assyrian Christian who chose to stay behind, how a statue of the Virgin Mary outside of one of Mosul's churches was destroyed and replaced with a black flag. All Muslims will be treated well, unless they are allied with oppressors or help criminals. Money taken from the government is now public. Whoever steals or loots faces amputations. Anyone who threatens or blackmails will face severe punishment (This section also quotes a verse from the Quran that says that criminals may be killed or crucified). All Muslims are encouraged to perform their prayers with the group. Drugs, alcohol, and cigarettes are banned. Rival political or armed groups are not tolerated. Police and military officers can repent, but anyone who insists upon apostasy faces death. Sharia law is implemented. Graves and shrines are not allowed, and will be destroyed. All women are told that stability is at home and they should not go outside unless necessary. They should be covered, in full Islamic dress. (41)

It's time to get real. What should we do about IS? If we had a president or prime minister or political leaders who had the guts to stand up and be counted on to do the right thing in the face of this barbarity their first move would be to recognize Iraqi Kurdistan as an independent country and make it a UN member state and a member of NATO.

Then move to expel Turkey from NATO membership as it is an ally of the Muslim Brotherhood. When Transparency International ranks Somalia as the most corrupt regime on earth why does Britain's foreign aid budget give them £110million (in 2014 and 2015) while the Somalian government is simultaneously arming Al Qaeda-backed terrorists? Why does another £24million go to Sudan, Nigeria and Libya? These are countries where Christians are being systematically wiped out by jihadi savagry. How about linking this blood money to the safety of Coptic Christians and their children being persecuted for blasphemy in Egypt and the preservation of their right to worship in Christian churches? Why are our own clergy not demanding this course of action from their pulpits instead of mouthing multicultural platitudes while their fellow Christians are being wiped out?

"Stay quiet and you'll be OK" said Mohammad Atta, the leader of the 9/11 plot, to the terrified passengers on the Boeing 767 about to crash into the North Tower. He lied, and they all died but that's the message coming in loud and clear from our politicians and broadcast media, just shut up and you might not die, as incrementally our freedoms are sacrificed in the vain hope of appeasing an implacable enemy.

CHAPTER FIVE

ONE SCHOOL OF THOUGHT

Nazi theory indeed specifically denies that such a thing as 'the truth' exists. ... The implied objective of this line of thought is a nightmare world in which the Leader, or some ruling clique, controls not only the future but the past. If the Leader says of such and such an event, "It never happened"—well, it never happened. If he says that two and two are five—well, two and two are five. This prospect frightens me much more than bombs.

George Orwell, Looking Back on the Spanish War (1943)

It started off with cultural Marxism, or Political Correctness as it is now known. It started off with jokes that can no longer be told and it led to self-censorship. It started off with press censorship and ended up with thought crime. Who would ever have thought it? There was once a time when comedies that employed the use of national stereotypes were hugely popular. *Love Thy Neighbour*, now condemned as "racist" and "unbroadcastable" by the Left once drew massive audiences amongst all races in the 1970s and paradoxically, is currently a bestseller on DVD in Nigeria and the Caribbean. Despite the fact that his upwardly mobile character Bill Reynolds was habitually referred to as "nignog" in the series and that he referred to the bigot played by Jack Smethurst as "honkey" Rudolph Walker insists the joke was always on the bigot: "These days, we can't take the piss out of each other and laugh," says Walker. "The whole climate in this country has changed. We have become very politically correct." Walker affirms from the evidence of his personal experience that when approached by older black people in Britain they often ask: "Why can't they bring it back?" The actor says: "Obviously, we know they can't bring it back in this climate. The classic example is that in black countries such as the West Indies and Nigeria, they play the series and people still kill themselves with laughter when they see it." (42)

Other classic comedies like Fawlty Towers have been the subject of censorship because of the use of the use of the words "nigger" or "wop". These shows were popular because they were funny; the laughter came because the use of stereotypes contained small elements of a truth that rang a bell with the experience of their audience. Because audiences laughed did it mean that the Third Reich was on the way back?

Not unless they could find a way of cloning Hitler and recreating Europe of the 1930s you would have thought, but that wasn't the way the intolerant Left saw it. Once jokes about the Irish were common among the general population and appeared on mainstream TV programmes like Spike Milligan's *Q* series or *The Dave Allen Show*. This morphed into it only being acceptable to tell these jokes against yourself, so you had to be Irish or Jewish or black. Thus Chris Rock, who is black, can do his: "it's not the blacks I'm scared of it's the niggers" shtick to a mixed race audience. Yet BBC's *Top Gear* presenter Jeremy Clarkson is threatened with imprisonment under race hate legislation for *almost* saying the 'N-word' during a show that was never broadcast. That segues into a *Celebrity Big Brother* contestant being thrown off the show for saying "negro" which, at a dizzying pace has now also become "racist".

A school headmistress with over 40 years experience felt the full force of Labour's hate crimes law after referring to a child as having "special needs" when a parent-governor said the pupil concerned would find the term "offensive". Janet Felkin was then subjected to a six-month Sussex police inquiry ably assisted by Brighton and Hove City Council and the Department for Education before it was found that there was no evidence of any disability hate crime. One might immediately ask what Sussex police were doing investigating what was said at a private meeting of school governors?

Why were police called to St George's Bickley CE Primary School, in Bromley, south London to interview nine-year-old Kyron Bradley, reported by teachers for using a ruler as a sword in a playground pretend game of Knights and Dragons?

The answer is that under Labour's truly Orwellian 2003 Criminal Justice Act, the definition of a "hate crime" became: "Any incident . . . which is perceived by the victim or any other person as being motivated by prejudice or hate." So whether an actual crime has been committed or not is irrelevant, what matters is that someone claims to have been offended.

It was the Ayatollah Khomeini who famously said "there are no jokes in Islam" and now there are no jokes on British television. The PC view that these programmes perpetuate stereotypes that could recreate the conditions, in the minds of the malleable unwashed, that could bring about a return of slavery or a new Holocaust should they be broadcast, didn't come out of thin air. At this point one might ask, is there anyone out there willing to stand up for free speech? We either have free speech or we do not. Using the 'N-word' is uncalled for in this day and age but in certain contexts; with reference to historical figures of the past, to literature or to discussions where words are not inciting violence in the context of their use, shouldn't the principle of free speech be paramount?

Those who don't like it are equally free to point out the error of any bigot's way and explain why such language is unacceptable in the modern era, but that's all. In using such a word on TV Clarkson would have revealed himself as a bigot and been forced to explain or apologise, but once what we can say to each other becomes ever more narrowly proscribed are we not a heartbeat away from The Inquisition, Stalin's gulags or the Islamic mutaween?

It's all about the law, a very powerful tool of the state. After race hate legislation was introduced in Britain humour got deadly serious when the politically correct could now insist that those who had laughed at such humour were now collectively racist. That was the insinuation of BBC stalwart Paul Merton when referring to the classic comedy *Til Death Us Do Part*, which Merton claimed would now be "unbroadcastable" in a BBC programme celebrating *Comedy Playhouse*. The undiscovered irony being that before the PC Left strangled comedy forever *Comedy Playhouse* had produced a long list of hits including *Steptoe and Son*, *Til Death Us Do Part*, *Are You Being Served*? as well as *It Ain't Half Hot Mum*, which will never again be shown on the BBC due to a ruling (was it from Greg Dyke?) that poking fun at different cultures, religions and sexual orientations is now beyond the pale in multicultural Britain. This despite the show's co-writer Jimmy Perry claiming it was the funniest show he ever created and: "the show I'm not allowed to talk about."

BBC comedy is now a contradiction in terms, doomed to fail because political correctness and real comedy are mutually exclusive. The cultural Marxists who now commission BBC comedy are in denial that any humorous quirks of nationalities or ethnicities can ever or ever did exist. The Marxist vision of all being equal or classless and the blunt instrument that will beat us all into correct thinking is the new fear of "racism", race hate law, equalities legislation and of course, fear of Islam. There is not enough space in this book to catalogue the BBC's failed attempts to produce a funny PC sitcom over the last 15 years and their excruciatingly dull efforts have all been comprehensively rejected by their captive audience. No one was surprised when beeboid Chris Sussman, the BBC's Executive Editor for Comedy, said that all jokes have to go through several layers of BBC bureaucracy before they can be broadcast on air in order to pre-empt any possibility of offence. What a joke, you might say, but then of course, you would be wrong.

"We have editorial policy advisers, we have legal advisers. I've been involved in a programme where it's gone all the way up to the Director-General," said Sussman. And so, just like Stalin had Trotsky retrospectively airbrushed out of portraits painted of the 1917 revolution so the PC zealots have begun the task of censoring what we *used* to laugh at, cutting lines from Fawlty Towers or Irish "racism" from Spike Milligan, making retrospective cuts in classic films like *Zulu* or Oscar-winning *Tom and Jerry* cartoons and now gleefully censoring offence even in historical contexts. Thus Guy Gibson's dog "nigger" was cut out of a dozen shots when *The Dam Busters* was shown one Saturday afternoon in order not to offend a hitherto non-offended audience. Of those Dam Buster cuts (on ITV), Index on Censorship commented: "Taking it out is unnecessary and ridiculous. It is a 50s film and it should be kept in context. The dog is also a very important part of the film, as its name is used as a codeword for one of the bombing runs". Ian McBride, the po-faced ITV executive responsible for broadcasting the film said that the company wanted to avoid offending its viewers, of course.

Following 9/11 there is one group no one will risk offending, and that's Islam. This fear is the ultimate hypocrisy of those who claim to support our freedoms and has quickly smothered almost every aspect of screen drama, as media commentator Nick Cohen noted: "One of the strangest features of mass culture over the past decade has been the near-total break between what thriller writers write and what spies do. Since 9/11, the fight against radical Islam has consumed the time of intelligence services and anti-terrorist police forces. Yet it barely features in spy fiction. The standard plot device remains the enemy within. The Bourne films were the most successful thrillers of the

2000s, and deservedly so. But it was not al-Qaeda but corrupt and unscrupulous officers in the CIA, whom Bourne had to fight. In the recent Bond films, 007 is also up against a cabal of western conspirators rather than a plausible foe. As soon as you see a government minister, or intelligence or police chief in television drama, meanwhile, you need only set your watch and count the minutes until the hero exposes him as the cancer at the heart of society. I watched the BBC's spy drama *Spooks* for no other reason than to marvel at how its hack writers avoided the Islamist in the room. In 2005, when real Islamists were bombing London, *Spooks* had environmentalists trying to destroy the capital. In 2006, it looked as if the BBC was facing the world as it was when it showed an Islamist cell planning an atrocity. The attempt at realism could not last. In the final twist, the Islamists turned out to be the tools of Mossad. According to the BBC, terrorism was a Jewish conspiracy, as white far right and Islamists groups had said after the bombing of the World Trade Centre." (43)

Celebrities like George Clooney will parade their faux-60s liberal consciousnesses alongside their Je Suis Charlie badges at awards ceremonies but how many of them would help get a film made about the dangers of radical Islam or show support at the Oscars for murdered filmmakers like Theo Van Gough or Finn Norgaard?

Author and blogger Mark Steyn summed this up perfectly: "Muslim lobby groups throughout the West are now using the pieties of political correctness to enforce a universal submission to Islam's self-evaluation. And their multiculti enablers seem happy to string along: Australian publishers decline novels on certain, ah, sensitive subjects; British editors insist forthcoming books are vacuumed of anything likely to attract the eye of wealthy Saudis who happen to have a flat in Mayfair. These are the books we will never read, the plays we will never see, the movies that will never be made... The lamps are going out all over the world - one distributor, one publisher, one silenced novelist, one cartoonist in hiding, one sued radio host, one murdered film director at a time. But it's more total than that. The Islamic enforcers will lead to a world where nothing is possible but dishonest art, which by definition cannot be art at all. And even the shallowest multiplex piffle will be lying to us: A few years ago, director Roland Emmerich made *2012*, a hit disaster movie in which human civilisation was suddenly destroyed by earthquakes and super volcanoes. As is mandatory for such films, the destruction of world landmarks was depicted. Many of the enormous monuments erected in the name of religion featured in the destruction. This was, according to the director, a reflection of his opposition to 'organised religion'. And so the statue of Christ the Redeemer in Rio de Janeiro was shown to roll down Mt Corcovado. The Sistine Chapel collapsed on to a group of red-hatted cardinals at prayer. St Peter's Basilica crumbled with the pope in its balcony and the falling masonry crushing thousands of the gathered faithful below. Notably, however, no Islamic holy site was destroyed on screen. In an interview, Emmerich said that he wanted to show the destruction of the Grand Mosque in Mecca, but was talked out of it because of potential reprisals. Pace George Clooney, no one will require you to "walk in fear", not yet. But you'll walk in non-fear to the movie theatre, and buy the Halal-compliant non-bacon butty and once in a while it'll occur to you that more and more areas in life don't seem even to be mentioned in public anymore. And then you'll sit back and enjoy latest the big-budget evasion." (44)

After the allies won the war against Nazi Germany there was an urgent initiative to rid German and Austrian society of the entrenched remains of Hitler's Nazi ideology. It was carried out by removing those who held National Socialist beliefs from their positions of power in the press, judiciary, culture and politics and by disbanding or banning the organizations associated with Nazism.

However, after the Cold War and the defeat of Communism no such effort was made to root out the sympathisers of an ideology reponsible for the mass murder of more than 20 million people. In Britain and America Marxist economists, historians and race theorists colonised schools, universities, trade unions, the press, politics and culture. Those who had stood for individual freedom, libertarianism and meritocracy became increasingly marginalised by those who now banged the drum again for the old totalitarianism. Their foes were those who "supported" capitalism; Christianity, the traditional family, science and the white men and women of the despised West.

Those the Left first target are the children in state schools, who must be brainwashed into "correct thinking". This return of "correct thinking" for schoolchildren reached its zenith under the New Labour stewardship of Tony Blair. Such was the politicisation of all aspects of public life under the cosh of Tony Blair and Harriet Harman that local education authorities were asked to monitor the opinions of three-year-old children for signs of racism. Labour's thought police were quick to target mostly white children in state schools as the reporting of racist incidents became recommended practice. Once initiated, Labour's totalitarian apparatus remained in place and operates to this day, as reported in a national daily newspaper: "Children as young as three are being branded racists, homophobes and bigots over playground taunts. Thousands of pupils are being reported for so-called hate crimes after using innocuous words such as 'Chinese boy', 'Somalian' or 'gay'. Teachers also log insults like 'doughnut' and 'fat bucket of KFC'. Even calling a pupil a 'girl' can be classified as abuse. Schools file the incidents for local education authorities. The details are also passed to Ofsted inspectors who are required to assess how teachers deal with bullying. Records of a child's 'prejudice-related' behaviour can be passed to their next school, potentially casting a shadow over their secondary education. Alleged offences by more than 4,000 pupils were logged in just 13 council areas – meaning the national total may stretch into the tens of thousands.

Civil liberties campaigners warned the practice this could have serious consequences for any children labelled as bigots: "These children have been tried and convicted in the court of political correctness and thought control without the aid of any defence or right to reply by a Left leaning teaching profession that sees no wrong in labelling the innocent as bigots without a hearing. In the same article it was revealed that: "Josie Appleton, of the Manifesto Club, a civil liberties group, said: 'Particularly worrying is the expansion of incident recording and reporting to ever-greater categories of prejudice, which seem limited only by the strange imagination of education officials. One primary school pupil calling another a girl suddenly becomes a sign of gender image prejudice, subjected to recording requirements more thorough than accompanying most burglaries. A reality check is urgently required.' (45)

Envy has always been the cannon of Marxism and its newest ammo became the accusation of racism. The West never got suckered into the madness and barbarity of post revolutionary Russian communism because it had the solid foundations of the Enlightenment to fall back on. A tradition of liberty, freedom, reason and democracy combined with the moral authority of Christianity and a homogenous population protected it from that prolonged bloodbath.

For the Marxists a non-revolutionary way to overthrow the West was now needed and the way to achieve this was through the use of hate crime and hate speech laws. In Leon Trotsky's *History of the Russian Revolution* (published in 1930), is the first documented use of the word "racist". Trotsky was, in one sense, much more lethal than his mass murderer boss Joe Stalin in that he managed to come up with a concept even more potent than the gulags… the criminalization of thought or motive.

For Trotsky hate crime and hate speech laws would be directed at one particular section of the population; traditionalists in the church, family, school, police, social work and universities. Trotsky's big idea was the introduction of laws that outlawed "inequality". In a denial that inequality can exist at all the law would be used to ban alleged discrimination against certain groups like homosexuals, the free press or institutions dominated by traditional "white" values. Any future Labour government will make it a legal duty to force public bodies to help reduce "inequality" caused by class as part of grander plans to improve social mobility.

The same sort of law pushed through in the dying days of the last Labour government known as "Harman's law" in the Equality Act 2010 was championed by the deputy Labour leader, Harriet Harman. This law was scrapped after the 2010 election but Labour plans to bring back their "Socialism in one clause" when they regain office. The similarities of Labour's plans to Trotsky's big ideas are striking.

Trotsky's initial targets were the Russian Slavic people, or "Slavophiles" as Trotsky called them; they were historically the section of the population who most valued their traditional families, their native culture and their way of life. Trotsky saw them as an obstacle blocking his internationalist plans for world domination. For Trotsky, Slavophiles had committed the crime of trying to protect a non-revolutionary way of life and were therefore "racists". The holocaust and the grotesque experience of Nazism and the Second World War managed to overshadow the origin of Trotsky's plot. Well-meaning liberals who used the word "racist" to identify those bigoted against certain racial groups and as a protector of racial minorities had fallen for the biggest lie of them all, from the co-creator of the biggest state murder machine in history.

The initial work of Trotsky was refined into a blunt instrument by Antonio Gramsci, a founding member of the Communist Party of Italy in 1921. Imprisoned in 1926 by Mussolini's Fascist government he spent the next eight years writing his *Prison*

Notebooks and becoming the most influential Marxist theorist of the twentieth century. Because Marxists are notable for getting *everything wrong* this was a disaster for the West. Gramsci believed that what the West knew as freedom and democracy must be destroyed because freedom was intrinsically linked to the even more despised capitalist system. Freedom and democracy, for Gramsci, was the fragile product of centuries of cultural, religious, and political poison.

Ignored was the fact that many brave men and women, from Martin Luther to the Suffragettes to the D-Day army had fought and died for this freedom. Gramsci wanted a "long march through the culture" to make the West susceptible to another glorious revolution like the one that took place in Russia in 1917. This meant the destruction of all traditional values, as outlined by Trotsky. Gramsci's long march must suffocate every western institution, tradition, and value; church, traditional education in schools, history, the media, the arts, government departments, finance, science and industry.

Everything of traditional value was to be undermined and changed. The traditional family unit, the traditional roles of men and women, the influence of Christianity in public life and "normal" sexual behaviour were to be replaced by the disaffected, the radical, the misfits; people of non-traditional sexual orientations, radically feminist women and, as the foot soldiers of this future revolution, culturally disaffected Muslims. The weapon that would lead all of their bourgeoisie enemies running for cover would be the accusation of "racism". And who would ever have believed that this little word could do more to enslave the free world than the 1917 revolution ever did. This "racist" end sum is now being played out across our now not so free world with the attempt to now attach "Islamophobia" to that proscribed category of offense.

America, once a beacon of small government and meritocracy, has been transformed by race double standards that are almost a requirement under the Obama administration. While at Harvard Law School Barack Obama defended law professor Derrick Bell, the creator of critical race theory and called opponents of affirmative action "racists". After graduation he taught courses about America's "Institutional Racism" at the University of Chicago Law School. As president, oath-sworn to defend the American Constitution, Obama has *attacked* the Constitution as "an outmoded, obsolete document written by white men". First Lady Michelle Obama clearly regards America as a racist, sexist, homophobic nation. She was a senior member of Third World Centre, a radical anti-racist group while studying at Princeton and despite poor test scores, was later admitted to Harvard Law School due to affirmative action… that means she was given preference because of the colour of her skin.

This new multicultural dogma was sown with the seeds of good intentions but what grew from it were the seeds of destruction, of western civilised values. As the distinguished conservative essayist Lawrence Auster concluded: "Multiculturalism is not the source of Muslim immigration. The source of it is our belief that we must not discriminate against other people on the basis of their culture, their ethnicity, their nationality, their religion. This is the idea of the 1965 Immigration Act, which was the idea of the 1964 Civil Rights Act applied to all of humanity: all discrimination is wrong, period. No one in today's society, including conservatives, feels comfortable identifying this utterly simple idea, because that would mean opposing it. To see how powerful the belief in non-discrimination is, consider this: Prior to World War II, would any Western country have considered admitting significant numbers of Muslim immigrants? Of course not; it would have been out of the question. The West had a concrete identity. It saw itself as white and in large part as Christian, and there was still active in the Western mind the knowledge that Islam was our historic adversary, as it has been for a thousand years, and radically alien. But today, the very notion of stopping Muslim immigration is out of the question, it can't even be thought." (46)

For the cultural Marxists (the politically correct) the idea that people are different from birth and can end up unequal is the antithesis of everything they hold dear. This is the red flag idea that Karl Marx, Stalin, Trotsky, Pol Pot and all of the other mass murderers of communist history demanded must be suppressed by the state, by state law…using their own equivalent of hate crime law or race hate law. Anti-colonialism became wrapped up in a hatred of Western science and was taken up by the new alliance of Marxism and Islam. The freedom to conduct academic research is, alongside the freedom of the press, the most important of all our freedoms. The progress of humanity depends on it. Without this freedom there can be no advances in medicine, technology, computing, gerontology or in any of the areas that create wealth and expand the breadth and accumulation of human knowledge. Yet many of our best universities are now under a sustained threat or have already capitulated in this new era of cultural Marxism, aided and abetted by race hate legislation.

Race hate laws now poison the civil discourse in Britain, where along with the rest of western Europe: Sweden, Norway, Canada and Australia the transformation of official state policy from historical/traditional national cultures to multiculturalism, underpinned by laws that criminalise "offensive" speech under hate speech legislation, has taken place.

In the 21st century science and scientists have again became the target of PC state dogma allowing the intolerant Left to block legitimate scientific research on genetic differences. James Watson, the Nobel prize-winning scientist and the genetic pioneer who unravelled DNA is the most high profile victim of this new thought crime. On a visit to Britain in 2007 Watson told *The Sunday Times* that Western economic policies towards African countries were based on the incorrect assumption that black people were as clever as their white counterparts when all scientific testing suggested that they were not. Watson was immediately threatened with investigation by the newly formed UK Commission for Human Rights and his lecture was cancelled at short notice. The research Watson was referring to was contained in the 1994 best seller, *The Bell Curve*, by Richard Herrnstein and Charles Murray. They used peer reviewed and tested statistical research to show that there is a racial divide in intelligence and that the IQ of black Americans scored consistently lower than other social groups. The accusation of "scientific racism" was levelled against the authors who contended that any positive discrimination on behalf of black Americans was a waste of money, a conclusion shared by another prominent geneticist, Arthur Jensen of Berkeley University in California.

Herrnstein and Murray's book was attacked not on the grounds of its scientific method but on its ideological unacceptability. One reviewer called it "academic Nazism" and the *New York Review of Books* claimed that it relied on "tainted" sources. Such was the hostility towards *The Bell Curve* from the Left/liberal media that Linda Gottfredson, a professor of sociology at the University of Delaware, felt obliged to draft a letter headed *Mainstream Science on Intelligence* to the *Wall Street Journal*. This was a public statement, signed by 51 university professors specialising in intelligence, supporting the validity of the concept of intelligence and IQ testing.

Professor Robert Plomin, from the Institute of Psychiatry at King's College London, carried out a long-term analysis of more than 11,000 twins born in England and Wales in the mid-1990s and proved that genes have a larger bearing on children's educational achievement than environmental factors do.

Plomin found that inherited intelligence may account for almost 60% of teenagers' scores in their GCSE examinations while other factors only account for perhaps one third.

Plomin must now run the gauntlet of those on the Left who would deny his academic freedom to publish such results. In a free society it should be completely valid, from a scientific point of view, to be able to speculate whether genetics affect the rate of development of different people separated by geographical distance. For those who accept Darwin's theory of evolutionary development this is an established fact, a fact denied by the intolerant Left. Another group who do *not* accept Darwin's evolutionary theory are the Islamists who have been given fertile new breeding ground in the colleges and universities of Britain.

A 2011 Home Office report found that more that 30% of those convicted of al-Qaida related terrorist activity had been radicalised at English universities. The report identified Taimour Abdulwahab al-Abdaly, the Stockholm suicide bomber who had a BSc in sports therapy from the University of Luton (now the University of Bedfordshire), the Detroit underpants bomber, Umar Farouk Abdulmutallab, who studied mechanical engineering at University College London and Abdulla Ahmed Ali and Assad Sarwar, the transatlantic liquid bomb plotters who attended City and Brunel Universities respectively.

In 2015 it was revealed that the serial beheader Mahammed Emwazi aka Jihadi John, was a graduate of the University of Westminster where radical Islamist preachers regularly urged sedition without a second look from the university authorities.

The Department for Business, which is in charge of universities, identified 40 English universities at particular risk of radical Islamic infiltration. The document raised particular concerns about the Federation of Student Islamic Societies (FOSIS) reinforcing the need to regard any organisation claiming to represent the interests of Muslims in Britain to be a tool of radical Islam. All of those named were radicalised through teachings and lectures given at UK institutions. Why are we allowing our universities to openly preach jihad in the same way we are allowing the mosques to preach jihad without any intervention? Here's another example of what has been going on unchecked throughout our academic institutions. On March 9th, 2013 The Islamic Education Research Academy (iERA), a hardline Islamist organization and terrorist front, held an event at University College London they called "Islam or Atheism: What makes more sense?". Those who attended this event were greeted with gender enforced segregated seating and separate entrances to the venue, women in through one door, men another, in total breach not only of the democratic norms of free speech, but also of established UCL policy. Those who refused to comply with the sharia seating arrangements were ordered out of the auditorium.

These protected groups are never censored by NUS activists, many of whom are Islamists themselves, or refused a platform. In 2009, Bilal Philips, was allowed to speak at Queen Mary College, London University. Philips had been last heard on Channel Four's *Dispatches* programme, saying: "The prophet Muhammad practically outlined the rules regarding marriage prior to puberty, with his practice he clarified what is permissible and that is why we shouldn't have any issues about an older man marrying a younger woman, which is looked down upon by this [Western] society today, but we know that Prophet Muhammad practiced it, it wasn't abuse or exploitation, it was marriage."

In 2012 The London School of Economics Student Union passed a motion prohibiting Islamophobia as "a form of racism expressed through the hatred or fear of Islam, Muslims, or Islamic culture and the stereotyping, demonization or harassment of Muslims, including but not limited to portraying Muslims as barbarians or terrorists or attacking the Quran as a manual of hatred." This surrender of free speech to the norms of Islamic blasphemy law meant that nothing even remotely critical of Islam could now be uttered in any debate on campus. This cultural genocide has been accompanied by hate crime legislation that actively persecutes the majority culture. Those who slavishly follow this agenda are a reminder to those, who can still recall recent history, that the fellow travellers of the Third Reich excused themselves personal responsibility for their actions by claiming "they were only following orders".

White bad/Islam good is the mantra of the Left where the only conflicts worth reporting are those where the white man can be blamed, especially true if the white man also happens to be American. At the apex of this cultural/suicidal pact is the axis of broadcast journalists and activist lawyers who seem determined to smooth a path towards the public's acceptance of an Islamic state without a fight. Their Quisling-like adherence to the discredited utopia of a future socialist state borders on treasonous. In June 2013 *The Guardian* newspaper deliberately leaked a massive swathe of top-secret documents stolen by the fugitive Edward Snowden which Andrew Parker, head of MI5, warned would help terrorist plots on the British mainland and be a "gift they need to evade us and strike at will".

He said there were several thousand Islamist extremists living in the UK who "see the British people as a legitimate target". The Guardian's editor Alan Rusbridger must have been well aware of the increasingly desperate measures that needed to be taken by MI5 and MI6 to stop Islamists killing innocent civilians. There have been 34 such plots since 9/11 and 7/7 including the Heathrow Airport plot to blow up transatlantic airliners that could have killed 5,000 passengers. Security officials said the leaks amounted to a "guide book", showing terrorists the best way to avoid detection when plotting an atrocity and is believed to have caused the greatest damage to western security apparatus in history. Parker revealed that the security services were working round the clock to stop the fanatics with MI5 "tackling threats on more fronts than ever before".

Most Leftists know nothing and want to know nothing about jihadist slaughters that do not involve the West - in Nigeria, Thailand, Philippines, Egypt, Algeria, Sudan, India, Pakistan, Russia, Somalia - and get angry if you bring them up. They think jihad only happens to deserving white men and women. When the next atrocity occurs on the British mainland, when a bomb goes off in a crowded shopping mall or an army barracks or maybe a school or university we need to remember this, because they will be nowhere to be seen, having scuttled off to watch the destruction unfold in their safe areas patrolled by the forces they profess to despise.

Just like journalists who know nothing about free speech or politicians who know nothing about democracy there are also lawyers who care nothing about justice and the rule of law.

The author and columnist Melanie Phillips summed up the way Britain's traditional liberty has been destroyed by this onslaught from the Left: "Its powers of self-government have been crippled by the EU. Its unique concept of liberty has been shrunk by European human rights law which makes freedom conditional on what judges say is to be permitted. The constitution has been dismembered, the House of Lords emasculated. Left-wing ideologues have all but destroyed the education system and the family unit, squashed dissent in the universities and become dominant in the law, medicine and other professions. And through the BBC, that state-licensed media behemoth dominating public debate with its Guardian 'group think' on every issue under the sun, they have managed to shunt the very centre of political gravity onto their own ground. The Press is, in fact, the last remaining bastion of free thinking that the Left has not managed to conquer. Until now." (47) In January 2015, after a year long enquiry costing £22 million, British soldiers were cleared of abusing Iraqi troops in a case brought by publically funded lawyers. Self-proclaimed socialist Phil Shiner's Public Interest Lawyers (PIL) and law firm Leigh Day were condemned for bringing baseless charges against British soldiers.

Defence Secretary Michael Fallon said in the Commons that these lawyers had made a 'shameful attempt to use our legal system to attack and falsely impugn our Armed Forces'. Fallon told MPs the lawyers' behaviour was 'shameful'. Shiner claimed that his clients had witnessed 'mutilations'. We now know that they made up these allegations. Yet neither Shiner nor Leigh Day will apologise. Outrageously, Public Interest Lawyers has been paid around £3 million for co-operating with the inquiry, which cost taxpayers a total of £31 million. Shiner himself insisted on a full inquiry, prolonging the innocent soldiers' ordeal for ten long years. The truth could have been established a decade ago, but lawyers acting for the detainees refused to co-operate with the original Ministry of Defence investigation. Labour has received tens of thousands of pounds in donations from one of the law firms who were criticised over the false claims that British soldiers were involved in torture and murder in Iraq. Leigh Day and Co gave the party or its MPs a total of £33,000 over two years, official records show. The law firm was criticised after the £31million Al-Sweady inquiry found the shocking allegations were, at the risk of repeating myself, 'wholly and entirely without merit' and based on 'deliberate and calculated lies'. Former defence minister Sir Nicholas Soames, wrote to Labour leader Ed Miliband calling on him to donate the same sum of money to charity for wounded military personnel. Official records show Leigh Day & Co gave £14,500 to Emily Thornberry which was declared in her register of interests on December 8. Miss

Thornberry was a senior ally of Mr Miliband's and the shadow Attorney General until she resigned over a 'sneering' row after posting on Twitter a picture of a house with a white van outside during the Rochdale by-election. The donation was to pay for a legal research assistant for Miss Thornberry's office.

A former senior Army interrogator, who served in Iraq and Afghanistan, told *The Sunday Telegraph*: 'There was an incident in 2008 when French soldiers were massacred and the bodies of four of them were mutilated. We had two of the suspects in detention and they were brought in for questioning. They murder women and children and all we can think about is did we shout in their ear and will we get investigated for that? One of the interrogators touched one of the suspects on the nose with an A4 piece of paper and he was investigated by the special investigation branch for abuse. Just for touching a detainee on the nose. The fact somebody could be investigated for that is to my mind incredible. It was ridiculous. These French soldiers had been horribly mutilated and yet it was the interrogator who was investigated.' Colonel Tim Collins, who made a celebrated eve-of-battle speech during the Iraq war, said he blamed 'ambulance-chasing lawyers' and 'play-it-safe judges' for the new rules on interrogation. He said: 'We are no longer able to carry out tactical questioning. That in itself brings risks to the lives of the people we deploy. These insurgents are not nice people. These are criminals. They behead people; they keep sex slaves. They are not normal people.' (48)

Littlejohn of the *Daily Mail* summed up what the majority of right-thinking people would have liked to shout from the rooftops: "this is simply part of the much wider human rights racket, a scandalous conspiracy by unscrupulous Left-wing lawyers designed to turn justice upside down. Most of the actions brought by the human rights parasites are part of a concerted assault on our institutions, aimed at demolishing traditional notions of fair play and common decency." (49)

This toxic atmosphere of intolerance created by the axis of Left/Islamic ideology is most virulent on social media. Brendan O'Neil editor of news website *Spiked* found himself shut out of a debate on abortion at Christ Church, Oxford, cancelled because what he referred to as "the Stepford students" protested that, as a man, he would endanger the "mental safety" of other students.

With the collapse of the traditional family, Christianity and the seemingly limitless migration of alien cultures into Britain a black hole has opened up in what used to be called traditional culture, and this hole has been filled by twittermob and online "Social Justice Warriors (SJW)" who have shut down "mansplaining" or "straightsplaining", that is the censoring of a heterosexual white male's right to speak on the grounds that his "privilege" has allowed him to gain more knowledge than the average SJW. Thus the bigoted and the ignorant who seek to proscribe free use of language in order to enforce their vision of equality, by censoring anything they find offensive, are empowered by equality legislation and race hate law. If these students are the cream of the crop, the hope for the future, then what hope for the continued existence of a free society? Commentating on this new and sinister use of twitter and Facebook columnist Rod Liddel remarked: "Out there in cyberspace is a moronic inferno whipped up by people determined to be outraged, legions of single-issue pressure groups maniacally insistent upon their cause and a perpetually angry tranche of The Great British Public that yearns to punish someone for saying something with which they might disagree and to which they gratefully take grave offence." (50)

The Left's dogma of non-offense has ensured that the only culture omitted from the multicultural curriculum now taught in state schools is that of white British culture. As parents listen to their children apeing gangsterrap patois when they arrive home at 4pm is it any wonder that they feel marginalised? White children bombarded with black history, racism awareness days and whole terms of Islamic study at school will inevitably despair, looking around for some institutional expression of cultural pride, to find only insinuated condemnation in the national curriculum for their collective racism and imperialist ancestry. A culture that no longer holds the values of freedom of any importance, no longer has time to remind its children that the British Empire didn't invent slavery, it abolished it, along with burning widows on funeral pyres, is finished.

Olivier Pètré Grenouilleau is a historian and a specialist in the history of slavery. Since 1999 he has been at the University of South Brittany and since 2007 at Sciences Po Paris. He was taken to court because, in his masterpiece *Les Traites Négrières* [The Slave Trades], he asserted that the slave trade was an invention of Islam, conducted with the active participation of African kingdoms, responsible for more fatalities than all the western nations involved in the trade combined.

I used to frequent the same pubs as the men who, like my father, served in the Royal Navy and Merchant Navy. The same generation who lost friends and relatives in actively opposing Nazism and Communism during and after the war, in the cause of freedom. This was an old culture of decency and manners, kindness and common sense, wisdom and banter, a generation despised by the toytown Marxists of Labour's brave new world. Their hate law legislation effectively ended that old world of free speech in Britain, laws New Labour enacted to stifle all dissent in the Left's bitter war against everything they hate and despise. Indigenous English, white, Christian, heterosexual family units. Without even the status of an "ethnic grouping" to fall back on minority white working-class children have little or nothing left to identify with and so gravitate to the dominant black or Islamic cultures they now find ruling the roost at their London schools. In less than 20 years what was once a safe, ordered society of intelligent and tolerant people who shared the collective norms of civilisation has been shattered into a warring, disordered maelstrom of Marxist agitation, race hate activism, black power anti-police entitlement groups and Islamic medievalists. Not a clash of civilisations but a war on civilisation.

CHAPTER SIX

NOT IN OUR NAME?

The clash we are witnessing around the world is not a clash of religions, or a clash of civilizations. It is a clash between two opposites, between two eras. It is a clash between a mentality that belongs to the Middle Ages and another mentality that belongs to the 21st century. It is a clash between civilization and backwardness, between the civilized and the primitive, between barbarity and rationality. It is a clash between freedom and oppression, between democracy and dictatorship. It is a clash between human rights, on the one hand, and the violation of these rights, on other hand. It is a clash between those who treat women like beasts, and those who treat them like human beings.

Interview with Arab-American psychiatrist Wafa Sultan on Al-Jazeera TV

The goal of Islamizing the British cities of Birmingham, Bradford, Derby, Dewsbury, Leeds, Leicester, Liverpool, Luton, Manchester and Sheffield may not be achieved until 2030 but what used to be known as the East End of London, Tower Hamlets, is already under Islamist control, thanks to the Labour Party.

This is the heart and soul of the capital: the old East End of the London docks, working-class pubs that stayed open during the blitz, West Ham United football club and the community spirit that held a nation together despite the bombs and fire unleashed by Hitler's blitz.

Today it is the area known locally as the "Islamic Republic of Tower Hamlets" where extremist Muslim preachers, also known locally as the "Tower Hamlets Taliban" issue death threats to women who refuse to wear Islamic veils. An area where streets that once housed the people who held the line on behalf of freedom are covered with posters declaring: "You are entering a Sharia controlled zone: Islamic rules enforced," and where advertising deemed offensive to Muslims (including any mention of The Holocaust) is vandalized or blacked out with spray paint. This is what was gained by Labour's accelerated multiculturalism.

Priceless was the look of shock on the face of Labour Home Secretary John Reid in 2006 when Muslim extremist Abu Izzadeen heckled him into cowed silence in east London, demanding: "How dare you come to a Muslim area". It was the look of a man face on with the reality of a new situation that had instantly laid waste to his multicultural illusions. It was a look that said it all: "Hell no, this cannot be happening!" But not for long, because John Reid is now safely out of it, ensconced in the House of Lords as Lord Reid, surrounded by liveried flunkies next to Labour's Lord Prescott. Not his problem anymore.

After Home Secretary Reid's speech and Islamic ambush Metropolitan police commissioner Sir Ian Blair that said it was "extraordinarily difficult" to clamp down on Islamic extremism without "offending large groups of Muslims". (51)

What he really meant was that in a multicultural state, wedded to human rights law and mass immigration, the indigenous people of Tower Hamlets were on their own and there was nothing the police could do to help them. The traditional residents of the old East End duly took note and then started to get the hell out.

As the 2011 census showed, Tower Hamlets had the largest population increase of any local authority in England and Wales between 2001 and 2011. The borough's population grew by 26.4 % from 201,100 to 254,100 in a single decade - more than twice the national increase of 12 %, thanks largely to Islamic immigration.

A 2015 study of the 2011 Census by the Muslim Council of Britain revealed that 66% of all school-age children in Tower Hamlets were now Muslims and that overall 34.5% of the population of Tower Hamlets is now Muslim, and doubling every decade.

How does that affect those who were born in Tower Hamlets, those who have been crowded out by an influx of Third World arrivals into their country, their home town, their streets, unasked for and without historical precedence.

According to the Office for National Statistics (2011), 600,000 white Britons have left London in the past 10 years. The latest census data shows the breakdown in telling detail: some London boroughs have lost a quarter of their population of white, British people. The number of white British resident in Redbridge, north London, for example, has fallen by 40,844 (to 96,253) during this period, while the *total* population of Redbridge has *risen* by more than 40,335 to 278,970.In Barking and Dagenham the white British population fell by almost one-third between 2001 and 2011. In Newham only 16.7% of the population in 2011 could be described as white British compared to an increasing Asian population now totalling 43.5% (9.8% Pakistani, 12.21% Bangladeshi). The Left's mantra of diversity will soon be challenged in these areas when, on current rates of white flight, there won't be enough white people left to give it any legitimacy. Mass Third World immigration would not, on its own, have been enough to facilitate the annexation of a London borough, but mass immigration combined with legislation demonising as racist any dissenter from this reverse colonisation has allowed the guests to completely change the house rules.

The mess Labour left cannot be reversed now and six years after Reid's wake-up call a national daily newspaper reported on the progress of "diversity" in Tower Hamlets: "Residents have grown used to the fact that the council-run libraries are stocked with books and DVDs containing the extremist rantings of banned Islamist preachers. There is a Muslim faith school where girls as young as 11 have to wear face-covering veils. There are plans to spend hundreds of thousands of pounds of municipal money to build a set of Islamic arches — the so-called 'hijab gates', which would look like a veil — at either end of Brick Lane, which is packed with Indian restaurants and clothes shops. And there have been allegations of corruption during council elections, with the names of hundreds of Bangladeshi 'ghost voters' suddenly appearing on the electoral register. But what many struggle to understand is how mainstream politicians are ignoring the corruption that is going on in the heart of our capital." (52)

In October, 2010 Bangladeshi-born Lutfur Rahman became the first directly elected mayor of Tower Hamlets. He was originally the official Labour candidate then elected Labour mayor but was deselected by the party after details of his links with the Islamic Forum of Europe (IFE), whose aim is to transform Britain into an Islamic state, became known. This de-selection would never have happened had not Jim Fitzpatrick, the Labour environment minister, had the courage to expose the IFE to a national Sunday newspaper. He said that the IFE were now a secret party within Labour: "They are acting almost as an entryist organisation, placing people within the political parties, recruiting members to those political parties, trying to get individuals selected and elected so they can exercise political influence and power, whether it's at local government level or national level, they are completely at odds with Labour's programme, with our support for secularism." (53) The evidence of corruption and gerrymandering was exposed by the press but did little to alter the outcome of the next local election, as described by a national Sunday newspaper: "Dumped by Labour, Mr Rahman ran as an independent and with the help of the Muslim vote romped to victory in what the *London Evening Standard* described as 'one of the nastiest campaigns in recent London political history'. Now in power, he has control over a £1.3 billion municipal budget. Rahman's aims may well not be the aims of traditional British politicians. A national Sunday newspaper revealed that: "The Islamists who run the Muslim show in Britain are already hard at work making sure that their ultimate success will come through the schools on a city by city basis. A major breaking story revealed a strategy called Operation Trojan Horse, ready to be implemented in Bradford, Manchester and Birmingham in order to Islamize the state school sector. "We have an obligation to our children to fulfil our roles and ensure these schools are run on Islamic principles," it said. "The first step of Trojan Horse is to identify poor-performing state schools in Muslim areas; then Salafist parents in each school are encouraged to complain that teachers are corrupting children with sex education, teaching about homosexuals, making their children say Christian prayers and mixed swimming and sports. The next steps are to 'parachute in' Muslim governors to drip-feed our ideal for a Muslim school and stir up staff to urge the council to investigate. The strategy stresses the importance of having an 'English face among the staff group to make it more believable'" (54)

Salafists and Deobandis preach jihad in British mosques and are the supporters of the hardline doctrines of Islamic State, who want sharia law to be supreme in Britain and the world. Deobandis are, inexplicably, allowed to run most British mosques and they are most associated with Sunni Muslims who are mainly from Pakistan. If anyone can be considered a fifth column in Britain, Salafists and Deobandis can. Their strategy worked like a charm in Birmingham as Balwant Bains, head teacher of Saltley School, resigned after opposing the demands of the schools' 12 out of 14 Muslim governors who insisted that Islamic studies be introduced to the curriculum, other "un-Islamic" subjects scrapped and only halal food be eaten, even though it is a non-faith school.

Such was the level of intimidation involved that an anonymous note was passed to Birmingham City council informing them that four more schools were on the sharia hit list including; Nansen Primary, Golden Hillock, Ladypool Primary and Oldknow Academy.

The head teachers at the first three schools named had all left their posts in recent years with the letter alleging that one of the heads had his car tyres slashed in the staff car park for opposing the Islamic takeover. In one of these schools, Oldknow Academy, a national Sunday newspaper found: "Children as young as six were told that white women were 'prostitutes' and urged to join in anti-Christian chants at a school embroiled in the Trojan Horse controversy. A report by the Education Funding Agency (EFA) into the Oldknow Academy primary school in Birmingham, says the school is "taking on the practices of an Islamic faith school and in this regard is not promoting community cohesion". (55)

In this *state funded school* Muslim teachers insisted on segregated classes with boys sitting at the front and girls at the back. All the girls had their heads covered. Christian children at the school were not allowed to celebrate Christmas; a Christmas card competition was scrapped and there were no Christmas parties or even a Christmas tree. Rehearsals for the school play, The Wizard of Oz, were stopped because children were told they were not allowed to sing during Ramadan (playing musical instruments is banned under Islamic law). The school prevented pupils from going on an exchange trip to a Catholic school but managed to fund three pilgrimages to Saudi Arabia, but only for Muslim pupils. These Islamic junkets cost £50,000 a trip of which £32,000 came from the school budget allowing staff and pupils to stay in 5-star hotels and spend £800 on tips. The EFA document revealed that non-Muslim staff were excluded from Friday assemblies so that pupils could be 'preached at'. Staff told inspectors: "that during Friday assembly occasionally words have been used such as 'white prostitute' and 'hellfire' which they felt were inappropriate for young children". Instead of supporting head teachers who were warning council officials that the Islamic takeover of their schools was proceeding apace officers colluded with Muslim governors then offered payoffs coupled with gagging orders for non-Muslim staff that the Muslim governors wanted rid of.

As yet, no action has been taken to change the five schools identified in the Trojan Horse plot to Islamize state schools in Birmingham. In Birmingham what we have now are wards like Washwood Heath where 86 % of children are Muslims and where nationally one in 12 school children are now Muslim, the direct result of Labour Party immigration policy. The rapid transformation of a low birth-rate white Christian nation into a majority Islamic one go hand in hand with Islamic attempts to infiltrate the state school system and attempts to defraud the electorate. In many British cities the local Labour Party organizations are now indistinguishable from Islamist cells operating in secret with the aim of overthrowing the democratic state. In 2005 Richard Mawrey QC, a senior judge, found six Muslim Labour councillors guilty of carrying out "massive, systematic and organised" postal voting fraud to win two wards during elections for the Birmingham city council. Declaring the results void, he barred the men from standing again in a by-election expected on May12. Judge Mawrey said the fraud was carried out with the full knowledge and cooperation of the local Labour Party in a scam that extended across the city of Birmingham and where applications for postal votes had soared from 28,000 to 70,000. The three Muslim Labour councillors representing the Bordesley Green ward, Shafaq Ahmed, Shah Jahan and Ayaz Khan all walked out of the hearing on the first day after Judge Mawrey refused an application for an adjournment. The petition against the three Aston councillors, Mohammed Islam, Muhammed Afzal and Mohammed Kazi was brought by the Liberal Democrats.

During the hearings, Judge Mawrey heard how the trio were caught operating a "vote-rigging factory". The West Midlands police described how they found Mr Islam, Mr Afzal and Mr Kazi handling unsealed postal ballots in a deserted warehouse in the city but later told the BBC that they *were not* pursuing a criminal case against the six convicted councillors, who were by then barred from standing again for election. Had the vote riggers been from outside of the protected grouping that is Islam would they have been treated so leniently? T. Dan Smith was heard rolling in his grave. These stories, revealing a serious attempt to corrupt the state education system and the democratic process, and they were both initially ignored by the police.

What had its beginnings with The Islamic Emirates Project, a lunatic fringe with little credibility has morphed into The Islamic Forum of Europe (IFE). Different name, same goal. The IFE has branches throughout Britain and most European countries; its youth wing appears to be based at the East London mosque in Tower Hamlets. The IFE believe they can transform Britain into an Islamic republic from the bottom up, working through schools, local councils and through the Labour Party. The Labour Party's inability to take action against Islamists within its ranks is a direct consequence of the paralysing fear that traditional Labour members have of being accused of racism.

Commenting on the Birmingham school row former Conservative chairman, Norman Tebbitt, came to this conclusion: "We have imported far too many immigrants who have come here not to live in our society, but to replicate here the society of their homelands. This is not a tirade against migration from the EU, which we are largely unable to control, but from the rest of the world, which we could have controlled if we had had the will to do so. However, even if suddenly the inward flow of those unwilling to adapt their society to ours were to be entirely cut off, it might already be too late to prevent the establishment of enclaves in which our values are treated with contempt, while foreign values and even laws are promoted. It is certainly true that nature abhors a vacuum and with the decline of Christianity leaving the structure of our values system with no foundation there is now a great emptiness in our society. The doctrine of multiculturalism is a nonesense. A society is defined by its culture, and rival cultures are bound to create rival societies within the same territory. That is what has now been forced into public view in Birmingham. Of course a tolerant dominant culture has no problem in tolerating or minority groups. Neither Judaism nor Buddhism are a threat to Christianity in Britain, but if our society loses confidence in its value system, it will not long remain dominant. For all the shouting and finger-pointing at Westminster, particularly that from the Labour Party – which bears responsibility for destabilising British society by its policy of unlimited, unrestricted, uncounted immigration fanned by unlimited welfare spending – I do not see any evidence yet that the scale of the problem is recognised, let alone that there is a realistic plan to deal with it." (56)

While Ofsted did nothing in Birmingham the Islamists were busy taking over a dozen or more state schools in Tower Hamlets.

Paul Burston, who edits the gay section in the London listings magazine *Time Out* has witnessed the changes in Tower Hamlets. He said: "In the past few years there have been more and more reports of homophobic incidents in Tower Hamlets, often involving attacks on gay men by gangs of young Bangladeshis. A large number of people have contacted me to tell me about all kinds of incidents, ranging from being stopped outside mosques and handed literature that is really horrible, to being verbally abused and physically attacked. But if you talk about it publicly then you are accused of fuelling Islamophobia. It is the idea that a potential thought-crime trumps a real crime that I find difficult to understand."

A Channel 4's *Dispatches* report employing covert filming by the programme's reporters found that: 'IFE activists boasted to undercover reporters that they had already "consolidated … a lot of influence and power" over Tower Hamlets, a London borough council with a £1 billion budget. Established that the group and its allies were awarded more than £10 million of taxpayers' money from government funds designed to "prevent violent extremism". One of the council's first acts was to tell schools that they should close for the Muslim festival of Eid, even where most of their pupils are not Muslim'. (57)

London mayor Ken Livingstone, (a supporter of Muslim Brotherhood leader Yusuf Al-Qaradawi) suggested of the *Dispatches* programme that it: "smacks of racism and Islamophobia. Of course Tower Hamlets council is not infiltrated by Islamists. Just because some people are Muslim and go to the mosque is not argument enough that they are Islamists, " said Livingstone omitting to mention that during his last term as mayor the East London Mosque was paid £500,000 by his London Development Agency.

The IFE campaigned hard to get Livingstone re-elected as mayor, just as they had campaigned for George Galloway, helping him to win a shock election victory in Bradford in 2005.

Galloway was heard throughout the campaign proclaiming: "Allah be praised!" through a megaphone…. Galloway is Scottish and was a tireless supporter of Saddam Hussein. The late Christopher Hitchens referred to Galloway as: "a pimp for, as well as a prostitute of, one of the foulest dictatorships of modern times." Galloway later admitted that the IFE had played a "decisive role" in his election victory, as indeed the IFE played a decisive role in getting Rahman elected as an "independent" mayor after being exposed as a supporter of the IFE. The IFE, bear with me, are *themselves* a front for Jamaat-e-Islami. This is a terrorist group, regarded as barbaric even by Islamists active in Pakistan and Bangladesh, but tolerated by the Labour party in Britain.

In March 2013 Abdul Quader Mollah, a leading Jamaat-e-Islami figure was given a life sentence by a Bangladeshi court for his role in atrocities committed in 1971. Known as the "Butcher of Mirpur," Mollah was convicted of beheading a poet, raping an 11-year old girl, and killing 344 people. For many Bangladeshis that life sentence in prison was a let off and protestors besieged Dhaka's main courthouse for weeks after the verdict. Of the ten people indicted for acts of genocide by the Bangladeshi war crimes tribunal, eight of them were from the Islamist movement, Jamaat-e-Islami. Bangladesh's official figures claim Pakistani soldiers and Jamaat collaborators killed three million people and raped 200,000 women at that time. One US official was quoted saying: "It is the most incredible, calculated thing since the days of the Nazis in Poland." Or perhaps, since the formation of the IS caliphate.

Yet under Rahman's tenure in office Jamaat thugs have been let loose to impose sharia zones all over Tower Hamlets. The East London mosque is the biggest in Britain and is under the control of the Islamic Forum of Europe who, let's repeat, oppose British freedom and democracy and want to impose sharia law on *everyone* in Britain.

Azad Ali is the IFE's community affairs coordinator, and he was quoted in the *Dispatches* report saying: "Democracy, if it means at the expense of not implementing the sharia, of course no one agrees with that".

When Gordon Brown was Prime Minister Azad Ali *was given a job at the British Treasury*. Jamaat, which has its worldwide HQ in Lahore in Pakistan, has been described as a cancer destroying secular Bangladesh, its method of operation is infiltration and intimidation. In Pakistan and Bangladesh Jamaat-e-Islami operates by inveigling members into positions of influence on the campuses of universities in order to spread its doctrine of hate and bigotry against non-Islamic minorities and anyone of a liberal disposition. Its structure is similar to that of communist revolutionary parties with members, strictly selected, organised into cells and moved up within local institutions. In Britain, members of Jamaat-e-Islami are known to have infiltrated British university campuses and the National Union of Students (NUS).

Despite worldwide condemnation of IS who were busily committing atrocities unseen since the darkest days of the Third Reich (burning infidels alive, plucking out eyes, beheading women and children) the National Union of Students, now seemingly a tool of hardline jihadis, *rejected* a call to condemn IS on the grounds that the motion was "islamophobic". In Bangladesh, a completely Muslim nation, Jamaat-e-Islami is busy silencing all opposition from within by crude intimidation that has allowed it to infiltrate the army, the air force and the civil service in order to permanently snuff out those who would oppose its extremism. In Bangladesh a courageous fight back has begun, but in Britain the useful idiots of the Left coupled with their racism/islamophobia doggerel allowed a major London borough to be infiltrated by a terrorist organisation.

Imagine, if you can, a scenario where at the height of the Second World War the British fascists (blackshirts) had announced that they were assisting a new political grouping to set up a pro-German zone in the middle of London. Yet this has been the Islamist tactics in Tower Hamlets where the politicians they regard as weak and easily manipulated have all rolled over to have their tummies tickled. Ed Miliband, former Labour Treasury minister and now Labour leader, believes that he has what it takes to be Britain's next prime minister. That is, if "what it takes" means ignorance, gullibility and weakness in the face of naked Islamist ambition aimed at destroying British democracy.

In 2010, the leader of the opposition and Labour's Harriet Harman MP attended a conference organized by the Mayor of London, Ken Livingstone, where Azad Ali spoke. Azad Ali was there as the chair of the Muslim Safety Forum, a group that had also been working with the Labour government and with their sanction, the Metropolitan Police, Crown Prosecution Service and the Home Office, but was in fact a front for Jamaat-el-Islami. Should Miliband ever be elected Prime Minister the supporters of Jamaat-el-Islami will be jumping for joy.

In 2012 Rahman, now set free from his Labour roots, but with the help of Labour councillors, changed council procedures so he could *personally* decide where all council grants over £1,000 went. This was achieved with his new adviser, Maium Miah, at the helm and suddenly guest hate preachers began to be rolled into the borough, all expenses paid. The IFE hosted a fundraising dinner for Interpal, a charity banned in the US for its links with the terror group Hamas (whose stated aim is the destruction of Israel). Other speakers at the mosque included the successor to Osama bin Laden as leader of Al Qaeda, Anwar al-Awlaki.

It appears that the East London Mosque is being run by the Islamic Forum of Europe who are being funded by council tax money diverted by its Islamist mayor in support of Islamic terrorists Jamaat-e-Islami. With council grant money firmly under his control the Labour Islamist mayor of what was once the old East End of London lost no time in distributing taxpayers' money to his close political allies. One of these groups, called The Island Bengali Welfare Association, based in a council flat on the Isle of Dogs, was given £91,000. That association was run by Maium Miah, who along with Rahman, was deciding who got the grant money. Come the elections of 2014 Rahman's use of public money to buy Muslim votes in Tower Hamlets could see Labour totally kicked out of the borough, which could then become a de facto terror state within a state situated slap bang next door to the City of London.

RAHMAN UPDATE

Rahman *was* re-elected mayor of Tower Hamlets but later, as reported extensively in the press (23/4/15), he has since been found guilty of electoral fraud, corruption and illegality by the election commissioner, Richard Mawrey.

Judge Mawrey ruled that the May 2014 mayoral election in Tower Hamlets be "voided" and new elections organised immediately. Rahman has been barred from standing in any new election and his election agent Alibor Choudhary has been stripped of his position as a councillor with immediate effect. Rahman was ordered to pay all the costs of the court and must make an immediate payment of £250,000 pounds. The judge said Rahman had made a successful career out of branding his critics racist and Islamaphobic "but those critics were not silenced and neither was this court."

Rahman was found guilty of making false statements about John Biggs, the Labour candidate for mayor, who he dubbed a racist. "No rational person could think Mr Biggs was a racist – it was a deliberate and dishonest campaign. Rahman and Choudhary are personally guilty of making false statements about a candidate," said judge Mawrey.

The judge also found that there had been clear evidence of electoral fraud including ghost voters and postal vote fraud with council grants handed out to Muslim groups in order to boost Rahman's popularity with grants being cut to non-Muslim charitable organisations such as the Alzheimer's Society.

One of Rahman's henchmen, who told the court that the atmosphere on election day at Tower Hamlets' polling stations had been "without intimidation" was proved to have cast his vote by post. The Met police now have a 200 page report detailing Rahman's extensive fraudulent and corrupt activity. He has yet to be arrested, in line with the nationwide tendency of the police to now turn a blind eye to crimes by Muslims, lest they also be accused of "Islamophobia."

I'm writing this sentence just before the closest general election in history. The Labour Party's introduction of postal voting on demand has brought with it massive electoral fraud, and may have cost the Conservatives a majority at the last election. It could be worse in 2015. Thousands of postal votes sent out to dual-nationality Pakistanis residing in Britain in 2010 ended up in Kashmir where they were "signed" on behalf of those who didn't speak English, then returned to Britain. Just a click on the mouse to the Electoral Commission, led by "long-term campaigner for women's rights" Jenny Watson who was appointed by Gordon Brown's Labour Government, and postal votes for made up voters will drop on the doorsteps of Labour strongholds in Oldham, Halifax and Tower Hamlets in 2015. Watson, despite her part-timer salary of £100,000 a year, has apparently been powerless to do anything about electoral fraud anywhere, requiring the High Court to step in and deal with the scandal at Tower Hamlets.

Shortly before the 2010 election, the police were investigating more than 50 cases of electoral fraud in principally Labour run areas but that number is now more than 80. In 2015 the Labour council election candidate Quesir Mahmood was arrested and bailed "on suspicion of electoral fraud and integrity issues".

The Lancashire Telegraph reported on April 29, 2015 that: "A police spokeswoman confirmed that the Monday arrests were made in connection with postal voting. Blackburn with Darwen, Burnley, Pendle and Hyndburn boroughs are on a list of 15 areas subject to strict monitoring by the UK's Electoral Commission over fears of election fraud, particularly involving postal voting." The alleged fraudsters are nearly always from Islamic backgrounds and the votes cast are invariably for the Labour Party, but rarely prosecuted by the police.

In a 2015 pre election interview Ed Miliband spelled out his plans for a post-election capitulation to Islamism. A future Labour Government, said Miliband, would change the law to make "Islamophobia" an aggravated crime. Miliband told Ahmed J Versi, the editor of *The Muslim News*: "We are going to make it an aggravated crime. We are going to make sure it is marked on people's records with the police to make sure they root out Islamophobia as a hate crime. We are going to change the law on this so we make it absolutely clear of our abhorrence of hate crime and Islamophobia. It will be the first time that the police will record Islamophobic attacks right across the country," he said. Brainwashing schoolchildren would be at the forefront of Miliband's intervention with children being branded "Islamophobic" as they are now branded "homophobic" or "racist" should they voice any criticism of the religion that demands jihad against non-Muslims from all of its followers.

Miliband outlined his objectives: "We will challenge prejudice before it grows, whether in schools, universities or on social media. And we will strengthen the law on disability, homophobic, and transphobic hate crime."

With Labour in power what has happened at Tower Hamlets will be replicated in cities across Britain with renewed vigour from the jihadis, now blessed with official state sanction. Those who oppose the new Tower Hamlets will be jailed as "Islamophobes" in Ed Miliband's brave new Labour world. When we look at Dewsbury in West Yorkshire we are looking at a snapshot of life as it will be lived in our Islamic cities after 2030. Once famous for the manufacture of woollen products, Dewsbury is now famous for its production of jihadists and suicide bombers, including three out of the four members of the 7/7 London Tube atrocity which killed 52 innocent people. Dewsbury also produced their leader, Mohammad Sidique Khan, the six Asians convicted of plotting to murder members of the EDL and Tahal Asma, Britain's youngest suicide bomber. Everywhere you look on the streets of Dewsbury are women dressed from head to toe in the niqab and mosques. The massive Markazi mosque, financed by Saudi Arabian cash and built on the grounds of a cricket club, now dominates the town. Savile Town, in Dewsbury, is the equivalent of a French Muslim ghetto with the number of Pakistani-Muslim residents living there just shy of 100%. The mosque is dominated by Tablighi Jamaat, a radical Islamist movement dedicated to erasing British cultural influences from Muslims. The sharia court in nearby Thornhill Lees dispenses Islamic justice to the residents of Dewsbury with English law regarded as incompatible with Islamic culture. Dewsbury is now racially segregated on Islamic and non-Islamic lines with ever greater numbers of jihadists emerging from it in ever greater numbers. Why are the security services allowing this radicalism to develop in Dewsbury and Tower Hamlets?

The answer comes from Andrew Gilligan whose impeccable journalistic efforts to expose corruption should receive the highest praise: "Terrified of being accused of racism, the authorities appear content to let Tower Hamlets stew in its own juice." (58)

However, being left alone to stew suited the Islamists at Tower Hamlets to a tee. It left them with a free hand to move onto the next stage of their grand plan, to flip their own corner of Britain into an Islamic state.

As every Marxist revolutionary knows, the successful transformation of society must begin with the education system and the brainwashing of those who will eventually become the footsoldiers of the new order, in this case, Islamic state UK.

Thus began, almost in tandem with Birmingham, the Tower Hamlets Islamists' attempt to influence children in state schools under their control in the London franchise of Trojan Horse. Again, the free press (curse them!) were on to the plot, as reported by a London daily newspaper:

"AS MANY as a dozen schools in the east London borough of Tower Hamlets face investigation after claims they have fallen under the influence of Islamic fundamentalists. According to government sources, officials at the Department for Education (DfE) are concerned that the situation may be worse than that uncovered in the 'Trojan Horse' scandal earlier this year, in which Islamic fundamentalists attempted to infiltrate secular schools in Birmingham. Emergency inspections of 21 schools in the city by the schools regulator Ofsted resulted in five schools being placed in special measures. 'Tower Hamlets is expected to be the next Birmingham, but even worse, because the problems surrounding Muslim fundamentalists imposing their views on education seem to be more embedded,' said a senior Whitehall source." (59)

Tower Hamlets is now the target destination for Islamists already inside Britain's flimsy garden gate and many more waiting to get in. In 2015, Bethnal Green Academy in Tower Hamlets had only one in four pupils with English as a first language, with most pupils coming from Pakistan or Bangladesh. Last year school inspectors carried out raids on seven schools in the borough fearing children were at risk of being radicalized, six of these schools were Islamic madrassahs. One of these madrassahs used to be known as John Cass's Foundation and Redcoat Church of England School, once judged "outstanding" but now found to be hosting the sermons of radical Islamic imams with the help of the school's own Islamic society. The Labour leadership have shut up about Tower Hamlets' Islamists but what they plan to do in power is shut everyone up who would demur from their groupthink on Islam. Behind the scenes Labour plans to brainwash a new generation of white working class children by labelling them "Islamophobic" or "racist" or "homophobic" through the schools.

It's not just our state schools under attack from anti-Western and pro-Islamic infiltration. All our state funded institutions are affected; but especially the universities, the broadcast media, Labour-run local councils and the civil service.

We saw from Trojan Horse in Birmingham and the corruption of Tower Hamlets that civil servants have no interest in preventing Islamic takeover in our institutions. Only the dogged integrity of Communities Secretary Eric Pickles was able to expose the rotten borough of Tower Hamlets and its Islamic/Labour mayor. If there is ever a future right of centre government in Britain it must take a leaf out of the Left's book, and purge on behalf of freedom. There must be a counter-multiculturalism strategy embarked upon in our schools, teacher training courses, universities, civil service and police, teaching that multiculturalism and Islamism is an ideology aimed at destroying *our* culture.

In tandem with this libertarian renaissance all laws that promote group rights and multiculturalism above the rights of the individual must be repealed. Sharia law has no place in any free society and it must be shouted from the rooftops that everyone is equal under the law and that none are more equal than others because of the colour of their skin or their religious beliefs. The Labour Party, unfortunately, are committed to a very different kind of British future.

As reported in the press Labour shadow Home Secretary, Yvette Cooper has unveiled the Left's new strategy to tackle the UK's "soaring rise in anti-Semitism, Islamophobia, homophobia and abuse of people with disabilities. The package includes making homophobic and disability hate crimes an aggravated criminal offence, ensuring that police treat such offences in the same way as racist hate crimes". (60)

Hand in hand with their strategy of targeting children as young as five through the schools, labelling and expelling those who can't adopt the correct multicultural mindset, Cooper outlined how changes to criminal records would highlight homophobia, disability or transgender offenses as well as anti-Semitism and Islamophobia.

For the record, Islam is not a race but a belief system open to all ethnicities. A fact lost on Labour Party ideologues who will spearhead a new PC troika alongside their ideological allies, the BBC, to clamp down on any criticism of perceived Muslim injustice in the same way Sweden has, with catastrophic results.

The police have already succumbed to Labour's cultural Marxism, post MacPherson. They now regularly employ the Regulation of Investigatory Powers Act (RIPA), a law introduced by Labour in 2000 to fight terrorism, but now used by the police to spy on journalists. The Metropolitan Police have accessed the phone records of more than 80 reporters and newspaper executives since 2012. How policing priorities will change under Labour will be a matter of fearful speculation for those who see our free society being dismantled piece by piece to accommodate the sensibilities of offended Islam but a good indication was the reaction of senior police officers to the Charlie Hebdo massacre of French journalists by Islamic terrorists.

As reported by the press, the National Counter-Terrorism Policing unit received a list of all UK newsagents that sold the memorial issue of Charlie Hebdo from distributor John Menzies then passed this list to the Association of Chief Police Officers (ACPO), who then wrote to police forces in those areas that included newsagents selling the magazines. Shopkeepers in Wales, Wiltshire and Cheshire then reported that police officers had approached them to demand that personal information on the readers of the Charlie Hebdo magazine should be passed over. These names and addresses were to be entered in a police database. The move to provide details of newsagents to local police was intended to "provide community reassurance", said Sir Peter Fahy, chief constable of Greater Manchester Police (GMP), in a letter to *The Guardian*.

Community reassurance for whom, one might ask? It seems that in the war against terrorism free speech is to be the Left's first target as the state ramps up its security apparatus to criminalise any dissent against the Islamization of Britain.

In February 2015 at a meeting in Westminster Harriet Harman gave assurances to Hacked Off supporters that if Labour wins the General Election in May it will impose full state-backed regulation of the press proposed by Labour's favourite judge, Lord Leveson. Harman insisted that: "We are absolutely committed to what Leveson proposed and we do not think that business as usual is acceptable". What is acceptable to Harman and Ed Miliband will be a whole new raft of measures designed to make the press politically correct. Thus Labour will finally get to do to the press what it did to the police, make it a tool of the Left. How will they do this?

By establishing a state-backed regulator of the press, underpinned by law, that would be able to oversee and punish the press by rewriting the editors' code so that newspapers are no longer in danger of printing "offensive" views and by issuing fines of up to £1million for those papers which have, for example, the temerity to run "offensive" leaders about immigration, welfare spending or Islam while rewarding "inoffensive" and PC papers with a government seal of approval. (And this year the award goes to *The Guardian*!) Here the dread hand of our PC/BBC would come into play as the "independent" system would itself be policed by Ofcom, run by political appointees and placemen. Hello Greg Dyke? Labour will also introduce Leveson's Complaint's Charter, a state-backed arbitration service that would hear complaints from "representative groups" and third parties offended by anything they might have read. How many of these groups will be Islamic, like the MCB? This is what the end of our free press will look like, and the beginning of sharia law. It is more than a scandal, more than a disgrace more of an outrage than any outrage in over 300 years of free British press history.

It would be the removal of free speech from Britain and its replacement by an ever narrowing range of permitted non-offensive opinions. This will be the real legacy of the Labour Party and its politically correct stooges who now run the BBC. The dictatorship of the Left that ran Soviet Russia could only survive because it abolished the free press and replaced it with its own state regulated version. What Labour intends to do to the press will make it easier for those who would enslave us, a tamed press would then act in the same way as the broadcasters do.

As former Muslim and author of *Cruel and Unusual Punishment*, Nonie Darwish attests: "The main concern of Muslim citizens in any Islamic state is staying safe, alive and away from being accused of doing or saying anything against Islamic teachings. In such an atmosphere of fear and distrust, harm can come not only from the government, but from friends, neighbours and even family members, who are protected from prosecution for killing anyone they regard as an apostate." (61)

If the Islamic world wanted Western democracy they would have accepted it with open arms in Iraq, they would have accepted the gift America gave them by deposing the despotic mass murderer Saddam Hussein and leaving the country the historically unique opportunity to live in freedom and replace theocratic fascism with democracy.

It almost bankrupted America but the penny eventually dropped that Arab Muslims don't want democracy at any price, what they want is sharia law. By allowing the mass migration of Muslims into Britain we have welcomed the unchangeable "diversity" of 7th Century medieval totalitarianism. Islam is the Gordian knot choking our multicultural society to death. We either surrender to the barbarity of sharia after an orgy of zero sum terrorism (as the Muslim population expands) or we recognise the incompatibility of Islamism with our free societies and deal with it, before it's too late.

Those who run our media won't believe they really want to kill us until we have the blade at our throats but as attempts to de-radicalise fanatics in Saudi Arabia have proved, you can't change the mind of Islamists. Once radicalised they stay radicalised. An American news report got the gist of it: "The Obama administration is scrambling to track down an Al Qaeda terrorist released from Guantanamo Bay years ago, offering a $5 million reward for information on him and placing him on a global terrorist list. Ibrahim al-Rubaysh was originally released in 2006 by the George W. Bush administration and put into a Saudi Arabian 'rehabilitation' program. However, al-Rubaysh returned to the battlefield and now serves as a top leader with Al Qaeda in the Arabian Peninsula — one of the most dangerous Al Qaeda affiliates." (62)

Charles Moore, then editor of *The Spectator*, wrote of the double standards our passive liberal elites applied to Islam: "The extent of the Islamic colonisation of Britain has been underlined with the news that the Muslim vote will be 'pivotal' in 82 constituencies in the forthcoming general election. According to a press release issued by the Muslim Public Affairs Committee (MPACUK), one of a myriad of front organisations dedicated to colonising Britain with the aid of the Tory/Labour immigration policy, the 82 constituencies have a Muslim population larger than the incumbent MPs' majority. As a result, the Muslims are organising through the network of at least 1,600 formal mosques which already exist in Britain."

The Islamists in our prisons, now being used as Al Qaeda recruiting offices, know they are at war; the Islamists who revel in their exploitation of our Human Rights Act know they are in a war; the foreign hate preachers who are furiously radicalising Muslim youth up and down the country know they are at war; the Islamists trying to take over our schools know they are at war and still the "moderate" Muslims make barely a sign or a gesture of protest as the news reports one Islamist atrocity after another.

Yet all we hear of from those in charge is that "most Muslims are not terrorists" or "Islam is the religion of Peace". This despite clear historical and current evidence (Charlie Hebdo, Jihadi John beheadings, Jordanian pilot burned alive) that since 9/11 almost every terrorist offence worldwide has been planned or committed by Muslim men aged between 19 and 35.

It is clear that our multicultural leaders are being played for fools by a death cult that still think the Sun revolves around the Earth. Under Barack Obama the same wool is being pulled over American eyes. Extensive research into the relationship of violence and mosques published in 2011, based on a study of 100 mosques over 15 states in the USA, found that 81% of mosques promoted violence and in 51% of mosques, extreme violence. Those mosques found to be non-violent had small congregations of less than 25 people, with those attracting more than 115 people habitually teaching extreme forms of violence. The evidence is always the same: as the Muslim population increases relative to the population as a whole so does the movement towards violence.

Of course the Left will accuse anyone suggesting a moratorium on immigration from Islamic nations or the rounding up and deportation of jihadis as "racists" or "fascists" and compare them to Hitler. Yet if we look at the history, the culture and the ideology of Islam the inescapable fact is that Islamism and Nazism are inescapably connected in a way Islam and freedom and democracy are not. It's not only the common thread of hatred for the Jews, hatred of our soft democratic systems, a belief in war and conquest and the enslavement of other races that binds the Nazi's to the Islamists. Islamists not only share National Socialist ambitions for world domination but go further, in their supremacist ideology over non-Muslims and doctrine of three choices: "conquest, convert or kill". When we see captives of IS being beheaded or burned alive no one is interested in the silent majority of the branch of Islam being represented by those doing the beheading. Beyond the propaganda of the BBC no one will accept the myth of "moderate" Muslims unless and until they take a stand themselves against the terrorists, by informing on the jihadis in their mosques and in their communities, which they are reluctant to do.

Why are mosques linked either to jihadi preachers or Muslims who have been radicalised not being shut down? Britain is not a Muslim country but Egypt is, and there 27,000 mosques have been closed by the government. As reported in *Al-Monitor*: "An Egyptian administrative court on Feb. 18 upheld the Ministry of Religious Endowments' decision issued in September 2013 to close down neighborhood places of worship of less than 80 square meters (861 square feet), a move intended to protect young people from the militancy and extremism that can prevail in such places, which lack the legal standing to hold Friday prayers." (63) In Britain and Europe the evidence shows that the bigger the mosque the more jihadists it produces. Either way we know where the the Salafist preachers are spreading hate.

Professor Tina Magaard has studied Arabic and read both the Koran and the hadiths. She draws the conclusion that it is not racism or socioeconomic factors that radicalize Muslim jihadis but straightforward exposure to Islam's holy scriptures: "What is striking is not in itself that one can find murderous passages in the Islamic texts, as such passages can also be found in other religions. But it is striking how much space these passages take up in the Islamic texts, and how much they focus on an us-and-them logic in which infidels and apostates are characterized as dirty, rotten, criminal, hypocritical and dangerous," she says. "It is also striking how much these texts demand that the reader fight the infidels, both with words and with the sword. In many passages, Muhammad plays a central role as one who encourages the use of violence, whether it comes to stonings, beheadings, acts of war or execution of critics and poets." (64)

ROTHERHAM

When Jack Straw was Home Secretary in Tony Blair's Labour government he never spoke out about the grooming of white English girls by Pakistani Muslims in his Blackburn constituency. In 2011, no longer in government and knowing he would not be standing in the next general election, Straw felt able to make a comment on what he knew to be true. When Mohammed Liaqat, 28, and Abid Saddique, 27, were jailed indefinitely at Nottingham Crown Court after being found guilty of having raped and sexually assaulted girls in Derby, Straw said on BBC's Newsnight programme that in some areas of the country Pakistani men: "target vulnerable young white girls" and that "they see these young women, white girls who are vulnerable, some of them in care ... who they think are easy meat". Straw is a Labour MP and like many other Labour MP's in the past and perhaps the majority of Labour MP's to come, relied on Muslim votes to be elected. He was immediately criticised by fellow Labour MP Keith Vaz, chairman of the Commons home affairs select committee, who said it was wrong to "stereotype a whole community".

Vaz is a Labour MP representing Leicester East and he also relies on Muslim support to get elected. On this occasion he did not accuse his Labour colleague of racism or Islamophobia. When Education Secretary Michael Gove, decided to appoint counter-terrorism police chief Peter Clarke to probe 25 Birmingham schools thought to be at risk from the Trojan Horse takeover he was immediately criticised by Labour MPs including Shabana Mahmood, MP for Birmingham Ladywood, and a Muslim, who described Clarke's appointment as "deeply provocative" and Khalid Mahmood, another Muslim Labour MP who represents Birmingham Perry Barr. Neither of these elected representatives seemed as eager for the truth to be revealed as apparently wanting not to offend Muslims in their constituencies. Just as disturbing, perhaps, was the reaction of Chris Sims, chief constable of West Midlands Police, who called Mr Clarke's appointment "desperately unfortunate". Sims was one of a number of chief constables appointed by Tony Blair's Labour administrations following the MacPherson report. This is just some of the background noise coming from official sources *prior* to the Rotherham report.

The Report

On the 4th of February, 2015, Louise Casey, a government official specialising in social welfare presented her report of inspection *Independent Inquiry into Child Sexual Exploitation in Rotherham (1997 – 2013)* to the government, detailing child abuse on a massive scale in Rotherham.

Her report found that: "In just over a third of cases, children affected by sexual exploitation were previously known to services because of child protection and neglect. It is hard to describe the appalling nature of the abuse that child victims suffered. They were raped by multiple perpetrators, trafficked to other towns and cities in the north of

England, abducted, beaten, and intimidated. There were examples of children who had been doused in petrol and threatened with being set alight, threatened with guns, made to witness brutally violent rapes and threatened they would be next if they told anyone. Girls, as young as 11, were raped by large numbers of male perpetrators. This abuse is not confined to the past but continues to this day. In May 2014, the caseload of the specialist child sexual exploitation team was 51. More CSE cases were held by other children's social care teams. There were 16 looked after children who were identified by children's social care as being at serious risk of sexual exploitation or having been sexually exploited. In 2013, the Police received 157 reports concerning child sexual exploitation in the borough. How could this happen in a civilized nation like Britain, how could elected officials, social workers and police be so blind not only to the truth but to what used to be known as "common decency" in allowing this corruption of English children to go on and do nothing?

The English author and columnist James Delingpole was moved to comment on the Rotherham case, asking: "**Q:** When is the sexual abuse of children culturally, socially and politically acceptable? **A:** When it's committed with industrial efficiency by organised gangs of mainly Pakistani men in English northern towns like Burnley, Oldham and Rotherham, of course. But obviously you're not allowed to admit this or you might sound racist. That's why, for example, in today's BBC report into the fact that at least 1400 children were subjected to 'appalling' sexual abuse in Rotherham between 1997 and 2013, you have to wade 20 paragraphs in before finally you discover the ethnic identity of the perpetrators. And even then, the embarrassing fact slips out only with the most blushing mealy-mouthedness: By far the majority of perpetrators of abuse were described as 'Asian' by the victims. Well hang on, a second. What this phrase seems to be hinting at is the possibility that the men involved *weren't* 'Asian' (note to US readers: Asian is UK PC-speak for Indians, Pakistanis, Bangladeshis, not Orientals) but that the victims mistakenly took them to be so. Is that actually the case or not? Let's have a look at the names of the Rotherham men found guilty by Sheffield Crown Court in 2010 of raping or sexually abusing girls as young as 12 shall we. Maybe that'll help: Zafran Ramzan, Razwan Razaq, Umar Razaq, Adil Hussain and Mohsin Khan. Nope. Absolutely no clues there, then...Still, let's suppose for a moment that the names of the gang members had been, say, John Smith, Barry Thorpe, Arthur Ramsbotham and Quentin Fforbes-Smythe. Are we seriously to believe that they would have been permitted to spend over a decade grooming, trafficking, drugging and raping young girls without arousing the concern of Rotherham Council's extensive social services department or the attentions of the local police? How many will continue to practice the Islamic "tradition" of having sex with underage English female kuffar (non-Muslim, regarded as subhuman by Islamists). The local authorities, in other words, knew exactly what was going on. Yet still they did nothing. Why? Well we've already answered that, pretty much. It's because the kind of politically correct, left-leaning and basically rather thick people that local authorities like Rotherham Council tend to have working for them are so paralysed by modish concerns about cultural sensitivity that they have made an obscene judgement call: better to allow at least 1400 kids to be hideously abused than to be thought guilty of the far greater crimes of being thought a bit racist or accidentally offending someone. Yep, these people really are that thick and warped. They've had it drilled into them that they must celebrate 'diversity' at every opportunity. And if that means letting a few Pakistani men rape kids, douse them with petrol and threaten them with guns, well who are we to judge? Quite possibly it's one of those vital cultural differences that we'll be trained better to understand when we attend our next Common Purpose course with some title like *Embracing the Other: Leadership Strategies For Multicultural Community Development*. Till then, let's not be quick to cast the first stone, eh? After all, there may be aspects of *our* culture that *they* find equally alien and troubling. The rule of law say; respect for women; children's rights; trendy Western liberal crap like that..." (65)

The trouble caused by those pesky journalists who have the nerve to report on the "cultural diversity" enriching us all, don't worry though, because Harriet Harman intends to stop all that offensive (to Muslims) reporting lark when Labour get back into power with the help of her favourite judge Lord Leveson and the chorus of Hacked Off celebs including Steve Coogan and Hugh Grant. Raymond Ibrahim is another troublesome chronicler of unpalatable truths, he recorded that: "Back in 2011, for example, Dr. Salih bin Fawzan, a prominent cleric and member of Saudi Arabia's highest religious council, issued a fatwa asserting that there is no minimum age for marriage and that girls can be married 'even if they are in the cradle.' Appearing in Saudi papers, the fatwa complained that 'Uninformed interference with Sharia rulings by the press and journalists is on the increase'—likely a reference to the justice ministry's advocacy—'posing dire consequences to society, including their interference with the question of marriage to small girls who have not reached maturity, and their demand that a minimum age be set for girls to marry'." (66) The abuse of underage white girls by Pakistani/Muslim men was already a well established fact among the ghetto's and enclaves embedding themselves across England by the time what was happening in Rotherham became public knowledge. At the heart of the Labour Party establishment, in Islington, Dianna Nammi of the Iranian and Kurdish Women's Rights Organisation (IKWRO) revealed that child brides as young as nine and at primary school are married off to older men in London's sharia courts. The *Islington Tribune* reported her saying that: "They are still expected to carry out their wifely duties, though, and that includes sleeping with their husband. They have to cook for them, wash their clothes, everything. They are still attending schools in Islington, struggling to do their primary school homework, and at the same time being practically raped by a middle-aged man regularly and being abused by their families. So they are a wife, but in a primary school uniform. The reason it doesn't get out is because they are too terrified to speak out, and also the control their families have over them is impossible to imagine if you're not going through it. The way it is covered up is so precise, almost unspeakable." (67)

Yet nothing was done, and Rotherham was allowed to happen when it could have been prevented. Jahangir Akhtar, was described in the Casey report into the sexual abuse, rape and prostitution of up to 2,000 mostly white English children by mostly Pakistani Muslim men, as an intimidating and "powerful figure" in Rotherham politics.

Aktar joined the Labour Party in 1990 and won election as a councillor before becoming the authority's deputy leader. The Rotherham abuse report indicated that the former taxi driver who had a criminal conviction for his role in a violent brawl also had "influence that extended to the police". Despite his criminal conviction, Aktar rose to become the police authority's crime panel vice-chairman. Jahangir Akhtar, is a cousin of Arshid Hussain, named as an alleged serial child abuser by victims of the Rotherham grooming gangs. Aktar lives a few doors from the alleged abuser's family home. Despite being accused of vile crimes by 18 young girls, Arshid Hussain was never even questioned by police. A report in *The Times* in 2014 accused Aktar of helping to arrange a deal where Hussain returned one of his alleged victims who had gone missing from home. Aktar would have been described as an "Asian" in the new PC-speak now used by the media, police and social services, which first obscures the fact that he is a Muslim and further obscures his Pakistani origin as being "south Asian" which also includes India and Bangladesh. The twist in this tale of incorrectness is that groups representing Sikh and Hindu communities have complained about the term "Asian" being used as a general description of the men involved in the grooming trials at Rochdale. When nine men were jailed in Rochdale for being part of a gang that groomed white English girls for sex were reported as being "Asian" The Ramadan Foundation strenuously objected that they were in fact "almost always of Pakistani origin" and that the term "Asian" was incorrect. A joint statement released by the Network of Sikh Organisations UK, the Hindu Forum of Britain, and The Sikh Media Monitoring Group UK said that grooming was "a significant problem for the British Pakistani community". (68)

In 2006 Google looked at the countries which made the most searches for pornographic items and Pakistan came in as the clear winner. Pakistan beat every other country in the world in searches per person for sex-related content with top searches being for horse sex since 2004, rape pictures between 2004 and 2009, rape sex since 2004 and child sex between 2004 and 2007. Pakistan has the most searches for "child sex video". (six of the top ten porn search nations happened to be Muslim countries; Egypt 2; Iran 4, Morocco 5, Saudi Arabia 7, Turkey 8.). This is the "cultural enrichment" of 7th century morality being imported to Britain. Such cultural norms are not reported in our broadcast media but a national daily newspaper was the only one in Britain to feature the Saudi preacher who raped and then tortured his five-year-old daughter to death. The paper reported that: "Lama al-Ghamdi died in October having suffered multiple injuries including a crushed skull, broken ribs and left arm, extensive bruising and burns. The child had also been repeatedly raped and then burned. Her father Fayhan al-Ghamdi, a prominent Islamist preacher who regularly appears on television in Saudi Arabia, served only a few months in jail despite admitting having used a cane and cables to inflict the injuries. Activists from the group Women to Drive said the preacher had doubted Lama's virginity and had her checked up by a medic. Randa al-Kaleeb, a social worker from the hospital where

Lama was admitted, said the girl's back was broken and that she had been repeatedly raped. Her injuries were then burned. Rather than the death penalty or a long prison sentence, the judge in the case ruled the prosecution could only seek 'blood money', according to activists. The money is compensation for the next of kin under Islamic law. Activists said the judge ruled the few months al-Ghamdi spent in prison since his arrest in November was sufficient punishment. He has reportedly agreed to pay £31,000 ($50,000), which is believed to have gone to Lama's mother. The amount is half that would have been paid if Lama had been a boy. Activists say under Islamic laws a father cannot be executed for murdering his children. Husbands can also not be executed for murdering their wives, the group say." (69)

The scores of men in these child sex trafficking gangs were Pakistani/Muslim and the girls sexually trafficked were non-Muslim. It was not even about race fundamentally because Islam is not a race; it's a religion/ideology. Identifying the men as "Asian" is a continuing multiculturalist cover-up of the codified Islamic culture of oppression and persecution of non-Muslims under sharia law, the ultimate sanction for this behaviour. Most "moderate" Muslims in Britain are probably unaware of the true meaning of the Koranic verses they recite in Arabic, it is probably this lack of complete understanding that keeps the lid on more religious extremism. However as more mosques are built and as Muslims become a larger and larger percentage of the UK population more of those who recite the verses will accept what they say as a literal word of command and act upon that word. This is the real reformation of Islam and this is the growing menace faced by all democratic European nations with increasing Muslim populations.

We have laws but, like the Rotherham council, our leaders fear to use them in case they are called "racists" but what we are up against now is a growing section of a growing section of the population with the same aims and methods of the foe we stood up to in 1940. This could all be nipped in the bud if our multiculturalist elite had the guts to instruct the police and security services to shut down mosques and religious schools which promoted jihad and prosecute and deport all jihadis with British passports. Instead, an industrial scale rape jihad with up to a million non-Muslim victims is allowed to rip unchecked across the towns and cities of England without much fuss from the police while they busy themselves arresting aging white male celebrities, allegedly guilty of fondling pubescent teenagers 40 years ago. The Labour Party has been thoroughly infiltrated by Islamists who are now directing it towards their goal of sharia law for Britain.

As the Muslim population increases those within the Labour Party who oppose this takeover will either leave or be silenced. This situation is far worse than when Labour faced being taken over by the Marxist Militant Tendency in the 1980s because those who opposed Militant within the Labour Party then were not hobbled by race hate legislation or the threat of being murdered. The irony of this situation will be lost on the Left until they themselves become some of the first victims of sharia law.

There are voices of reason among British Muslims and when they do speak out it is with criticism of the insanity of the Left's multiculturalism that has allowed radical Islam to flourish.

Dr Taj Hargey is an imam at the Oxford Islamic Congregation. He is one of the few Muslims willing to speak out, despite the dangers, to say that Islam itself is linked to the grooming of under-age white girls in our towns and cities. After an Oxford court delivered guilty verdicts on seven members of a Muslim child sex ring who forced under age girls to commit acts of extreme depravity a national newspaper reported on the case: "Their victims, aged between 11 and 15, were groomed and plied with alcohol and drugs before being sexually assaulted and forced into prostitution. They targeted 'out of control' teenagers. Dr Hargey said that the case brought shame on the city and the community and is a set back for cross community harmony. The activities of the Oxford sex ring are 'bound up with religion and race' because all the men - though of different nationalities - were Muslim and they 'deliberately targeted vulnerable white girls, whom they appeared to regard as easy meat, to use one of their revealing, racist phrases', Dr Hargey said. That attitude has been promoted by religious leaders, he believes. 'On one level, most imams in the UK are simply using their puritanical sermons to promote the wearing of the hijab and even the burka among their female adherents. But the dire result can be the brutish misogyny we see in the Oxford sex ring.' People tiptoe around the issues and refuse to discuss the problems exposed by the scandals such as those 'from Rochdale to Oxford, and Telford to Derby', he wrote. In all cases the perpetrators were Muslim men and the victims were under-age white girls. To pretend it is not a problem in the Islamic community is 'ideological denial', Dr Hargey said. 'But then part of the reason this scandal happened at all is precisely because of such politically correct thinking. All the agencies of the state, including the police, the social services and the care system, seemed eager to ignore the sickening exploitation that was happening before their eyes. 'Terrified of accusations of racism, desperate not to undermine the official creed of cultural diversity, they took no action against obvious abuse.' The men were allowed, he said, to come and go from care homes by the authorities, and if the situation had been reversed with gangs of white men preying on Muslim teenagers 'the state's agencies would have acted with greater alacrity.' (70) This article appeared before the Rotherham scandal happened but no lessons were learned. What has happened since is that what happened at Rotherham and elsewhere has been replaced in the headlines by an alleged "Westminster paedophile sex ring" where dead former politicians like Leon Brittan and Second World War heroes like Lord Bramall are hounded by the political police. Despite a million potential victims it seems that the Left will overlook any atrocity committed under the umbrella of "diversity" rather than relinquish multiculturalism as a means of strengthening its Stalinist grip on Britain. The label "diversity" should come with a health warning like "this means anti-Western civilisation" as should the BBC. As James Delingpole points out: "The left wing *Daily Mirror* meanwhile decided to hail the northern Muslim stronghold of Bradford the 'second-most peaceful of Britain's top ten cities' - in contradiction of a survey which suggested quite the opposite. But the BBC is the worst. For as long as I can remember, it has been talking up the 'Far Right' threat, not just in its news bulletins but even in its dramas with neo-Nazis and their ilk often being invoked as the sinister bad guys in thriller series from *The Professionals* to *Bonekickers* and *Spooks*. If the 'Far Right' really is the pre-eminent menace in Britain today, though, it has a funny way of showing it. How many schoolgirls has it raped, recently? How many people has it killed or maimed? How many bombs has it exploded? The grand total for all the above, I believe, is as near as makes no difference to zero. Now this isn't to say that the boot-boys who join these fascistic organisations are the loveliest of people nor that they don't hold racist views. But it seems to me that if we are to use our limited resources to address the most pressing problems of our time, we ought to bend our attentions to those dangers which are most clear and present rather than to politically correct chimeras like 'Islamophobia' and the 'spectre of the Far Right'. (The clue for the latter is in the name: a spectre is, by nature, ghostly, insubstantial). Otherwise what will happen is what is already happening now: you get the police turning a blind eye to antisocial behaviour by the Muslim 'community', the better to concentrate on arresting louts from the English Defence League or dads (both white and Sikh) who have had the temerity to try to take action against the gangs which have been raping their daughters. And you get a media culture which fails in its duty to expose, without fear or favour, corruption and wrongdoing wherever they are found. As we have reported before, those 1400 victims of the Rotherham rape gangs are just the tip of the iceberg. The first case involved girls trafficked and raped by Muslim gangs dates as far back as 1989. We also know that this has been going on in towns and cities across Britain, from genteel Henley-on-Thames to Telford to parts of Norfolk. A scandal like this on so epic a scale ought to be meat and drink to any half-way decent reporter, even in an organisation as ideologically-blinkered as the BBC. How can it not be a major story that over a period of 25 years communities across the country have been terrorised by gangs operating with near impunity, for all the world as if they were bandits on the lawless North West Frontier, not citizens of a liberal democracy? Why is not the BBC devoting its still fairly lavish resources to harrying all the bent councillors and police chiefs who have turned a blind eye to the problem and who have yet refused to resign? And how, in all conscience, can it be so insensitive as to insult its licence-fee-paying listeners by preaching to them a gospel which most of them know not to be true: that a 'far right backlash' that *might* happen is more worthy of our attention than a spate of rapes, bombings and murders that actually *has* happened, is continuing to happen, and will go on happening for as long as our politically correct establishment (of which the BBC is chief Cultural Commissar) goes on ducking the issue for fear of sounding 'Islamophobic'?" (71)

The Second World War was a war worth fighting because our very freedoms, won after 1000 years of struggle, were at stake. Then, our leaders didn't constantly make reference to the number of Germans who weren't members of the Nazi Party before throwing in the towel. Are we to surrender to an ideology/religion without being able to make an honest assessment of the true nature of the culture that awaits us compared to the one we are being asked to give up?

If Islamic teaching and culture is tolerant of what we would call paedophilia because such practices are approved of in their holy scriptures and Muslim men are told in their mosques that sex is permissible with non-Muslim kuffar girls, who are regarded as subhuman "whores" by their religion or "easy meat" (as Labour MP Jack Straw described it) aren't we entitled to know why? Tragically, because we are living in the liar's paradise of multicultural Britain, we cannot even reference cause and effect. We cannot say this Islamic religious racism is unacceptable and shut down all the mosques where imams are using literal interpretations of a medieval text to inform their Friday prayers. We cannot expel these imams, we cannot insist that imams hold prayers in English or not at all and we cannot deport those Pakistani/ Muslim convicted rapists back to their country of origin.

So what do our multicultural politicians do in response to 1400 Muslim rapes in Rotherham and possibly up to a million Muslim rapes of mostly white children elsewhere in Britain? They decide to follow plans devised by the Personal, Social, Health and Economic Education (PSHE) Association, set up in 2006 by Tony Blair's Labour Party, to ensure that *all* children in our state schools are forced to learn about rape and sexual consent from the age of 11. Thus, what used to be known as "childhood" in England has been wiped away, along with free speech in order to appease Islamic "culture". Where will this appeasement get us in the long run? There are clues and precedents around the world so let the clock tick on to 2030 and we can imagine finding ourselves in a situation similar to the one which now appears normal in the Philippines. As reported: "The Philippines has a major Muslim population in its southern most regions, particularly on the Island of Mindanao. The Muslims have been clamoring for their own land there, like they do in pretty much any other country they inhabit, and the Philippine Government, obviously not having learned from their former saviors, the U.S., that you do NOT negotiate with terrorists, have given in more and more over time. As a result, any time the Muslims want something, they take over a city or blow up a Mall, which has happened on several occasions this year alone. The results? The Philippine government caves and gives them more of what they want. Part of caving in the Philippines has been the recognition of certain Islamic laws, particularly, in the case of molesting children. The Philippines, a Christian nation, with strong Western ties and an ally of the U.S., actually now allows for girls who have achieved puberty to be married off to men of any age. *The Muslim Family Code of Philippines states, 'Any Muslim male at least 15 years of age and any Muslim female of the age of puberty or upwards and not suffering from any impediment under the provisions of this Code may contract marriage. A female is presumed to have attained puberty upon reaching the age of fifteen.* This allows an escape clause for pedophiles, and the golden parachute was taken this week by Filipino rock star, Freddie Aguilar. Aguilar is 60 years old, but has a penchant for underage girls. His recent fling is only 16 years old, and Aguilar admits to having been with the girl since she was 15, though rumours are circulating that he's been with her since she was only 14. With authorities hot on his tail, seeking prosecution for child molestation, Aguilar took legal counsel and converted to Islam. Again, since the Philippine Government recognizes men's rights to marry children under Sharia law, and now that Aguilar claims protection under Islam, he is untouchable. Aguilar is not the first pedophile to take advantage of Sharia laws being allowed in traditionally non-Muslim nations to avoid prosecution for molesting children. He is merely the first big named celebrity to do so. This is the danger of Sharia, coming to a democracy near you that people are missing. It's not only Muslims who think it is okay to have sex with children that you'll have to worry about. It's the predators already having sex with children, like Aguilar, who will be provided protection from prosecution merely by a profession of faith in Allah." (72)

The Left have looked at the atrocities committed by the fascists in World War Two and drawn completely the wrong conclusion. Instead of opposing intolerance in all its guises it has turned on its own people and attacked the very culture, national pride, history and homogeneity that allowed evil to be defeated in the first place. Instead of embracing decency and family they have instead adopted the same kind of superstitious, hate filled, violent ideology that brought the world to war in the first place.

As director of the Middle East Forum, Daniel Pipes wrote: "Muslims are entitled to equal rights and responsibilities but not to special privileges. They must fit into the existing order, not remake Western societies in the Islamist mould. Increasing freedom is welcome, regressing to the medieval norms of the Sharia is not."

If our Muslim minorities have no fear of raping non-Muslim (infidel) women and children in non-Muslim countries, countries where most have only *recently* arrived (after

1997) just what do indigenous English people have to look forward to when Muslim births outnumber Christian births in 2030 or when Muslims themselves become the majority grouping in Britain circa 2050?

To prevent this ultimate nightmare scenario from happening we must act now before it is too late and to prevent horrific violence further down the road to 2050.

Britain must halt all immigration from Islamic countries, at least until there is integration and an acceptance of Western values by those Muslims already here. We must deport all imams preaching jihad from British mosques and allow them to fight deportation from beyond our borders. Any expression of support for jihad and sharia law must become illegal with those found promoting sharia or jihad deported from Britain. As a first step towards this we must scrap the Human Rights Act and the sway it holds over our sovereign parliament.

This policy is being belatedly pursued now in France where between 2001 and 2010, France deported 129 of its "citizens" while over the same period the UK deported just nine alleged jihadis who actually *posed a threat to national security.*

The Islamists that France deported were kicked out for merely *making disparaging remarks about the country* rather than planning terrorist attacks. France, despite waking up late to its mortal peril after Charlie Hebdo, has now slashed welfare benefits to immigrants by 83% and with a tougher line on deportation may be in better shape than Britain by 2030. In Britain it took judges 10 years to agree the deportation of Abu Qatada, one of al-Qaeda's most dangerous terrorists, despite Qatada's own mother calling for his removal!

The law of the land in Britain must ultimately be decided by our own people and not by left-wing European judges. As a first step to saving ourselves from sharia law Britain must withdraw from the European Court of Human Rights (ECHR) and then from the European Union itself. Only then can we begin the mammoth task of removing from British soil those who would destroy us and our way of life and then protecting that way of life with border controls. We cannot prevent Britain from becoming an Islamic nation while we remain a member of the European Union, without control of our own borders. The British government must call on all Islamic advocacy groups to renounce any intention now or in the future to replace English law with Islamic sharia and this intention should be backed by verifiable action to monitor what is taught in British mosques. Why must one of the most advanced nations on earth kowtow to an utterly failed culture whose people will risk their lives in wooden rafts to gain entry to our utterly successful culture? Any mosque that fails to comply with this request, or is found to be teaching sharia law must be reclassified as a political, not religious, organization and made accountable to the laws which all political groups are held. Any group or mosque that continues to teach political Islam should be closed and the imams prosecuted and deported. Without deportation for those who preach jihad we can only substitute increased surveillance and banning orders for real action, which means the end of free speech for all of us.

Instead, what we are gradually doing is stripping down every aspect of our free society and dismantling the institutions that made us free in the first place so that we can continue with EU directed multiculturalism and Islamic immigration.

Like the Red Queen cutting off the wrong heads the state is contorting itself into repressive knots in its attempts to square the circle of multiculturalism and Islam.

CHAPTER SEVEN

STRONG HORSE TACTICS

An Islamic regime must be serious in every field. There are no jokes in Islam. There is no humour in Islam. There is no fun in Islam.
Ayatollah Khomeini

Why was *The Sun* columnist Katie Hopkins threatened with hate crime law because of an inane remark about "sweaty jocks" when protestors with placards reading "Behead those who insult Islam" were not charged with incitement to violence? These double standards are baked in the pie of multiculturalism along with the fear of provoking Muslim rage. This tolerance is regarded as weakness by traditional Islamic culture, which respects not our decadent pansy permissiveness but the "strong horse" of Islam, and will carry on pushing back our man made laws if it thinks it can achieve its goal.

The goal of almost all those who represent Muslims in *any* religious, official or quasi-official capacity in Britain is the enforcement of an Islamic caliphate ruled by sharia law. Some think they can get it by deceiving our liberal elites into believing they share multicultural values; others are just gathering strength until the numbers make sense before using the electoral process, hand in hand with terrorism, to abolish democracy. Examples of this strong horse mentality are everywhere reported in the national press: "Abu Waleed, 35, a leading preacher for a group banned last week for incitement to terrorism, was seen earlier this month at a barbecue in the Welsh capital where the banner of the Isis terror group – the Al Qaeda splinter group which the trio are fighting for – was flying. Jobless Waleed – whose real name is Shahid Janjua – lives in a council house in Hounslow, West London, and claims benefits for himself, his wife and three disabled children. Waleed rants about a future Britain under Islamic law: 'The kaffir [non-believer], when he walks down the street, he has to wear a red belt around his neck, and he has to have his forehead shaved, and he has to wear two shoes that are different from one another. 'He [the non-believer] is not allowed to walk on the pavement, he has to walk in the middle of the road, and he has to ride a mule.' He says that under a British sharia state, non-Muslims will pay a tax called jiziya for protection. He continues: 'We are the ones who want to work for the sake of Allah, to establish the manifestation of Islam, and make sure David Cameron comes on his hands and knees, and gives us the jiziya.' (73)

Lord Carlisle, the Lib Dem peer compared Waleed's views to: "the worst views and actions of Adolf Hitler." So why was Waleed not arrested for incitement to religious hatred? Do our establishment figures think that because he called Kate Middleton a "whore" and said she and the Queen would be forced to wear the veil that he wasn't seriously representing what is now mainstream thought among a significant section of British Muslims? Compare the treatment of Waleed to that of BNP member Michael Coleman. Coleman blogged on his computer, accusing Stoke-on-Trent city council of: "flooding this city with Muslims and blacks, a complete population replacement programme. Darkies in, whites out". Police were called in by Labour city councillor Joy Garner, who had been asked by a member of the public to read the blogs.

Coleman was arrested and ended up with an eight month prison sentence (suspended) with 240 hours of community service. I would be that last person to defend the BNP but what we really need to know is why Coleman ended up with a criminal record for publishing "racist" articles on his blog when those who publically said they wanted to "slay those who insult Islam" do not.

Coleman was protesting against mass immigration and if that was the reason for his conviction in the courts then the courts are sending us all a clear message that we better not make a peep about the unasked for millions flooding into Britain or we might face jail. His use of the word "darkies" is unfortunate but also one of a number of words and epithets that are steadily coming to be regarded as "racist" by the Left.

On TV a Celebrity Big Brother (how ironic) contestant was removed for his use of the newly minted racist word "negro" to which "coloured" and "darkies" must now be added, say the race hate activists. Gradually the Left and their PC enablers are restricting and controlling even our use of language for the purposes of closing down any criticism of its immigration agenda. Such is the speed of this transition that even liberals are beginning to get uneasy about the way threats of prosecution or actual prosecutions are applied to people in situations which appear to be ever more extreme. Take Brendan O'Neill of *The Daily Telegraph*, on the Coleman controversy. He pays ritual obeisance to the horror of Coleman's views and the use of "darkies", calls him a moron, but then writes: "The councillor who kick-started the legal action against Coleman said something very interesting – he said the reason Coleman had to be punished and turned into a criminal for writing those blog posts is because the views they expressed are 'not acceptable to the overwhelming majority of local people'. That is true; the vast majority of Britons find racist ideas and language disgusting. But are we really going to start threatening with imprisonment people who express opinions that the 'overwhelming majority' consider to be unacceptable? Will that include radical political views, edgy social arguments, hare-brained religious beliefs? The fact that in Britain in 2012 a man has been given a suspended jail sentence and 240 hours' community service for saying something that is offensive to the 'overwhelming majority' should give us all serious pause for thought, and make us ask what gives us the right to slam Putin's Russia for likewise banging up punkish singers who, according to polls, also offended an 'overwhelming majority' of Russians." (74)

Those who watch a crime being committed without reporting it are classed as accomplices under English law and we must assume this applies to "moderate" Muslims. Those who class themselves as "moderate" Muslims, like the Muslim Council of Britain (MCB) are anything but. Broadcasters should be doubly wary of any group claiming to represent Muslims in any official capacity, as police advisors, as advocates of sharia courts and community leaders. They are always Islamists seeking sharia law and Islamic supremacy.

An article for *The Daily Mail*, in January 2014, described how "one of Britain's leading Muslims" Javed Khan the Pakistani born head of Victim Support, a Government-backed and taxpayer funded charity for the victims by crime, had been accused of taking an gang of eight men armed with automatic rifles back to Pakistan to settle a land dispute in the village of Haveli Bagal. In March 2014 Khan was appointed head of Britain's largest children's charity Barnardo's, the main provider of child sexual exploitation services in the UK. Barnado's now stands accused of knowing all about the child sex scandal in Rotherham but of doing nothing about it.

Barnardo's had contact with hundreds, if not thousands, of children who went on to become victims of Muslim rape gangs. Some of these victims' stories are told in Barnardo's own report which *never mentions* the religious or ethnic identity of the rapists.

In his 2014 report *Easy Meat: Multiculturalism, Islam and Child Sex Slavery* ... author Peter McCloughlin lists numerous occasions when Barnardo's could have spoken up about Rotherham's Muslim rape gangs but chose not to. Why, when local Labour MP Ann Cryer raised the issue of Muslim rape gangs in her Keighly constituency in 2003 did her *own party* accuse her of racism and why did Barnado's not back her up? Why, when a Channel Four documentary on the subject was shelved at the request of the chief constable of West Yorkshire police, did Barnado's not demand that it be shown and why were the police so keen not to have it broadcast in the first place?

When interviewed by Eamonn Holmes on Sky news Javed Khan repeatedly refused to call for the resignation of South Yorkshire police commissioner (and former head of Rotherham council children's services) Shaun Wright while seeming to show little interest in condemning the institutions that allowed this mass child rape to occur.

This was the Left's multiculturalism rotting right out in the open for once and it stank to high heaven.

Better than asking how many of the Pakistani community of Rotherham knew that white children were being passed about and raped right in front of them shouldn't we instead be asking how many *didn't* know?

All cultures are not equal and if that ever needed proof then Rotherham was the place to come with witnesses. Try passing a child around a white working-class community of the kind I grew up in and the perpetrators would have been either arrested or hospitalised.

Yet, pass a white child around for rape in a Muslim/Pakistani community and what it appears you get is a cover up from representatives of the dominant culture who appear to regard the abuse of white children as acceptable.

The Islamic immigrants who voted with their feet and decided to move en masse to Britain after 1997 crossed many borders to get here. They made a conscious decision to come to a country whose people had defended freedom from tyranny and whose society, as a result, was safe and prosperous and happy. They came to Britain, presumably, to enjoy the rewards of those sacrifices made by this indigenous people over hundreds of years of hardship, leaving behind countries that had none of these freedoms. Countries with no free speech; no freedom of conscience; no freedom of religion; no freedom or equality under the law. Countries with feudal economic systems, eternal tribal hatreds and medieval laws permitting female genital mutilation and pre-pubescent sex.

So why did our politicians permit these new arrivals, with their hands held out begging to be let in, to set about agitating to change irrevocably the land which had given them everything they had asked for, and more? The Left's criminalisation of free speech and of British history leaves us unable to say what we know is true, that our native culture is infinitely superior to Islamic culture and that the Left, in combining with Islam, is guilty of the most heinous treason.

Lady Warsi, former Coalition cabinet minister and Tory grandee resigned from the Government over its "morally indefensible" position over Gaza. The Muslim peer has worked with the Organisation of Islamic Cooperation, which wants a worldwide ban on insulting religion, a de facto Islamic blasphemy law that would end free speech.

While in government Warsi supported the UN Human Rights Council Resolution 16/18, which would have effectively criminalised any criticism of Islam and then appeared on television in Paris after the Charlie Hebdo murders, saying that they were "an attack on Islam". Baroness Warsi, the first Muslim woman to sit in Cabinet has acted as a facilitator for radical Islamists by handing official posts to people linked to Islamist groups. One radical given a leg up by Warsi is Muddassar Ahmed, a former senior activist in the Muslim Public Affairs Committee (MPAC), a militant Islamist and anti-Semitic group, banned from many universities as a hate organisation. During Ahmed's time at MPAC they campaigned heavily against Lorna Fitzsimons, the former Labour MP for Rochdale who lost her seat by a handful of votes after MPAC activists distributed thousands of leaflets to local Muslim voters saying they should get rid of her because she was "Jewish" (though she is not).

MPAC states that all Muslims are "at war" and that "every Muslim who does not participate in that war is committing a major sin". Thanks to Warsi he now sits with other Islamic radicals like Fiyaz Mughal (of the discredited Tell Mama) on an influential Government working group making policy on "anti-Muslim hatred". Mughal, through his

Tell Mama group, given £375,000 by the taxpayer, wants to influence police forces up and down the country and shut down debate on the real aims of Islam in Britain by, according to his website: "providing training to police forces on understanding the language of anti-Muslim hate."

Mughal's goal is to bring about a new blasphemy law in Britain that would equate any criticism of Islam with racism. After the jihadi murder of Lee Rigby, Mughal's Tell Mama group were exposed by *The Daily Telegraph*'s Andrew Gilligan for making up evidence about a "wave of attacks on Muslims" which had never, in fact, taken place. Mughal hopes to change police and the Crown Prosecution Service (CPS) guidelines to criminalise criticism of Islam not only in the press but also on social media where he asserts that tougher sentences are needed to tackle "Islamophobic crime". Despite being completely discredited by Gilligan's thorough detective work Tell Mama are now working directly with the Association of Chief Police Officers (ACAPO). Have any of them read Gilligan?

The moral cowardice being shown by our political elite in the face of naked Islamic attempts at entryism was also the focus of a considered article by former *Spectator* editor Charles Moore. (Outraged Muslims subsequently demanded he be sacked for this outrageous display of free speechery). Moore said: "Four days ago, six Muslim men were sentenced at the Old Bailey for a plot to blow up an EDL rally. The news was received quietly, though it was a horrifying enterprise. No one spoke of 'white-phobia'. Imagine the hugely greater coverage if the story had been the other way round. All journalists experience this disparity. If we attack the EDL for being racist, fascist and pro-violence, we can do so with impunity, although we are not being strictly accurate. If we make similar remarks about Islamist organisations, we will be accused of being racist ourselves. 'Human rights' will be thrown at us. We shall also – this has happened to me more than once – be subject to 'lawfare', a blizzard of solicitors' letters claiming damages for usually imagined libels. Many powerful people in the Civil Service, local government, politics and the police, far from backing up our attacks on extremism, will tut-tut at our 'provocative' comments. Much more important – from the point of view of the general public – you frequently find that Muslim groups like Tell Mama get taxpayers' money (though, in its case, this is now coming to an end). You discover that leading figures of respectable officialdom share conference platforms with dubious groups. You learn that Muslim charities with blatantly political aims and Islamist links have been let off lightly by the Charity Commission. And you notice that many bigwigs in Muslim groups are decorated with public honours. Fiyaz Mughal, for example, who runs Tell Mama, has an OBE. Obviously it would be half-laughable, half-disgusting, if activists of the EDL were indulged in this way; yet they are, in fact, less extreme than some of those Muslims who are." (75)

These are the Muslim groups financed by the Labour governments of 1997-2010.

The Muslim Council of Britain (MCB) Part of The Muslim Brotherhood, a global Islamist organisation dedicated to establishing a global caliphate ruled by sharia law. The UK branch (MCB) was set up with the support and funding of Tony Blair's Labour government, who handed out over £550,985 to it and related Islamic groups over a period of three years (from the Department of Communities and Local Government).

The MCB are, like almost all representatives of Islam in Britain, Islamists, whose aim is the overthrow of democracy in Britain and its replacement with sharia law. One of the MCB's first acts in 2007 was to publish a policy document called *Towards Greater Understanding* advising local authorities how to deal with Muslim pupils in state schools. In this document was a list of changes that the MCB wanted, and still want, to see imposed on British schools.

Prayers: Schools should provide (1) extra "water cans or bottles" for washing before prayers (2) prayer facilities, separate ones for boys and girls. Schools should make available "a suitable external visitor, a teacher or an older pupil" to lead communal Friday prayers and give the sermon.

Toilets: Water available in water cans or bottles for cleansing purposes. Social customs: No touching hands with members of the opposite sex, students or teachers.

Holidays: Vacation days for all on the two major Muslim holidays, the Eids. During Ramadan all children, not just Muslim ones, should celebrate "the spirit and values of Ramadan through collective worship."

Ramadan: No exams during this month and only halal meals must be eaten. (The MCB are clearly determined for Ramadan to become a part of the British calendar, watch out for this if Labour return to power).

Clothing: *Everyone,* including non-Muslim children must wear hijabs and jilbabs (a long outer garment down to the ankles). In swimming pools, Muslim children should wear modest swimwear (for girls, full leotards and leggings). Islamic amulets must be permitted.

Sports: Sex-segregation where there is physical contact with other team players, as in basketball and football, or when exposed, as in swimming.

Music: Should be limited to "the human voice and non-tuneable percussion instruments such as drums." (There is no music in Islam).

Dancing: No dancing allowed unless it is done in a single-sex environment and does not "involve sexual connotations and messages."

Teacher training: Staff should undergo Islamic awareness training (the most sinister policy of all).

Art: Muslim pupils must be exempt from producing "three dimensional figurative imagery of humans."

Religious instruction: Pictures of any prophets (including Jesus) prohibited.

Languages: Arabic should be made available to all students.

The ringleader of the Birmingham Trojan Horse plot Tahir Alam wrote this detailed blueprint for the radical Islamisation of secular state schools for the MCB. Alam, who later surfaced as chair of governors at Park View School in the city, called for "girls [to] be covered except for their hands and faces", advocated gender segregation in some school activities, and attacked a "multicultural approach" to collective worship. Just join the dots and you can see how the real picture emerges.

The MCB's Islamist agenda is controlled by Jamaat-e-Islami a genocidal Islamist organisation and the banned Islamist terror group The Muslim Brotherhood.

Despite managing only 3.4% of British mosques and despite a 2007 survey that showed 94% of British Muslims did not believe that the MCB represented their views and despite their links to government being cut in 2009 after they signed a declaration *supporting* violence against British armed forces, they *still* pull the wool over the eyes of our political elites. The BBC still regard the MCB as the "go to" official voice of Muslims on their news and online services and are quick to surrender licence fee money if perceived "offence" is caused. In 2009, former *Daily Telegraph* editor Charles Moore stated on the

BBC's *Question Time* programme: "The Muslim Council of Britain, which is the umbrella organisation for all Muslim groups in this country, I've gone to them many times, and I said will you condemn the killing and kidnapping of British soldiers in Iraq and Afghanistan, and they won't. But there is a bigger, another step that they take, they say it is actually a good thing, even an Islamic thing, to kill or kidnap British soldiers." Moore had been debating the protests in Luton of a group of Islamic extremists led by Adnan Choudery during a homecoming parade by the Royal Anglian Regiment. They had heckled the troops and waved placards which read "Butchers of Basra". The MCB sued and, instead of defending an easily winnable action, the BBC caved in, paid out £30,000 (later raised to £45,000) and apologized. The BBC paid libel damages simply for broadcasting Charles Moore's comment despite the fact that Muhammad Abdul Bari, of the Muslim Council of Britain, who sued, was never even mentioned by name.

Yet still the MCB are perceived as representatives of Britain's Muslims. The Ministry of Defence, insanely, uses the MCB to sponsor and approve all Muslim chaplains serving in Britain's armed forces, NHS hospitals and prisons. The result is the commonly voiced concern that Islam now runs Britain's prisons, not the guards, with MCB sponsored Muslim Chaplains being paid £100 for every non-Muslim they convert. And Christian chaplains are where, doing what? Following concerns over Islamic radicalisation in prisons researchers visited HMP Whitemoor between 2009 and 2010 to interview staff and inmates and found that more than a third of prisoners were now Muslims, compared with 11% across all jails. This was due to intimidation from Muslim gangs and the conversion of non-Muslims, including many sex-offenders, by prison chaplains.

Why are those who run HMP's not advocating the need to separate Muslim prisoners from others and close down all mosques in our prisons? Muslim prisoners should have no special privileges and be subject to deportation after their sentences have been served if they have been convicted of jihadi activity or its promotion.

It takes *The American Thinker* to uncover the obvious: "It seems that every time the government or other agencies take any concrete or real action against Islamic extremists - or even against Islamic terrorists - in the UK, the MCB has a serious problem with it. For example: i) The MCB had a problem with the actions against Islamic terrorists in the UK between 2005 and 2010. It said that such actions 'could cause [or did cause] extremism within the community'. ii) The MCB had a problem with the investigations and actions against the Islamization of British schools. It said such investigations and actions 'could cause [or did cause] extremism in the Muslim community'. iii) The MCB had a problem with the emphasis on the Muslim and Pakistani nature of sexual-grooming gangs. It said such an emphasis 'could cause [or did cause] extremism in the Muslim community'. It's almost as if the MCB doesn't want any action — of any kind — to be taken. Now why would an organization which is part of the Muslim Brotherhood - a worldwide Islamist movement - not want any action to be taken against any section (extreme or otherwise) of the Muslim community...? Do I really need to answer that?" (76)

Sharia Watch is an organisation, led by former Labour Party candidate Anne Marie Waters, that seeks to expose "movements in Britain which advocate and support the advancement of sharia law in British society". (The group was created in response to the news that Britain's Law Society is now offering guidance for sharia law in Britain!) In its launch document it was heavily critical of the Muslim Council of Britain (MCB), saying that: "Sharia Watch UK believes that the MCB is itself an extremist organisation." Other Islamic organisations listed and suspected of being fronts for Islamic extremism were: the Islamic Sharia Council, the Muslim Association of Britain, the Federation of Student Islamic Societies, the Cordoba Foundation, the British Muslim Initiative, the Green Lane Mosque, the East London Mosque/London Muslim Centre, the Islamic Forum of Europe, iEngage, the Islam Channel, the Islamic Human Rights Commission, the London Central Mosque (Regent's Park Mosque). Like a bloated spider at the centre of this tangled web of jihad sits The Muslim Brotherhood and its plans for "jihad by stealth", with non-Muslims duped into believing the MCB's red herring of Muslim victimology.

Potentially the culmination of this *dawa* (spread of Islam) has been the actions of President Barack Obama and the plot to *dawa* America. In 1995, Yusuf al-Qaradawi, the spiritual leader of the Muslim Brotherhood, told a Muslim Arab Youth Association convention in Toledo, Ohio: "We will conquer Europe, we will conquer America! Not through the sword, but through dawa."

The Holy Land Foundation, based in Texas, used to be the largest Islamic charity in the United States. On 7th November 2001 a document written in Arabic and called "The

Project", a long term plan to convert all countries to Islam and overthrow all Western democracies, was found in a house that belonged to Youssef Nada, director of the Al-Taqwa bank of Lugano of which Sheik Yousef Al-Qaradawi was the fourth largest shareholder. The tactics recommended in this document were very clear.

a) Avoid open alliances with terrorist organizations to give the appearance of moderation.

b) Involve Muslims in democratically elected institutions at all levels including government, NGOs, private organizations and unions.

c) Support jihad movements across the Muslim world.

d) Have a constant campaign to incite Muslim hatred against Jews and reject any discussions about reconciliation or coexistence with them.

This was the Muslim Brotherhood's real agenda for change, the wolf in sheep's clothing among the real sheep. In 2007, federal prosecutors brought charges against the organization for funding Hamas and other Islamic terrorist organizations (just before Obama came to power). The Holy Land Foundation's assets were frozen and the charity was shut down by the U.S. government after it proved it was funding Hamas.

The 2008 trial of the charity's leadership was the biggest terrorism funding prosecution in US history and the result was that in 2009 the Foundation's leadership were all given life sentences for funneling $12 million to Hamas. During the course of the 2008 United States v Holy Land Foundation terrorist finance trial evidence was presented to the court showing the extent to which The Muslim Brotherhood had infiltrated American institutions and its control of *all* major Muslim organizations in America, including the Council on American Islamic Relations (CAIR) and the Islamic Society of North America (ISNA). A document titled *An Explanatory Memorandum: On the General Strategic Goal for the Group,* was particularly damning for The Muslim Brotherhood's "moderate" image.

Written in 1991 by senior Hamas strategist Mohamed Akram (Hamas are dedicated in their charter to the genocidal destruction of Israel and the establishment of a worldwide caliphate ruled by sharia law), and also on the Muslim Brotherhood's board of directors in North America, the Explanatory Memorandum explained that the Muslim Brotherhood movement in the US is a front to establish itself as a "moderate" grouping which, once established, would begin a "grand jihad" in America, eliminating and destroying Western civilization from within its own borders and "sabotaging its miserable house by their hands and the hands of the believers so that it is eliminated."

Before the election of Barack Obama and before Eric Holder became attorney general the Dallas US attorney's office intended to prosecute the named co-conspirators, that was *before* Barack Obama decided to stop the process moving forward. Here was *dawa* running rings round elected officials, but more was to come. In 2011 the Obama Administration removed all references to Islam in connection with any examination of Islamic jihad terror activity from all FBI and national security training manuals. Dwight C. Holton, former U.S. attorney for the District of Oregon, confirmed on behalf of his boss, attorney general Eric Holder, that all FBI training materials would be purged of any references to the wider motives and goals of jihadi terrorists.

"I want to be perfectly clear about this: training materials that portray Islam as a religion of violence or with a tendency towards violence are wrong, they are offensive, and they are contrary to everything that this president, this attorney general and Department of Justice stands for. They will not be tolerated," he said. The Muslim Brotherhood exulted in this victory for the cause of "stealth jihad" while across the Atlantic the British arm of the Brotherhood, the Muslim Council of Britain continued with its own *dawa* along with the rest of the spreading tentacles of stealth jihadists.

The Cordoba Foundation, an independent research organisation which advises leading Muslim groups and which was founded by Anas al-Tikriti, former president of the Muslim Association of Britain, has received 'anti-extremist' funding. The group was given £38,000 by Tower Hamlets council in East London in 2007

The Islamic Foundation found by the BBC's Panorama to be an outpost of militant Islamist ideology was set up by members of Pakistan's Jamaat-i-Islami opposition party, which campaigns for Pakistan to become an Islamic state governed by sharia law.

An all-Party Parliamentary Group on Islamophobia was linked to **iEngage**, an organisation of Islamists which called on the Government to revoke a ban on an imam who said that 'every Muslim should be a terrorist'.

Lambeth Council gave public money to the **STREET** project, run by Abdul Haqq Baker, the chairman of the Brixton Mosque and Islamic Cultural Centre. Baker is an adherent of hardline Salafism, a form of Islam opposed to liberal democracy and man-made law.

Government money was given to Birmingham's Green Lane and Central mosques who allowed radical Islamists to openly preach hatred of the West and its freedoms. Among suggestions from the main speakers was a suicide bomb attack on the Queen for awarding a knighthood to Salman Rushdie. The Met also employed as an anti-terrorism adviser Mohamed Ali Harrath, who was wanted by Interpol because of his links to an Islamic terror organisation.

CAGE In February, 2015 "human rights" group CAGE, held a press conference where heavily bearded research director Asim Qureshi spoke live on the BBC and without interruption. The subject was Jihadi John, the beheader of IS videos, now unmasked as Mohammed Emwazi but described by Qureshi as an "extremely kind" and "beautiful young man". For three years CAGE had been in close contact with Emwazi before he left Britain to fight in Syria in 2012. Qureshi waxed lyrical about Jihad John while spitting bile against the injustices of Britain's "war on terror". There was no hint of remorse for the victims of Emwazi, only the usual Islamic victimhood on parade from Qureshi, who lives with his partner in a £500,000 house in Surrey. In 2006, Qureshi was filmed outside the US embassy in London addressing a rally organised by the extremist group Hizb-ut-Tahrir where he said: "When we see the example of our brothers and sisters fighting in Chechnya, Iraq, Palestine, Kashmir, Afghanistan, then we know where the example lies. We know that it is incumbent upon all of us to support the jihad of our brothers and sisters in these countries when they are facing the oppression of the West. Allahu Akbar! Allahu Akbar!" In an interview on Russia Today, Qureshi said he wanted the imposition of sharia law, including the stoning to death of adulterers. On the platform with Qureshi was a member of the hard left Socialist Workers Party (SWP) signalling the alignment of the hard Left with hardline Islam.

CAGE portray themselves as a human rights group and by doing so dupe gullible liberals into financing their activities.

Over a period of six years £305,000 was donated by the Joseph Rowntree Charitable Trust, a Quaker-run fund set up by the York-based chocolate maker. The Anita Roddick foundation has also made considerable donations. In 2006 Birmingham-born Moazzam Begg joined CAGE as its "outreach director". Begg had been arrested in Pakistan in 2002 for alleged terrorist related activity then sent to Guantanamo Bay where he claimed to have been the "victim" of 300 interrogations.

Despite having admitted to "visiting" terror training camps in Afghanistan, Begg was awarded £1million compensation by the British Government and later worked for *The Guardian* which, as we shall see, is heavily linked to the BBC's *Newsnight* just as the BBC and The Labour Party are heavily linked to each other.

While the "religion of peace" rhetoric continues to rattle round Whitehall our citizens are being edged ever closer to an Islamic bloodbath on the streets of England.

Paranoia, exaggeration? Not even the current, nominally Conservative, government has even begun to realise just how fast Islamist infiltration has progressed within the seat of government.

In 2010 classified papers, presented to new Coalition ministers on the Cabinet's home affairs committee, gave *official* guidance to ministers about Islamic groups openly operating in Britain like Hizb ut-Tahrir, which wants to turn Britain into an Islamic dictatorship run by sharia law or al-Muhajiroun who praised the 9/11 murderers of more than 3,500 people as "magnificent". Their advice was that individuals *do not* go on to commit acts of terrorism or become radicalised and that *too much* weight had been given to ideological factors, like Islam and its radical preachers and unsupervised mosques. The document further suggests that the government *co-operate* with these Islamic organisations rather than try to boycott or close them down. This advice, still being followed by Nick Clegg and some of his Cabinet colleagues, was written with the help of the Labour Party's favourite Islamist, Mohammed Abdul Aziz. Patently this policy was naivety in all its multicultural glory or there were people *inside* the home office writing this taqiyya who needed a second or even a first look from our security services.

Melanie Phillips in her prescient work *Londonistan,* described the changing face of the capital under New Labour: "London had become the hub of the European terror networks. Its large and fluid Muslim and Arab population fostered the growth of myriad radical Islamist publications spitting hatred of the West, and its banks were used for fund-raising accounts funnelling money into extremist and terrorist organizations. Terrorists wanted in other countries were given safe haven in the United Kingdom and left free to foment hatred against the West. Extremist groups such as Hizb ut-Tahrir remained legal, despite being banned in many European and many Muslim countries. Radicals such as

Abu Qatada, Omar Bakri Mohammed, Abu Hamza and Mohammed al-Massari were allowed to preach incitement to violence, raise money and recruit members for the jihad. An astonishing procession of UK-based terrorists turned out to have been responsible for attacks upon America, Israel and many other countries.

When Abu Hamza was finally jailed in February 2006 for soliciting murder and inciting racial hatred, an astounded British public suddenly discovered that for years he had been allowed to operate from his London mosque as a key figure in the global terrorist movement while the British authorities sat on their hands. Not only had he openly incited murder and racial hatred, but he had amassed inside his mosque a huge arsenal of weapons to be used in terrorist training camps in Britain. Worse still, through his preaching of jihad he had radicalized an unquantifiable number of British Muslims, including three of the London bombers." (77)

It took Britain's pesky free press, in the form of Andrew Gilligan, to take that second look, and he noted that: "The papers are understood to have been prepared with the involvement of Mohammed Abdul Aziz, a controversial paid ministerial adviser to the Communities Department. Mr Aziz is an honorary trustee of the hardline East London Mosque, which has hosted dozens of hate and extremist preachers, including Anwar al-Awlaki, a cleric cited as an inspiration by the perpetrators of 9/11 and many other terrorist attacks. The mosque is the headquarters of, and closely linked to, a secretive, fundamentalist network, the Islamic Forum of Europe – which believes in transforming 'the very infrastructure of society, its institutions, its culture, its political order and its creed ... from ignorance to Islam'. Mr Aziz is a former officer of the IFE's youth wing'." (78)

The penny still hasn't dropped among the "see no Islam" multiculti juveniles running Britain that *everyone* who works for any organisation representing Islam is likely an *Islamist* working for the establishment of an Islamist state in Britain under sharia law. What they will say in public is that they are loyal British Muslims and know nothing about terrorism, but behind the façade and the taqiyya (Islamic sanctioned lies) is a common determination to replace our democratic system with sharia law. This is a war on freedom but until we acknowledge that we are at war and identify the enemy it is a war we cannot hope to win while taqiyya compliant politicians roll out the red carpet for the new Islamic state in Britain.

Take the three schoolgirls, Shamima Begum, Amira Abase and Kadiza Sultana, who bunked off from the Muslim dominated Bethnal Green Academy in London to become the Jihadi rape-brides of psychopathic Islamic State killers in Syria. The BBC gave us blanket coverage on the fate of these "victims" with Labour MP Keith Vaz quick to hop on the BBC bandwagon, demanding that police answer the accusations of the father of one of the girls, Abase Hussen, that it was somehow the fault of the police and British society that she went missing in the first place.

In front of Vaz's parliamentary committee Hussen, clutching his daughter's Teddy bear, denied even knowing what Islamic radicalisation was: "As for me, I don't know the symptoms even — what radicalisation is," he told doe-eyed MPs. Then slowly the truth emerged (thanks again to our pesky free press) a few weeks later when this article appeared in a national daily: "His face twisted in fury, Abase Hussen punches his fist into the air and launches into an Islamic war cry.'Burn, burn USA,' he yells from his prime spot at the front of one of the most notorious rallies in recent times. Once the crowd is whipped into a fever, an American flag is set on fire and held aloft by a fanatic. Video footage shows Mr Hussen desperately trying to hold the burning flag as the chanting behind him intensifies. He manages to grab the flag briefly before being forced to drop it because of the power of the smoke and flames. As the remainder of the flag burns on the ground, Mr Hussen chants 'Allahu Akbar'. He pushes the palm of his hand repeatedly toward the embers, rejoicing at the destruction of the stars and stripes. Mr Hussen – the father of one of the three schoolgirls who fled Britain to join Islamic State – then turns his attention to a burning Israeli flag on the floor and begins to chant and gesture toward it. He is one of a dozen fanatics standing behind a banner which proclaims: 'The followers of Mohammed will conquer America.' Behind him, hundreds of fanatics repeatedly chant incendiary slogans while holding menacing black jihadi flags. Among the rabble-rousers was notorious hate preacher Anjem Choudary, who has led a number of Islamist groups that were subsequently banned. Alongside him stood Michael Adebowale, one of the two Muslim converts who murdered and almost beheaded Fusilier Lee Rigby in the name of Allah eight months later. But last month Mr Hussen gave evidence to Parliament refusing to accept any responsibility for the three schoolgirls' actions, instead seeking to blame the police, teachers, Turkish officials and others." (79)

On April 2, 2015 BBC news reported that a politics student from Rochdale, Waheed Ahmed, 21, was arrested leading eight of his relatives towards the Syrian border in an apparent attempt to join Islamic State. No surprise there, it's the duty of all Muslims to go on a jihad against the unbelievers (us). They were the biggest family unit so far caught trying to join the IS jihadis and included an auntie, male cousins and four children aged from one to 11 years old. Where was the father, the head of this jihadi family when this was all going on?

He was shaking hands with Labour leader Ed Miliband, he was trying to get the Labour Party elected to run the country, he is an elected Labour councillor in Rochdale called Shakil Ahmed and of course he was "shocked" by what had happened to his family. When informed that his son had been arrested on suspicion of him being an Islamist militant Ahmed replied: "I don't believe my son was on his way to join Islamic State. I was shocked, worried and extremely upset to hear that my son has been arrested. It's a total mystery to me why he's there, as I was under the impression he was on a work placement in Birmingham." Naturally, and in order to clear up any future misunderstandings on the issue of travelling abroad to commit jihad we must demand that our politicians enact laws to cancel the citizenship or residency status of anyone who leaves the country for the purpose of engaging in jihad activity, and ensure refusal of reentry into Britain after that jihad activity. Furthermore anyone found to be plotting, financing, or in any way attempting to carry out jihad attacks should be immediately deported. Those who fail to inform the authorities about jihadis in their family would have their family assets seized and their citizenship revoked.

The Labour Party policy of open door immigration was an attempt to gerrymander the electorate by importing a new class of foreign voters who would be more inclined to vote Labour than the untrustworthy and collectively "racist" white working class of England. Their plan succeeded beyond the wildest dreams and will bear the rotten fruit of mass unrest, economic bankruptcy and religious violence before 2030.

Research published by the University of Manchester and widely reported in the press on 30 January, 2015 revealed that in the London constituencies of East Ham and Brent

North, the majority of the people voting will be new immigrants. Another survey, by anti-racism organisation the Runnymede Trust, found that in the 2010 election 68% of migrants voted Labour. The Manchester study went on to say that those born overseas could hold the balance of power in at least 70 seats as more than four million foreign voters, now one in ten of the electorate, become crucial after the 2015 General Election. Most of these voters are from Pakistan, Bangladesh and India, nations where Britons do not have the right to vote, most of them are Muslims. That's an increase of more than half a million foreign born voters since the 2010 election and with the Muslim birth rate now one in ten of all new births in England and Wales we can conclude that the Islamisation of Britain in now within touching distance, thanks to Labour's policy of mass migration. Other conclusions to be drawn are that The Conservative Party may never again win a majority after the 2015 election.

In 2009 a leading London newspaper published an article by Andrew Neather, a government advisor who wrote speeches for Tony Blair, Jack Straw and David Blunkett. The article was about a policy document published by the Home Office, then headed by Jack Straw, in January 2001. The paper, *Migration: An Economic and Social Analysis*, was produced by a New Labour think-tank, the Performance and Innovation Unit. Its author was a civil servant Jonathan Portes, sometime speech writer for Gordon Brown and a senior aide to Cabinet Secretary Gus O'Donnell. Neather claimed that in the drafts he read of this policy document there was an obvious political purpose to the new initiative: "that mass immigration was the way that the Government was going to make the UK truly multicultural". After discussions during the process of the paper's creation, Neather said that he had come away with a belief that what the New Labour leadership wanted was: "to rub the Right's nose in diversity and render their arguments out of date". (80) This was Gramsci in action and finally the eternal student activists of the Labour Party would have their chance to change the nature of British society; in 1997 mass immigration began that unstoppable change. As Paul Mason, the BBC Newsnight economics editor (who spoke at a Socialist Workers Party conference in 2007), said: "If I ever own a dog I will call him Gramsci". What could be bettered as a tool of revolution than the pseudo-revolutionaries running the British Labour Party.

That change began as soon as the new Blair/Brown government were in power with the removal of Britain's Primary Purpose law, brought in by the Conservative government in 1993. This law had ensured that a new British citizen could not also bring his wife and dependents over from Pakistan or Bangladesh to live unless he could prove that the purpose of the marriage wasn't just to get round immigration laws.

The move led to an immediate stampede of foreign spouses into Britain, an increase of 50% within 10 years of the primary purpose law being abolished in 1997. The rule change was warmly welcomed by Keith Vaz, the Labour MP for Leicester East, who said: "This is an historic decision. Jack Straw should be congratulated on this move. Thousands of people separated under this cruel and malicious rule will now be treated with the respect they deserve. Today's announcement is the first step towards restoring justice to Britain's immigration policy." Vaz is only the vanguard of a new breed of Labour MPs who will soon represent majority Muslim constituencies.

John Major's Conservatives won in 1992 with a slim majority of 21 seats, winning 336 to Labour's 271 with the Liberal Democrats securing 20 seats. But Britain today is very different to 1992. The ethnic minority vote, which the Conservative Party has traditionally struggled to attract, is now bigger and carries more electoral weight. Would Major still have won in 1992 with today's electoral demographics?

British Future used electoral data from 1992 and census figures from 1991 and 2011 to conduct a hypothetical "re-run" of the '92 election's key marginals with ethnic minority populations as they are today. Their research showed that Major would have lost 22 seats to Labour, leading to a hung parliament. They concluded: "Demographic shifts would have cost Major's Conservatives seats up and down the country, including in Brentford, Birmingham Edgbaston, Bolton, Luton, Southampton, Corby, Chester and Norwich. Our projections are hypothetical, of course: 1992 is not 2011, nor is it 2015 when the next election will be fought. What the projections do illustrate, however, is an important point for Conservatives. The Britain that goes to the polls in 2015 will look very different to the Britain that last returned an outright majority for the Conservative Party." (81) A similar study by the Runnymede Trust had similar results: "Black and minority ethnic people remain highly supportive of the Labour Party, with 68% (two-thirds) voting Labour. The Conservatives and Liberal Democrats – coalition partners in the current government – got only 16% and 14% of the BME vote respectively." (82)

In the British general election on May 7, 2015 more than 4 million voters, making up 10% of the entire electorate will have been born overseas. By 2019 Britain will have the same number of potential Muslim voters as France had when it held its last presidential election on May 6, 2012. That will be the tipping point for the Conservative party. On that day François Hollande was swept to victory on a tide of immigrant votes that made him first Socialist president of France since 1995, his victory in the polls was due to Muslims who voted for him in overwhelming numbers. That vote may well be looked upon by future generations as the beginning of the end for democratic, republican France, marking the first time that Muslims decided a presidential election in a major western European country. In France as in Britain the Muslim population continues its remorseless rise and as the vast majority of Muslims vote for socialist political parties will libertarian or conservative parties ever find themselves in power again in Britain and France?

According to an *Opinionway* survey of 10,000 French voters for the Paris-based newspaper *Le Figaro*, 93% of French Muslims voted for Hollande on May 6, with only 7% of French Muslims voting for the conservative president, Nicolas Sarkozy. At least 2 million Muslims voted in the 2012 French election so, based on the *Opinionway* survey, roughly 1.7 million Muslim votes went to Hollande rather than to Sarkozy. In the election itself Hollande only beat Sarkozy by 1.1 million votes. This means that Muslims cast the votes that placed Hollande into power in France. Here's a snapshot of the electoral future of Britain after 2019 based on what has just happened in France. The Muslim population of France during the 2012 election was already at 10% of the total population and during the campaign they were already making political demands. The candidate who caved into these demands was the eventual winner, Francois Hollande. He offered an amnesty to *all* of the illegal Muslim immigrants then living in France, estimated at almost half a million then promised to change French electoral laws so that Muslim residents *without* French citizenship would be allowed to vote in future elections. Thus the socialists were able to consolidate power both locally and nationally with the help of the Muslim vote. We have seen the way this is playing out in France already with the rise of anti-Semitism and the murder of free speech at the offices of Charlie Hebdo. Of course the useful idiots of Socialism are only a stepping stone to the real objective as the cultural Marxism (political correctness) of the Left is the real Trojan Horse that allows and defends jihad and the looming destruction of our civilisation. Muslims vote wholeheartedly for socialist parties that promote multiculturalism because their representatives, the Islamists, know that is the way to achieve the Islamization of Europe and the implementation of sharia law. Socialists only serve their purpose until the Islamists have the demographic clout to form their own political parties at which juncture the socialists will have served their turn, and will then be dispensed with, alongside the rest of the infidels on the chopping block. As Melanie Phillips wrote in *Londonistan*: "Mike Gapes, MP for the east London suburb of Ilford South, told the House of Commons how Muslim groups were trying to unseat him because he was an officer of the Parliamentary Labour Friends of Israel and supported both a two-state solution in the Middle East and the government's anti-terrorist legislation. After being harangued and harassed in the street with taunts of "Racist," "Murderer" and "How many children have you killed today?" he was sent a distorted digest of his views by Inayat Bunglawala, the public affairs officer of the Muslim Council of Britain, and his constituent, with the implied threat that this would be used to persuade Ilford's Muslims not to vote for him. Gapes was interviewed by Faisal Bodi for the BBC Radio program *The World Tonight*. Unknown to Gapes, as he subsequently told the Commons, Bodi was a Hamas supporter who had previously written an article published in the *Guardian* stating that Israel had no right to exist. The Bodi item transmitted by the BBC show allowed Gapes's opponents to state without challenge that he was an "Islamophobe" and "a proven enemy of Muslims." Following complaints, the BBC decided not to use Bodi again; after which he wrote a two-page attack published in the *Guardian,* singling out Gapes for having gotten Bodi "banned" by the BBC. (83) After the industrial scale abuse of up to a million children by mostly Muslim men in mostly northern Labour-held seats, where is the outcry from Labour MP's? The Islamists know full well that they can rely on the silence of the Labour lambs to help pave their way to an Islamic state in Britain.

CHAPTER EIGHT

THE BBC

The Palestinian people do not exist. ... in reality there is no difference between Jordanians, Palestinians, Syrians and Lebanese. Only for political and tactical reasons do we speak today about the existence of a Palestinian people, since Arab national interests demand that we posit the existence of a distinct 'Palestinian people' to oppose Zionism. For tactical reasons, Jordan ... cannot raise claims to Haifa and Jaffa, while as a Palestinian, I can undoubtedly demand Haifa, Jaffa, Beer-Sheva and Jerusalem. However, the moment we reclaim our right to all of Palestine, we will not wait even a minute to unite Palestine and Jordan.
PLO leader Zuheir Mohsen (speaking in 1977) on the invention of Palestine as part of the struggle against Israel

Broadly speaking the Labour Party and your taxpayer funded national opinion former, the BBC, is run by a cabal of unreconstructed student radicals who never lost faith in the propaganda drip fed to them by their Marxist lecturers in the 70s and 80s. Many are followers of the Frankfurt school that waved the red flag for the tactics of Gramsci and Marcuse, a blueprint for controlling organisations funded by the state.

This is the class warfare of Ralph Miliband; taught to students of History, Philosophy, Sociology, Politics and Economics. The Left's utopian vision of one great melting pot of humanity with the whole world hand in hand, like the old Coca-Cola advert, required the overthrow of capitalism and the destruction of Western values to sustain it.

The problem was that after the fall of the Berlin Wall no one wanted the Left's crackpot socialist version of reality anymore, capitalism having already (inconveniently) taken half of the Third World out of poverty. No one, except for the Islamists that is, whose hatred for everything the West stood for qualified them as the Left's last ally in their great totalitarian crusade. Thus was created a new axis of religious and ideological mania, revolutionaries who wanted to rule the world, a second Hitler/Stalin pact of insanity. For the Marxist Left in the Labour Party and the BBC the mass migration of Third World poor to suckle at the teat of Britain's welfare state was just payment for the imagined injustices of the detested British Empire and the white men who administered it.

Of course, those who would have to deal with this influx were never going to be politicians or BBC producers, now nicely tucked away with gold plated pensions. Their salaries allowed them to neatly sidestep all the pleasures that diversity could bring.

That penance would fall on the working-class, whose Victorian ancestors had endured an industrial slavery every bit as harsh as the one experienced by transported Africans. Hard graft had financed their meagre safety net over six post war decades and yet they were about to be on the receiving end of the new Left's war on the old white working class, who had dared to vote for Margaret Thatcher.

As former BBC correspondent Robin Aitken noted, being anything other than left-wing at the BBC makes you very lonely: "The General Election of 1992 put things into sharp focus. The BBC had privately rejoiced at the downfall of Thatcher in 1990 and there was widespread expectation of a Labour victory. But that optimism was misplaced. Neil Kinnock failed to convince the voters. On Election night, the atmosphere in the newsroom was one of palpable deflation. A young female producer was in tears." (84)

On January 7, 2014 the BBC broadcast what they called *The Truth about Immigration*. This was to be the corporation's "come clean" response to criticism that the BBC had singularly failed to provide any form of critical debate balancing the Labour Party's open door immigration policies during the largest population movement in British history, 1997-2010.

Based on official government statistics (ONS), of the 5.5 million immigrants who became permanent new residents in Britain between 1997 and 2010, less than 30% came from Europe. After more than a decade without any critique of this massive historical change this 30% was, apparently, what the BBC were *now* willing to discuss. What the BBC still resolutely refuses to discuss is the other 70% of permanent new immigrants who came from *outside* the EU during this period, mostly from Islamic nations. Nick Robinson's programme never once mentioned the biggest issue that must now be faced, the economic and social consequences of Muslim demographics. In this respect the programme was a continuation of the de facto way that the BBC had worked with the Labour Party to facilitate Britain's transformation by mass migration between 1997 and 2010. With that transformation now well on the way to completion it seems that the corporation has now switched function to act as a de facto conduit for the Left's second and final act, the Islamic transformation of Britain.

As Ed West, author of *The Diversity Illusion*, noted: "From 1997 to 2004 almost no one dared say anything about this influx for fear of being shot down; on the BBC archives you can see how even very modest criticism by the Tories – comments that would be pretty vanilla by today's standards – were presented by the BBC as 'racism rows', while government claims about the need for opening the borders were presented as unarguable economic facts." (85)

The claims made by Channel Five executive David Elstein that the BBC had a "vested interest" in mass immigration because it meant more people paying the licence fee were ignored but with a third of the proverbial cat almost out of the bag and after years of silence on the subject some senior members of the BBC, with pensions and severance pay safely banked, were now able to finally say what they felt they could not while employed by the corporation.

Peter Sissons was a news and current affairs anchorman at the BBC for over 20 years until his retirement in 2009. His view of the corporation is unequivocal: "At the core of the BBC, in its very DNA, is a way of thinking that is firmly of the Left. By far the most popular and widely read newspapers at the BBC are The Guardian and The Independent. Producers refer to them routinely for the line to take on running stories, and for inspiration on which items to cover. In the later stages of my career, I lost count of the number of times I asked a producer for a brief on a story, only to be handed a copy of The Guardian and told 'it's all in there'. If you want to read one of the few copies of the Daily Mail that find their way into the BBC newsroom, they are difficult to track down, and you would be advised not to make too much of a show of reading them. Wrap them in brown paper or a copy of The Guardian, would be my advice. I am in no doubt that the majority of BBC staff vote for political parties of the Left. But it's impossible to do anything but guess at the numbers whose beliefs are on the Right or even Centre-Right. This is because the one thing guaranteed to damage your career prospects at the BBC is letting it be known that you are at odds with the prevailing and deep-rooted BBC attitude towards Life, the Universe, and Everything." (86)

While still in the post of director-general Mark Thompson admitted that: "In the BBC I joined 30 years ago there was, in much of current affairs, in terms of people's personal politics, which were quite vocal, a massive bias to the left." (87) Former news director, Helen Boaden, said the BBC had a "deep liberal bias" in its coverage of immigration when she took up the role in 2004. (88) So there it is, from the horse's mouth, the BBC is institutionally left-wing and pro-immigration.

In July 2013 a BBC Trust commissioned report found that the BBC had failed in its duty to provide "breadth and diversity of opinion" on issues like Europe and immigration, with the caveat that all was now well and the bias was now a thing of the past.

For the BBC the past is a foreign country but for Britain so is the future, a place where things will be done very differently. Even lefty comedian and actor Rik Mayall was eventually sidelined by the leftier-than-thou BBC elite. As Mayall noted before his untimely death: "You have to be black, homosexual and a woman to work at the BBC. The BBC banned Adrian and I from being on TV, for being heterosexual or known to disagree with the (Labour) Government." (89)

When we look at the BBC and its senior employees the links between that taxpayer funded institution and the Labour Party are hard to ignore.

Greg Dyke

Appointed BBC Director General (2000-2004) by the Labour government of Tony Blair he walked through the doors of broadcasting house and pronounced it "hideously white". A lifelong Labour supporter and activist Dyke had stood as a Labour candidate for the Greater London Council in 1977. In the run up to the 1997 election he reportedly donated over £50,000 to the Labour Party. Robin Aitken, former BBC Business and Economics correspondent recalled a run-in with Dyke. "My colleagues had elected me to the BBC Forum, designed to improve communication between management and staff. At one meeting, director-general John Birt seemed nonplussed when I raised the issue of Left-wing bias. He asked Jenny Abramsky, a senior news executive, to answer. Her reply was short and dismissive; my fears, she said, were unfounded. I was wrong to raise them. At a Forum meeting in December 2000, I suggested to Greg Dyke, the new director-general, that there should be an internal inquiry into bias. Dyke, a Labour Party donor and member, along with BBC chairman Gavyn Davies, mumbled a muddled reply. As he left the meeting, I overheard him demand angrily of his PA: "Who was that f****r?" (90)

Gavyn Davies

Appointed BBC Chairman 2001-2004. Davies was a lifelong Labour Party member and financial supporter. From 1974 to 1979 he worked as an adviser to two Labour governments. From 1992 to 1997 he was an adviser to the Labour chancellor, Gordon Brown, his close personal friend. His wife, Sue Nye, was Gordon Brown's private secretary.

Sir Michael Lyons

Appointed chairman of the newly established BBC Trust in 2007 by the Labour government. The Trust was, laughably, set up to represent the interests of licence fee payers and ignore, sorry... deal with complaints. Before that he had been paid around £500,000 to carry out a few studies for Labour chancellor Gordon Brown and before that he was a Labour councillor in several authorities and Labour chief executive of Birmingham City Council. Are you getting the picture so far? All the top posts at the Beeb nicely filled by Labour Party placemen. More to come though...here's more Labour/Beeboid big guns.

Bill Bush

Was Ken Livingston's chief of staff and right hand man at the ultra PC loony bin that was the Greater London Council (GLC). From there where else to go? In 1990 he became head of political research and analysis, at the BBC.

He then became head of research for Labour Prime Minister Tony Blair and is believed to have been a major influence on the "benefits" of open-door immigration. Bush later became special adviser to New Labour culture minister Tessa Jowell. As Minister for Culture, Media and Sport, Jowell and Bush were in charge of back scratching Government policy towards the BBC including huge increases in the licence fee.

Ed Richards

An adviser to Gordon Brown then became controller of corporate strategy at the BBC until 1999. Through the revolving door he left the BBC in 1999 to become Tony Blair's senior policy adviser on media. Richards was a key policymaker based at No10 during the 2002 general election, responsible for drawing up political strategy. Obviously, that strategy didn't include immigration control. While at Downing Street, he helped draft the act which established the broadcasting regulator OFCOM and then in 2006, amazingly, became chief executive of the very same quango, at a salary reported to be £392,056 (including benefits and pension entitlement). OFCOM is responsible for ignoring...sorry, adjudicating complaints against the BBC. So that's the BBC's Band of Brothers nicely sorted, from the top. No right of centre comment or opinion at these echelons but surely some room for intellectual diversity further down the food chain? You would think, but no, read on.

James Purnell

Another of Tony Blair's advisers, then a Labour MP and then work and pensions minister. He was BBC head of corporate planning before he became a Downing Street adviser in 1997. Prior to then he worked for the Institute of Public Policy Research, the left wing think-tank often used by the BBC. Now back via the revolving door between the BBC and the Labour Party as new director of strategy and digital media after being appointed to the post in February 2013.

Chris Bryant

Bryant joined the Labour Party in 1966 and from 1993 to 1998 served as a Labour councillor in Hackney. In 1997 he stood unsuccessfully as a Labour candidate for Wycombe and then joined the BBC in 1998 as head of European affairs. In 2000 he was selected for the Rhondda seat and finally became Labour MP for Rhondda.

Celia Barlow

Labour MP for Hove and parliamentary private secretary to the minister for climate change. She joined the Labour Party and then her first trade union when she was 16. Between 1983 and 1995 was a BBC Westminster reporter and then BBC home news editor.

Michael Crick

Former BBC Newsnight political editor, also a lifelong Labour man who joined the party aged 15 and was selected as a potential parliamentary candidate.

Martin Sixsmith

Joined the BBC in 1980 and worked as a foreign correspondent in Brussels, Geneva,

Moscow and Washington. Following the 1997 election he left the BBC to work for the Labour government as director of communications. He was press secretary to Harriet Harman and Alistair Darling before leaving, mind the doors! He returned to the Labour government in 2001 as director of communications for the Department of Transport and is now working for the BBC, again.

Charlie Whelan

A key Labour activist and spin doctor for Gordon Brown as well as a commentator and political journalist for BBC Radio Five.

Phil Woolas

Labour MP for Oldham and Saddleworth and Immigration Minister until he was sacked for telling lies. From 1988 - 1990 he was a producer on the BBC's *Newsnight* programme.

A word, at this point, about BBC current affairs in general. Robin Aitken courageously struggled to raise his concerns about left-wing bias with senior BBC management and ended up having to leave the corporation. He recalls. "Alongside specific interviews and programmes I thought demonstrated bias, I recounted the story of Steve Richards and John Kampfner, BBC current affairs presenters who both subsequently became political editors of the *New Statesman*. About two months later I received a response. After discussing my letter with (Greg) Dyke and Richard Sambrook, then director of news, they concluded I 'did not provide conclusive evidence of systematic bias'. I was disappointed. It wasn't just the slightly patronising tone of the reply, but the way my concerns were dismissed on the say-so of a senior BBC executive. What would the BBC have said if the Metropolitan Police, faced with accusations of racism, had held a brief internal inquiry that concluded that there was no problem?"

Denis MacShane

Or Denis McShame as he is sometimes known now. Worked for the BBC from 1969 to 1977 as a newsreader and reporter. Became Labour MP for Rotherham in 1994 and Labour minister of state for Europe from 2002 to 2005. Was sacked after fiddling his expenses and ended up doing time at HMP Belmarsh.

Lance Price

Joined the BBC as a trainee journalist and worked there for 17 years then left in 1998 to work as Alistair Campbell's assistant in Downing Street. In 2000 he became the Labour Party's director of communications. He is now a freelance journalist working for the *Guardian* and the BBC, mind the doors! Sam Jaffa, BBC North America correspondent, stood as Labour candidate for Eastleigh in 2001, Rory Cellan Jones, married to Diane Coyle who managed to combine her job as a BBC Trustee with that of adviser to the Labour shadow business secretary.

Sue Inglish

Sue Inglish, the BBC's head of political programmes is paid more than £150,000 a year, and chaired the broadcasters' panel during the negotiations over the proposed TV debates prior to the 2015 general election. David Cameron had rejected the idea of a head-to-head debate with Ed Miliband and said he wanted to take part in a single seven-way debate with the other party leaders. The BBC, leading the pack of other broadcasters, insisted the debates "will go ahead" apparently happy to see the Prime Minister "empty chaired" in a farcical and partisan "head-to-head" debate with Ed Miliband. (Would the BBC have threatened to "empty chair" Miliband, I wonder?) Sue Inglish is married to John Underwood, who was an important Labour Party spin doctor in the 1990s.

The BBC is considered by many observers to be biased against Israel and has been the subject of several studies and critical articles including The Balen Report which senior BBC executives killed off by spending £200,000 of licence payers' money on a High Court action to stop its publication. "Islam must not be offended at any price, although Christians are fair game because they do nothing about it if they are offended," said Peter Sissons, who spent 20 years at the BBC reading and reporting the news. Here are some of the BBC's Middle East correspondents in "unbiased" action.

Orla Guerin

Was a candidate for the Irish Labour Party before reporting from the Middle East. In 2004, in a rare reaction from Jerusalem, Israeli minister Natan Sharansky wrote to the BBC that Guerin had not only set a new standard for biased journalism but that her reporting: "has also raised concerns that it was tainted by anti-Semitism." Sharansky referred to the case of a Palestinian youth set to blow himself up as a suicide bomber. Whereas other major world media outlets reporting on this case focused on the use of children by Palestinian terror groups, Guerin's main theme was that viewers should be outraged that the Israelis had paraded a child in front of the international media. Sharansky noted that he did not recall a single BBC report that ever showed: "the ways and means in which the Palestinian authorities stage events for the media or direct the media to stories that serve Palestinian advocacy goals." In 2006 Guerin reported that the town of Bint Jbeil in Lebanon had been "wiped out" by the Israeli air force. At the same time, Alex Thompson, of Channel 4 News, correctly reported: "the suburbs are pretty much untouched by the Israeli attack and invasion". Currently a BBC Middle East correspondent, based in Cairo.

Jehad "Jon" Donnison

Changed his name to Jehad and then back to Jon. BBC "war reporter" Donnison makes constant use of social media but blundered by tweeting a photograph of an injured child from Syria indicating she was from Gaza. At the time Donnison was the BBC's Gaza correspondent but added, "Heartbreaking" to the front of a message he retweeted from Hazem Balousha, a Palestinian "journalist and social activist". Balousha had posted a picture of a young girl lying on a hospital bed with bloodied clothes, along with the words "Pain in #Gaza". Donnison's tweet went out to his 7,971 followers on the social networking site and he was soon hit with a barrage of outraged responses. The website *bbcwatch.org* highlighted the error and wrote: "Up to now, it may have been possible to put down Jon Donnison's frequently problematic reporting to a lack of knowledge and understanding of the region. However, his decision to promote deliberate misinformation – either knowingly or as a result of a complete failure to check facts – indicates that he is not merely naive. Donnison has rendered himself no longer fit for the purpose of accurate and impartial reporting from the Middle East in accordance with the BBC's legal obligations." The BBC's politically correct grovelling in its report on the Lindt café hostage killings by an Islamist in Sydney, Australia was nauseating. If you read the report on the BBC website, as the drama unfolded, you would have been at a loss as to why it was happening at all as there was no mention of Islam for a full 16 paragraphs.
The author of the report was the BBC's very own Middle East headbanger Jehad Jon Donnison, now strangely exiled in Australia but still as "unbiased" as ever. My complaint to the BBC produced the usual "nothing to see here, move on" reply from Nicola Maguire at BBC complaints. *"I understand you had concerns the report failed to mention*

the Islamic motive and I note your comments regarding Jon Donnison. The report to which you refer was the 'Latest' information on the siege and thus this was the focus of the report" she usefully explained. No mention of the Islamic motive in the "Latest" or any other report actually, Nicola. The BBC are not too keen on reporting any atrocities in the name of Islam, despite the fact that Christianity is well on the way to being wiped out entirely in the Middle East. *The Commentator* wryly noted the BBC line on dead Christians: "A February 2012 BBC report on a church attack in Nigeria that left three Christians dead, including a toddler, objectively states the bare bone facts in one sentence. Then it jumps to apparently the *really* big news that 'the bombing sparked a riot by Christian youths, with reports that at least two Muslims were killed in the violence. The two men were dragged off their bikes after being stopped at a roadblock set up by the rioters, police said. A row of Muslim-owned shops was also burned...' The report goes on and on, with an entire section about 'very angry' Christians till one confuses victims with persecutors, forgetting what the Christians are 'very angry' about in the first place: nonstop terror attacks on their churches and the slaughter of their women and children."
(91)

Barbara Plett

In 2004, BBC Middle East correspondent Barbara Plett said she "started to cry" as Yasser Arafat left the West Bank to go to France for cancer treatment. BBC governors ruled her comments "breached the requirements of due impartiality". The corporation's head of editorial complaints originally cleared the edition of *From Our Own Correspondent* of breaching BBC impartiality guidelines, but in 2005 upheld the complaint of bias against Plett. Her reward for this complete error of judgement and pro-Palestinian bias was to be appointed the BBC's chief correspondent in Pakistan and later to an even better job at the UN.

Not one of the BBC's Middle East correspondents made any mention of what became known as the Itamar massacre of 2012 when two Palestinian terrorists stabbed to death a family of five Israelis, including a baby girl in her crib, in their family home. It took a select committee to wring an apology out of the BBC's head of news, who blamed it on a "very busy news period". The story, had by chance, came to the attention of the committee via an American website under the headline "Dead Jews is No News".

One wonders what the reaction of the "even-handed" BBC's Middle East news team would have been had the victims been a Palestinian family in Gaza.

The BBC's Middle East reporters were doubtless student left-wingers once, supporters of a romantic vision of Marxism which they linked to Third World struggles, allowing them to bask in a fake solidarity with the "world's oppressed" shoulder to shoulder against "imperialism". The end result; anti-Semitic and anti-Western hatred which make peace in the Middle East an impossibility and nuclear calamity likely in the none too distant future. The real victims of the BBC's pseudo revolutionary posturing are the thousands of women, children, pacifists and apostates who have been sacrificed to accommodate their retarded student activism playacted out on the small screen at taxpayers' expense.

Newsnight

Newsnight deserves its own category. The BBC's flagship current affairs programme has over the years morphed into a fully fledged Guardian/Labour Party campaigning organisation. Newsnight's editor, Ian Katz, was "Mr Guardian" working for the Labour supporting paper for 13 years before becoming deputy editor then editor of *Newsnight*. Katz's appointment came hard on the heels of Allegra Stratton's appointment as *Newsnight*'s political editor, Stratton was previously the *Guardian*'s political correspondent. *Newsnight*'s new economics editor Duncan Weldon has had almost no journalistic experience and appears to be an unalloyed political appointee.

He was a TUC economics advisor, Labour Party researcher and former adviser to Labour's deputy leader Harriet Harman before being hand picked for *Newsnight* ahead of seemingly "less able" candidates like Gillian Tett, the highly respected *Financial Times* economics correspondent. If in doubt they can always call in BBC Economics editor Robert Peston, son of Labour peer Maurice Peston. For those of us who wonder how any publically funded organization, with a charter that obliges it to remain impartial, can get away with this the answer is provided by former BBC business editor, Jeff Randall. This is how BBC editorial policy is formulated: "It's a bit like walking into a Sunday meeting of the Flat Earth Society. As they discuss great issues of the day, they discuss them from the point of view that the Earth is flat. If someone says, 'No, no, no, the Earth is round!', they think this person is an extremist. That's what it's like for someone with my right-of-centre views working inside the BBC."

Then there is Newsnight's regular presenter, Kirsty Wark, close friend of former Labour Scottish First Minister Jack McConnell (which of course had nothing to do with him making use of her holiday home abroad) and *Newsnight* presenter Stephanie Flanders, who had close personal links with Labour's Ed Miliband and Ed Balls. Little wonder Jeremy Paxman gave in and departed, probably waved off by *Newsnight* producer Lizzie Watson, daughter of former Labour minister Margaret Hodge. Paxman was replaced by Evan Davis, who was noted for barely being able to contain his excitable Tory bashing personality when he presented the BBC's *Today* show. Little has changed on *Newsnight*. When the Marxists gained power in Greece, he tweeted: "In honour of the Syriza victory, I shall not be wearing a tie on @BBCNewsnight this evening." Openly gay, only someone completely ignorant of the Muslim Brotherhood's attitude towards homosexuals could have said to the Egyptian Ambassador: "come on, the Muslim Brotherhood aren't ISIS, are they?" I wrote to the BBC with some basic historical facts about the Brotherhood. "No, they are not ISIS, they are much more dangerous, they are the parent of all Islamist terrorist groups. The Muslim Brotherhood's aim is exactly the same as Islamic State, to restore the worldwide Islamic Caliphate. The founder of the Muslim Brotherhood Hassan al-Banna admired Hitler's hatred of the Jews and wrote to Hitler expressing his desire to collaborate with him. When Hitler came to power the Nazis financially supported al-Banna helping him to grow the Muslim Brotherhood into an ally in the Middle East." This was their reply (17 February, 2015).

With regards to your comments about Evan Davis's interview with Nasser Kamel, Egyptian Ambassador to the UK, we understand that you were concerned about his remarks about the Muslim Brotherhood not being ISIS, as you feel this betrayed his lack of knowledge of the organisation and their aims.

Evan was asking whether the Egyptian government was using the threat from ISIS to crack down on more legitimate organisations such as the Muslim Brotherhood. We're aware that the Brotherhood are a controversial organisation however, in the context of this discussion, Evan was trying to gauge whether Egypt was using ISIS as some sort of smoke screen to hide their real intentions towards the Muslim Brotherhood. Thank you again for contacting us,

BBC Complaints team

www.bbc.co.uk/complaints

Please note: this email is sent from an unmonitored address so please don't reply. If necessary please contact us through our webform (please include your case reference number).

This reply revealed all you need to know about what is going on inside the BBC and their pro-Islamic agenda. The Muslim Brotherhood is a genocidal organisation committed to the destruction not only of Israel but of the Jewish race and, as I mentioned, the establishment of a worldwide caliphate under sharia law. The Muslim Brotherhood regard the equally genocidal Hamas as their armed wing. Mohammad Morsi was the first, fraudulently elected, Muslim Brotherhood president of Egypt. In office he disgraced himself at a rally in his hometown in the Nile Delta by not only repeating the mantra that Jews were "descended from apes and pigs" but also that, "We must never forget, brothers, to nurse our children and our grandchildren on hatred for them: for Zionists, for Jews," then demanded that Egyptian children "must feed on hatred; hatred must continue," he said. "The hatred must go on for Allah and as a form of worshiping him." On June 30th, 2013, the first anniversary of Muhammad Morsi's "election" as their president, Egyptians, sickened by the Muslim Brotherhood's one year stewardship of their nation, took to the streets in their millions to oust both. They were the largest demonstrations ever seen in Egypt. The Brotherhood have since been declared a terrorist organisation in Egypt, yet as far as those running Middle East commentary on *Newsnight* or the BBC are concerned "more legitimate organisations such as the Muslim Brotherhood" are regarded as being in the vanguard of opposition to Zionism and the hated Israeli government. This is the same mindset that now dictates the way the BBC looks at Islam.

The BBC clearly regard The Muslim Brotherhood as being, incredibly, on the side of the people, while the Egyptian government, manfully trying to deal with this totalitarian entity, are looked on as the perpetrators of an illegal military coup.

If the police could be nailed as institutionally racist then when is the institutionally Leftist BBC going to face similar scrutiny? Most troubling is the potential infiltration of the BBC by Islamists in the same way as Islamism has spread throughout Muslim communities. Labour supporting Andrew Marr has admitted that: "The BBC is a publicly-funded urban organization with an abnormally large proportion of younger people, of people in ethnic minorities and almost certainly of gay people, compared with the population at large".

What is more troubling is the potential infiltration of the BBC by Islamists in the same way as Islamism has become the leading voice of Islam. Among the large proportion of young people now being recruited into the BBC are those with Muslim backgrounds, many more are showing up in front of camera as reporters and many more are being hired as producers A detailed look at programming from the BBC's Religion and Ethics department revealed that since 2001 the BBC had made 41 faith programmes on Islam, compared with just five on Hinduism and one on Sikhism prompting complaints from Hindu and Sikh leaders that the BBC was biased in favour of Britain's Muslim community.

Up until 1985 a political vetting procedure (introduced by the Cabinet Committee on Subversive Activities in 1948) was in place that could have exposed those with political views outside the scope of the ballot box. It also served to dampen down what has now become known as "extremism" among the wider staff. As a journalist, I am well aware how the political views of the wider staff can filter through to influence what is produced in print or on screen.

Reporter Secunder Kermani who has close links with IS fighters, used his "contacts" to secure an interview with a 27-year-old British Pakistani, calling himself Awlaki, named after Anwar al-Awlaki, the dead Al Qaeda preacher. It was broadcast on *Newsnight* and criticised by former security minister Dame Pauline Neville-Jones who said the interview should not have been broadcast. That cut no ice with *Newsnight* editor Ian Katz and Secundar Kermani is now a regular contributor on *Newsnight*, despite his unconventional journalistic qualifications. He is described on his profile as a "multimedia journalist" and a former presenter of The Islam Channel.

Sharia Watch is an organisation, led by former Labour Party candidate Anne Marie Waters, that seeks to expose "movements in Britain which advocate and support the advancement of sharia law in British society" in its launch document it identified Islamic organisations suspected of being fronts for Islamic extremism. High on the list was The Islam Channel. A look at his twitter feed also confirms that Kermani is in constant communication with a range of jihadis. Would Kermani have been allowed anywhere near a publicly funded monopoly broadcaster had the vetting procedure still been in place? When called out on Kermani's background the BBC delivered the usual obfuscation from their dhimmi department of complaints. I quote:

Thank you for contacting us regarding 'Newsnight' broadcast on 16 February. We understand that you were unhappy with Secundar Kermani's report from Copenhagen as you believe he was insinuating that those who worked for Charlie Hebdo had in some way 'had it coming" for insulting Muslims. Although we appreciate your feelings, Secundar was in no way condoning the attack. In his report he stated that the attack in Copenhagen wasn't simply anti-Semitic. He pointed out the outrage amongst some Muslims following the publication of images of Mohammed in a Danish cartoon as well as the Charlie Hebdo attack. Secundar's report was matter of fact and was not taking any kind of line regarding the attacks. Thanks again for taking the trouble to share your views with us.

Kind regards

Richard Carey

BBC Complaints.

BBC bias is dangerous, not only for the British electorate, force fed a narrow range of left-liberal opinions disguised as objective reporting, but for those at the sharp end of Islamic violence. When it comes to the threat of Islam, BBC journalists reporting the Middle East are seemingly untouchable, an elite cadre of self regarding "anti-imperialists", as they see it. When they collectively help to bring down the one Western-style democracy in the Middle East what will be left? The sharp edge of Islamic imperialism may not be as obliging.

Such is the corruption of BBC editorial news values, now clearly to the left of Britain's most left-wing daily *The Guardian*, that the encroachment of Islamism on the streets of Britain is selectively ignored by its news and online outlets. During the anti-Israel protests of 2014 a group of young Muslims from the East End of London blocked the Blackwall Tunnel and beside the Palestinian flag, flew the black flag of Jihad. A Guardian reporter went to see what was happening as the police were clearly reluctant to intervene. They reported: "When the estate was approached last night, a group of about

20 Asian youths swore at Guardian journalists and told them to leave the area immediately. One youth threatened to smash a camera. When a passerby tried to take a picture of the flag on a phone, one of the gang asked him if he was Jewish. The passerby replied: "Would it make a difference?" The youth said: "Yes, it fucking would." Asked if the flag was an ISIS flag, one local man said: "It is just the flag of Allah." But another man asked: "So what if it is?" (92)

As Europe is flooded with more Islamic migrants from Libya and North Africa and as the Muslim population grows the first victims will be the Jews. It is ironic that the asylum, human rights and immigration laws created by the EU as a response to Hitler's Final Solution now pose the greatest danger of manufacturing the very situation these laws were designed to prevent. The EU bureauocrats should have studied the law of unintended consequences, because Europe has now imported more than 20 million Muslims and a new epidemic of anti-Semitism. By ignoring what was happening to Jews on its doorstep the EU has made a grave error, one that they will never be able to correct. Today, in the Maghreb, the Jews have been driven out of Algeria and Libya completely. In 1948 there were 140,000 Jews in Algeria, today there are none. In Libya there were 38,000, today there are none. The Arab hatred of Jews is just as shocking. Before the First World War the population of Baghdad was one third Jewish, today there are no Jewish families left in the whole of Iraq. In Egypt where the Jewish population once numbered 80,000, in 2014 and after the rule of the Muslim Brotherhood, just 12 Jews remained. In Lebanon the 20,000 Jews who lived there in 1948 are all gone as are the 30,000 that once lived in Syria. Judenrein, as it was once known in Nazi Germany.

The July, 2014 anti-Semitic marches in London, in response to the Israeli reaction to the Palestinian/Hamas rocket attacks from Gaza, shocked many. "Hitler was right" was a placard openly carried by one Palestinian supporter, unmolested by police. Did the toxic brew of anti-Israeli hysteria created in London and Paris help fuel the Charlie Hebdo massacre six months later? Who knows, but Douglas Murray watched this new anti-Semitism unfolding in London: "Thousands of anti-Semites have today succeeded in bringing central London to an almost total standstill. They marched though the centre of the city before congregating to scream outside the Israeli Embassy in Kensington. It was interesting to watch this rather non-diverse crowd pass. Most of the women seem to be

wearing headscarves or the burka, while their men-folk were naturally more appropriately dressed for a sweltering summer day. But what a picture. These are the people who stayed at home throughout the Syrian civil war, stayed at home when ISIS rampaged across Iraq, stayed at home when Boko Haram and Al-Shabaab carried out their atrocities across central Africa and showed no concern whatsoever when the Muslim Brotherhood was running Egypt into the ground. Yet they pretend to care about Muslims." (93)
Similar protests by Islamic radicals aligned with the Left in Paris led to many incidents, including the siege of a Parisian synagogue by a Muslim mob. In France, Jewish travellers are now told not to wear headgear or jewelry that identifies them as Jews, like many must have during the Nazi occupation. However, this new wave of anti-Semitism is not a welling up of outrage from the indigenous populations of Britain, France and Germany, it's a welling up of anti-Semitism from mostly Muslim immigrants who have rejected assimilation. The Jews are, historically and culturally, their favoured scapegoats and victims. This hatred for Jews and Israel has bubbled up from the toleration of radical Islamist imams and ideologues brought to Europe by mass immigration and the collaboration of the broadcast media who legitimated it. The Islamists have found succour and support from leftist intellectual elites, whose hatred of Israel matches that of terrorist groups Hamas or Hezbollah.

As Douglas Murray concluded: "When historians look back on Europe in this era, they will rub their eyes in disbelief. ISIS is carrying out actual genocide, ethnic and religious cleansing on the people of Syria and Iraq. Their exact ideological soul-mates in Hamas, Hezbollah and al-Qaeda are doing everything they can to set light to the same region. Right now the western states are finally talking of intervening in Iraq to stop ISIS wiping out the ancient Yazidi and Christians communities of Iraq. Yet we do nothing to stop the same murderous ideology thriving here." (94) Could some of these leftist intellectuals now in charge of the BBC also be responsible for the rise of anti-Semitism in Britain? Douglas Davis, the London correspondent of the Jerusalem Post thinks so: "I am convinced the BBC has become the principal agent for reinfecting British society with the virus of anti-Semitism", he told *The Spectator*.

As far as Israel is concerned very little of what led to the founding of this nation is ever given a sympathetic hearing on the BBC or in our schools, which no longer teach

Holocaust history in heavily Muslim populated areas, fearing offence and violence. Would the BBC ever think to cover any of the issues outlined by Professor Benny Morris in his book *One State, Two States: Resolving the Israel/Palestine Conflict*?

Writing soon after the Gaza crisis that provoked the London/Paris anti-Israeli rallies Morris noted: "television doesn't show this bigger picture; images can't elucidate ideas. It shows mighty Israel crushing bedraggled Gaza. Western TV screens never show Hamas – not a gunman, or a rocket launched at Tel Aviv, not a fighter shelling a nearby kibbutz. In these past few weeks, it has seemed as if Israel's F-16s and Merkava tanks and 155mm artillery have been fighting only wailing mothers, mangled children, run-down concrete slums. Not Hamasniks. Not the 3,000 rockets reaching out for Tel Aviv, Jerusalem, Beersheba. Not mortar bombs crashing into kibbutz dining halls. Not rockets fired at Israel from Gaza hospitals and schools, designed to provoke Israeli counterfire that could then be screened as an atrocity. In the shambles of this war, a few basic facts about the contenders have been lost: Israel is a Western liberal democracy, where Arabs have the vote and, like Jews, are not detained in the middle of the night for what they think or say. While there is a violent, right-wing fringe, Israelis remains basically tolerant, even in wartime, even under terrorist provocation. Their country is a scientific, technological and artistic powerhouse, in large measure because it is an open society. On the other side are a range of fanatical Muslim organisations that are totalitarian. Hamas holds Gaza's population as a hostage in an iron grip and is intolerant of all "others" – Jews, homosexuals, socialists. How many Christians have remained in Gaza since the violent 2007 Hamas takeover?" (95)

The conflict continues because it is part of an Islamic war of ethnic hatred and religious supremacy against Israel now and the rest of the non-Islamic world later. How many BBC reports from the recent Gaza conflict even referenced the offers of peace made by Israel to settle the conflict over the years? All rebuffed because of Arab unwillingness to co-exist with a democratic, non-Arab and non-Islamic race. The conflict continues because Arabs hate Jews more than they want peace.

Only three years separated the end of the Holocaust and the first wave of Arab attacks on Israel, a tiny strip of land, roughly the size of Wales. At its narrowest point it is three miles wide and only 60 miles wide at its widest; backed against the Mediterranean and surrounded by 22 hostile Arab/Islamic dictatorships who have a combined area 640 times that of Israel's where a population of 13 million Jews face off 250 million Arabs who are themselves part of a worldwide Umma of more than 1.5 billion Muslims. Yet making peace with the people of this tiny speck of land, the one Western-style democracy in a sea of totalitarian Islam, cannot be contemplated by Arab neighbours who are dedicated to Israel's destruction. Israel is the West's canary in the coalmine, once destroyed the next on the list will be non-Muslim states in Europe, yet that context is presented by the BBC as often as it shows Hamas fighters on our screens. How many viewers are even aware that Israel's greatest enemy is the terrorist organization Hamas, heirs of the PLO and sworn to Israel's destruction? When have the BBC's cabal of Middle East correspondents *ever* made reference to the Covenant of Hamas, issued on August 18, 1988?

For those licence fee payers undoubtedly in the dark, the Hamas Covenant is a comprehensive manifesto comprised of 36 separate articles, all of which promote the basic goal of destroying the state of Israel by Jihad (Islamic Holy War). It says: "The Islamic Resistance Movement is a distinguished Palestinian movement, whose allegiance is to Allah, and whose way of life is Islam. It strives to raise the banner of Allah over every inch of Palestine." (Article 6)

On the Destruction of Israel, it says: "Israel will exist and will continue to exist until Islam will obliterate it, just as it obliterated others before it." On the rejection of any negotiated peace settlement, it says: "[Peace] initiatives, and so-called peaceful solutions and international conferences are in contradiction to the principles of the Islamic Resistance Movement... Those conferences are no more than a means to appoint the infidels as arbitrators in the lands of Islam... There is no solution for the Palestinian problem except by Jihad. Initiatives, proposals and international conferences are but a waste of time, an exercise in futility." (Article 13)

John Howard Kuntsler, author and anti-globalisation campaigner says it as he sees it: "Israel has all the proof it needs that world opinion will never consider its right to exist important. The Obama White House, and a lot of the US News Media, portray the Hamas-Israel conflict as something like an amateur soccer match, with the uneven score (40-odd Israeli soldiers killed versus 1000-plus Palestinians, mostly civilians) showing that the contest is unfair, that Israel has 'gone too far,' that they have entered the same moral zone as Hitler, Stalin, and Pol Pot, carrying out a 'genocide.' Of course, this is a real hot war, not a diversity training exercise, or a self-esteem course, or any sort of the kindergarten psychotherapy that has come to form the basis of American thought and policy. And a vicious world opinion uses America's own moral fecklessness the way Hamas uses women and babies to shield its rocket installations. Apparently world opinion also doesn't take seriously Israel's founding maxim, 'never again,' meaning that Israelis will not passively wait for world opinion to save them from an enemy that plainly and clearly seeks to annihilate them, as happened in 1933-45. The Hamas organization is explicitly dedicated to the destruction of Israel. That is not a rhetorical gimmick; it is its declared unwavering primary goal. The claim that Israel seeks to annihilate the Palestinians is simply a lie. Israel seeks to stop rocket attacks and tunnel invasions, and as long as Hamas is dedicated to those actions, they can expect a forceful Israeli reaction. The sealed border of Gaza has been part of that reaction, to counteract the traffic in war materials and the ready supply of suicide bombers who, Hamas declares, 'love death more than the Israelis love life.'" (96)

Real facts about the Palestinian independence struggle, or Yasser Arafat who founded the PLO in 1964, rarely see the light of day as billions of pounds/dollars/euros are pumped into the West bank and Gaza by gullible Western governments, without any tangible return on their investment.

None of the UNWRA history books will record that the Israeli leadership twice offered Yasser Arafat and the Palestine Authority, at Camp David in 1999 under Ehud Barak and under Ehud Olmert in 2008, 95% of Judea and Samaria (West Bank) in return for a final peace settlement.

Middle East expert Efraim Karsh, professor of Middle East and Mediterranean studies at King's College will, I can safely say, never be employed as a BBC Middle East reporter. His demystification of PLO leader Yasser Arafat is clinical: "For all his rhetoric about Palestinian independence, Arafat had never been as interested in the attainment of statehood as in the violence attending its pursuit. In the late 1970s, he told his close friend and collaborator, the Romanian dictator Nicolai Ceausescu, that the Palestinians lacked the tradition, unity, and discipline to become a formal state, and that a Palestinian state would be a failure from the first day. Once given control of the Palestinian population in the West Bank and Gaza as part of the Oslo process, he made this bleak prognosis a self-fulfilling prophecy, establishing a repressive and corrupt regime in the worst tradition of Arab dictatorships where the rule of the gun prevailed over the rule of law and where large sums of money donated by the international community for the benefit of the civilian Palestinian population were diverted to funding racist incitement, buying weaponry, and filling secret bank accounts. Extensive protection and racketeering networks run by PA officials proliferated while the national budget was plundered at will by PLO veterans and Arafat cronies (in May 1997, for example, the first-ever report by the PA's comptroller stated that $325 million, out of the 1996 budget of $800 million had been "wasted" by Palestinian ministers and agencies or embezzled by officials). Arafat himself held a secret Tel Aviv bank account accessible only to him and his personal advisor Muhammad Rashid, in which he insisted that Israel deposit the tax receipts collected on imports to the Palestinian territories (rather than transfer them directly to the PA). In 1994-2000, nearly eleven billion shekels (about US$2.5 billion) were reportedly paid into this account, of which only a small, unspecified part reached its designated audience. Had Arafat set the PLO from the start on the path to peace and reconciliation instead of turning it into one of the most murderous and corrupt terrorist organizations in modern times, a Palestinian state could have been established in the late 1960s or the early 1970s; in 1979, as a corollary to the Egyptian-Israeli peace treaty; by May 1999, as part of the Oslo process; or at the very latest, with the Camp David summit of July 2000. Had Abbas abandoned his predecessors' rejectionist path, a Palestinian state could have been established after the Annapolis summit of November 2007, or during President Obama's first term after Benjamin Netanyahu broke with the longstanding Likud precept by publicly accepting in June 2009 the two-state solution and agreeing to the establishment of a Palestinian state. But then, the attainment of statehood would have shattered Palestinian leaders' pan-Arab and Islamist delusions, not to mention the kleptocratic paradise established on the backs of their long suffering subjects. It would have transformed the Palestinians in one fell swoop from the world's ultimate victim into an ordinary (and most likely failing) nation-state thus terminating decades of unprecedented international indulgence." (97)

The death of Arafat and the uncovering of a vast network of corruption did nothing to open the eyes of the West who continued to pour taxpayer relief aid into Gaza and the West Bank without even basic checks on what these vast sums were financing. Emanuele Ottolenghi a senior fellow at the Foundation for Defense of Democracies (FDD) and Jonathan Schanzer vice-president for Research at FDD at least questioned where the money went: "Despite Europe's worst economic crisis in recent memory, the European Parliament (EP) has just decided to raise Europe's aid to the Palestinians by €100 million, 30% more than previous years. At the end of tough negotiations among the European Union's institutions over the 2012 budget, the EP somehow made room for an additional €18 billion over the €129 billion cap imposed by expenditures-wary EU member states. Among the additional line items is that extra €100 million for the Palestinians. The EU has been a financial backer of the Palestinian cause since 1971, when its institutional predecessor, the European Community, started funding The United Nations Relief and Works Agency (UNRWA), the UN agency in charge of underwriting Palestinian refugees and their descendants. UNRWA is a bottomless pit of international aid – designed to keep Palestinian refugees in limbo, rather than resettling them, as the UN has done for every other displaced population in history. UNRWA is a waste of money by definition, even under the most stringent accountancy standards, since its raison d'être is to perpetuate the Palestinian refugee problem instead of solving it. EU support dramatically increased in 1994, when the signing of the Oslo Accords seemed to offer a promise of Palestinian-Israeli peace, with huge sums ploughed into Palestinian state-building. From its outset, the Palestinian Authority was rife with corruption and wastefulness, but the wastefulness never drove off donors. From 1994 to 2009, the EU donated €4.26 billion to the Palestinian Authority through various channels – and this figure does not take into account individual EU member states' donations to the PA. In 2006 the Islamist terrorist organisation Hamas won 44% of the popular vote in the Palestinian Authority elections." (98)

In 2013 *The Sunday Times* leaked an unpublished report from the European Court of Auditors that revealed more than €2 billion had been embezzled by corrupt Palestinian officials. Ruthie Blum, author of *To Hell in a Handbasket* responded with a look at the way EU bureauocrats hand out vast sums of taxpayers' money without any democratic accountability and the "gratitude" shown by cynical Islamists who receive it. In her article *Palestinian Corruption: Restating the Obvious*, she said: "Kudos to this week's Sunday Times for revealing the contents of a report on Palestinian spending of European aid. The aim of its report, then, was not to investigate the Palestinians per se. Rather, it was to examine the extent to which the EU has been keeping an eye on how the Palestinians have been utilizing the nearly €2 billion transferred to the Gaza Strip and West Bank from Brussels between 2008 and 2012. It should come of no surprise that the EU did not pass inspection on this score. As the report determined, there have been no serious attempts to reduce the risk of "funds [in the hands of the Palestinian Authority] not being used for their intended purpose." This "intended purpose" was to provide the Palestinian leadership with the money required to reform society and build democratic institutions, towards full-fledged statehood. More specific and immediate needs that have to be met, ostensibly through international funding, include matters like paying the salaries of public-sector employees. Lo and behold, no matter how many millions of euros and dollars flow into the PA, Palestinian society does not reform, democratic institutions are not built, and salaries are not paid. The legacy left by Palestine Liberation Organization chief Yasser Arafat is not only that of combining terror with talk of peace as the means to putting an end to the State of Israel, after all. Pocketing foreign cash is another time-honoured tradition in Ramallah that carries on unhindered. It is the latter that is the focus of the Court of Auditors' report. But to blame the EU for its lack of control over the money trail, the auditors had to acknowledge that the Palestinians have been lying about it with impunity. This is not how they worded their criticisms, of course. Even the logical conclusion that emerges from the Sunday Times article must have caused them no small degree of ill ease, as is indicated by their having declined to comment for the piece. If so, the reason is a lot more transparent than Palestinian allocation of funds. The premise on which the EU bases its policy towards the Palestinians is that every aspect of their plight is due to Israeli 'occupation' - that, had they not been 'robbed' of their 'national identity,' they would have turned Ramallah into Silicon Valley by now. That this has been proved again and again to be a totally false premise is of no consequence. As George Orwell pointed out, 'People can foresee the future only when it coincides with their own wishes, and the most grossly obvious facts can be ignored when they are unwelcome.' The Palestinian leaders have been literally capitalizing on this Western mindset. Their underlings in the street, on the other hand, rarely catch a glimpse of the gold - other than when being rewarded for horrific acts of violence that they are educated and encouraged to commit. Meanwhile, happy to rake in the dough, the PA makes no bones about its disdain and loathing for its sugar daddies overseas."(99) The money that the EU and UNWRA gleefully ships by the truckload to those who would destroy them should instead be going to finance the one project that could lead to reconciliation in the Middle East, namely ending anti-Semitism and hatred of the infidel and the Jew being openly taught to Arab children through the schools in Gaza and the West Bank. In Gaza, schoolbooks bought with EU aid money show maps of the Middle East omitting Israel. Teachers, being paid by the UN and the EU, openly advocate jihad. The Arabs have to learn that they must live peacefully with their Jewish neighbours or catastrophe looms beyond yet another generation of jihadis and suicide bombers, graduating from the UNWRA Academy of jihad. If the EU cannot ensure this one fundamental first step on a long road to a safer Middle East then all aid should be withdrawn from UNWRA funded schools.

Isn't it long overdue that some action is taken to prevent the promotion of jihad using funds channelled from the United Nations via UNWRA to jihadi sympathisers? How long until sanity prevails and jihad as it is traditionally understood, to involve warfare against non-Muslims, is declared a crime against humanity at the U.N.

Why is the EU or America's financial leverage not being used so that if the UN refuses to agree to a detoxification of Arab schools then it will leave the UN and allow its army of taxpayer funded jihadi sympathisers to go and look for real work. Without this action the charge of "Zionism" will join the Left's war cry of "racism" as the streets of our English cities become battlegrounds in a proxy war of Islamic fanatics.

The anti-Israel organisation Amnesty International, which now backs Taliban supporters like Moazzem Begg rather than real prisoners of conscience, has accused Europe's governments of "Islamophobia", but there was no mention in their 2012 report of Muslims being unwilling to assimilate in Western societies.

In May 2011 Amnesty hosted what can only be described as an anti-Israeli hatefest in London. It featured Islamist Abd al-Bari Atwan, who says he wants Iran to nuke Israel. "If the Iranian missiles strike Israel, by Allah, I will go to Trafalgar Square and dance with delight," he said.

Thanks to Barack Obama's appeasement of Iran he may not have long to wait as Iran makes rapid progress towards developing nuclear weapons that will be able to wipe out every major city in Europe. Then again, if you think what's happening now is appeasement just wait until Iran is threatening London or Paris with annihilation as their apologists and killers multiply under Iran's nuclear umbrella.

CHAPTER NINE

BLACK FLAG OVER EUROPE

If the people of this religion [Islam] are asked about the proof for the soundness of their religion, they flare up, get angry and spill the blood of whoever confronts them with this question. They forbid rational speculation, and strive to kill their adversaries. This is why truth became thoroughly silenced and concealed.
Muhammad ibn Zakariyā Rāzī (865 – 925 AD) Persian physician, alchemist, chemist, philosopher, and scholar

The establishment of Islamic no-go zones in Europe's major capitals is the first stage of a long term goal to build the house of sharia on the ruins of democracy. It relies on the protection of multicultural politicians, mass immigration, race hate law, a cowed media and fearful locals...and it is succeeding in almost all major European cities.
As predicted by Peter Hammond in his book *Slavery, Terrorism and Islam* once the Muslim population of any country grows beyond 10% of its total population so do their demands involving the use of violence. Hammond said: "When Muslims approach 10% of the population they tend to increase lawlessness as a means of complaint about their condition. In Paris, we are already seeing car burnings. Any non-Muslim action upsets Islam and results in uprisings and threats, such as in Amsterdam, with opposition to Mohammad cartoons and films about Islam. Such tensions are seen daily, particularly in Muslim sections." What we are seeing all over Europe now is the accelerating Islamization of multicultural societies in tandem with the accelerating rate of Islamic immigration.

FRANCE
Peter Hammond wrote the words above in 2005, when the Muslim population of France was officially 7.5% of the total population. His prophetic words were hammered home by the massacre of Charlie Hebdo's editorial staff in 2015 for daring to publish cartoons of

the Muslim prophet. In 2005, research conducted by France's domestic intelligence network, the Renseignements Generaux, revealed that French police dared not go into more than 150 no-go zones across the country without reinforcements. In these areas Arab gangs were able to deal drugs and burn synagogues at will and without retribution from the authorities. In line with all EU multicultural states French law prohibits the collection of official statistics about the race or the religion of its citizens but by October 2011 a number of studies, including a 2,200-page report, *Banlieue de la République* (Suburbs of the Republic) found that Seine-Saint-Denis a Paris suburb, and other no-go areas had become "separate Islamic societies" cut off from the French state where Islamic sharia law had effectively displaced French civil law and where radical Muslim preachers were allowed a free hand in promoting the creation of a supremacist Muslim society in France, ruled by sharia law.

In France the Muslim minority live in ghettos or banlieues and despite now making up 10% of the population overall these ghettos contain almost 100% Muslim inhabitants living under sharia law. The police don't dare enter the ghettos, where there are no facilities for the non-Muslim; no courts, no shops and no schools other than madrassas, where only the Koran is taught. In 2014, a *Newsweek* poll reported that one in six French citizens sympathised with the Islamist militant group Islamic State, also known as IS. The poll of European attitudes towards the group, carried out by ICM for Russian news agency *Rossiya Segodnya*, revealed that 16% of French citizens have a positive opinion of ISIS (or IS). That's the Islamic State which has been called "the real Islam" by leading Dutch political figures. That's the IS of forced conversions and beheadings, mass rape of women and murder of children, of atrocities against Yazidis and Christians, blinding with red hot pokers and burning alive those who refuse to convert. This percentage who admire IS increases among younger respondents, spiking at 27% for those aged 18-24. Mass immigration from Islamic nations has seen the traditional enlightened tolerance of French values being replaced by barbaric totalitarianism. "This is the ideology of young French Muslims from immigrant backgrounds," said *Newsweek*'s France Correspondent, Anne-Elizabeth Moutet.

IS has the support of more than quarter of all young people living in France today. The BBC/Comres survey found similar attitudes among British Muslims, this is the Islamic future of Britain, just a few years behind France.

In 2013, Elisabeth Schemla, one of France's most admired journalists and former editor of left-wing magazine *Le Nouvel Observateur*, published an investigation on French Islam entitled *Islam, l'épreuve française* which in translation means Islam: The French Test. She found that there are at least 7 million Muslims in France but that about one third of that community, at least 2 million people, "is embracing radical Islam."

This was happening because there was no check or monitor on the activities of imams in France, who were radicalising Muslim youth from a growing number of French mosques. It was clear to her that a tipping point had been reached in France where the rapidly expanding number of French citizens who had been converted to jihadis were now in open revolt against the authorities and the democratic process, demanding separate laws, territory and adherence to Islamic blasphemy laws.

She believed the end result would be civil strife or war in France. The Charlie Hebdo killings may have proved her point. After the killings reports came from schools all across Paris of Muslim children refusing to honour the minute's silence called for in respect of the Hebdo dead, with some children shouting abuse or support for the killers in class. During the silence cries of "Allahu Akbar were also heard from the Fresnes prison, south of Paris. Latest Pew surveys point to the Muslim population of France having reached 6.5 million in 2014, roughly 10% of the country's total population of 66 million. France has more Muslims than any other country in Europe and is the first nation to see its Muslim population go through the crucial 10% barrier, at which point civil unrest may lead to chronic terror attacks and widespread Muslim militia violence.

Germany has the next biggest Muslim population, now closing in on 10%, and in 2010 the police union in North Rhine-Westphalia needed to bring in Turkish police to help control Turkish-Muslim populations rioting in their major cities. Behind France and Germany it is Britain who has the largest Muslim population in Europe, fast expanding towards the 10% French total, potentially already beyond that as more than one million extra non EU (mostly Muslim) migrants have arrived in Britain since 2011.

Before the Hebdo murders a Paris survey found that three quarters of Jews were already considering emigration from France as the Muslim population set fire to the banlieues in an orgy of destruction. On May 6, 2012, the day France elected Francois Hollande as their next president with 51.7% of the vote, more than 5,000 French Jews participated in an Aliyah (immigration of Jews to Israel) fair in Paris. The annual event, run by the Jewish Agency, normally attracts about 2,000 visitors. Maybe they smelled something rotten in the French air, something wicked this way coming. They were right.

It was on May 19th, 2012, that Mohamed Merah went on the rampage in Toulouse, murdering three off-duty French paratroopers and then three children and their teacher outside a Jewish school. The picture of the one of his victims, Myriam Monsenego, an angelic blonde 8-year-old, couldn't fail to break the most hardened heart. She was hauled up by her hair then shot in the head by Merah while he filmed the act on portable video camera equipment strapped to his body. Speaking just hours after Merah was reported killed, the soon to be gone French president Nicolas Sarkozy, announced: "The Islamic faith has nothing to do with the insane motivations of this man. Before deciding to target Jewish children he targeted other Muslims." The media in France slavishly followed Sarkozy's "lone wolf" line… but only until statements given to police by Merah during the siege were inconveniently leaked to the press.

French Prosecutor François Molins then hurriedly convened a news conference to confirm that Merah had boasted that he *was* an Islamic warrior… on a mission to avenge the deaths of Palestinian children and opposed to France's law banning the Islamic facial veil known as the niqab. Molins told the press that Merah had said: "He has no regrets, except not having more time to kill more people, and he boasts that he has brought France to its knees." Also noted was Merah's stated aim that he wanted to kill French Arab soldiers because they were 'traitors to their religion' and that he hated Jews and that Jews had to be 'removed form the face of the earth' and his only regret was that he did not have 'the opportunity to kill more Jews.'" (100)

It then came to light that Merah had visited Pakistan in 2010, where he had been stopped by Afghan police who handed him over to US forces who in turn passed him over to the French authorities… who allowed him to return to France. It was also acknowledged that France's version of MI5 (DCRI) was aware of this trip and suspected him of radical Islamist activity. French Interior Minister Claude Gueant confirmed that intelligence officials had questioned Merah in November 2011 and asked him to explain the reason for his visit to Pakistan. Incredibly, Merah had shown them holiday snaps to prove he had been there as a tourist! And they believed him…and waved him off back to France, to murder the innocent.

After the Hebdo murders in 2015 more than 15,000 Jews decided they had had enough of Muslim "cultural enrichment" and decided to pack their bags and leave France for Israel, while many more decided to come to Britain. Unfortunately, a snap *Jewish Chronicle* survey then found that almost 20% of British Jews were, by that stage, considering emigration themselves. Where do we run to after the 10% barrier is broken? It isn't just the Jews that feel unsafe though. French polls show that that more than 70% of French people are afraid of the rise of Islam in France and they expect that France will become a country under submission to Islam in the near future. Yet all voices critical of the demonstrable results of mass Islamic immigration are demonised by the state.

It appears no one is safe now in France, not even "BB" 1960s film icon Brigitte Bardot, who has been on trial five times for insulting Muslims and "inciting racial hatred." Bardot has written: "I am fed up with being under the thumb of this population which is destroying us, destroying our country." The prosecutor in her fifth trial, Anne de Fontette, wanted a jail term. What crimes has Bardot committed in the former land of liberty where hate speech law, so deftly manipulated by Islamists, now trumps free speech? In 2004, in her book, *A Cry in the Silence*, Bardot wrote: "Over the last twenty years, we have given in to a subterranean, dangerous, and uncontrolled infiltration, which not only resists adjusting to our laws and customs but which will, as the years pass, attempt to impose its own". Bardot,78, is caricatured by the left wing press in France as an eccentric animal rights activist but she also has the courage to speak the truth as she sees it and those who, like her, remember what it was like to be truly free become a diminishing number as the years go by. As will those who remember an almost perfect age of modern enlightenment when individual rights, freedom to speak without fear of offense and the separation of religion and the state were the accepted norms.

A secret vote by an EU committee has seen Marine Le Pen, another "far right" leader who opposes Islamic immigration, stripped of her European Parliamentary immunity so that she can now face "racism" charges over comments she made comparing Muslim street prayers to an occupation of French territory during World War Two. Le Pen has repeated the remarks first made in 2010 and says she stands behind them.

SWEDEN

In Sweden the situation is at an equally critical impasse. Statistics collated from official government records published by The Swedish Social Insurance Agency and Sweden's National Board of Health and Welfare in 2011 show the nation locked in a colossal multicultural meltdown. As long ago as 2002, Swedish economist Lars Jansson estimated that immigration cost Swedish taxpayers about $27 billion annually and that fully 74% of immigrant-group members in Sweden lived off the taxpayers.

Like Britain and France, Sweden does not keep specific welfare payment data for Muslims, but estimates from available government welfare statistics on "foreign-born" indicate that between 70 to 80% of *all* Sweden's welfare allocation goes to Muslims. This figure was confirmed by Jan Tullberg, a researcher from the Stockholm School of Economics, who published a book on the cost to Sweden of Muslim immigration. Tullberg estimated the outlay to be around Kr250 billion (Swedish kroner) each year, that's roughly 7% of Sweden's Gross Domestic Product (GDP) for 2013. Some commentators have theorized that by dividing Kr250 billion by 9.7 million people you come to a figure of Kr 26,000 per Swede per year (before tax) being paid to unproductive Muslims, that's the average monthly wage in Sweden.

Sweden is now in the middle of the biggest population increase in its history with roughly 100,000 non-Western immigrants arriving every year, mainly Muslim refugees from Syria and Somalia, yet a 2014 study from Gothenburg University found that eight out of ten Swedes now believe they won't get a state pension enough to live on after retiring. Swedes have commented that whoever comes to the country claiming to be from Syria gets permanent residency status and is then allowed to bring in their whole family. Links to the classic *Two Ronnies* comedy used to begin "and in an unrelated item" so here is one from Sweden. The Swedish Migration Board announced in 2014 that it needs massively increased funding to pay for the costs associated with asylum and migration, an additional total of Kr48 billion was requested for 2014 and for the next four years after that, an extra £18.5 billion. What worries the average Swede even more than the sequestration of their wages is the way their once homogenous and peaceful society has changed over the last decade.

In the first seven months of 2013, over 1,000 Swedish women reported being raped by Muslim immigrants in the capital city of Stockholm. Over 300 of those were under the age of 15 with a large proportion of the increase including the rape of pre-teen girls. The number of rapes is up 16% compared to 2012 numbers.

Race hate law means that the BRÅ (The Swedish National Council for Crime Prevention) cannot refer to Muslims as the perpetrators of these crimes, though senior police and government sources will confirm it anonymously. The BRÅ website states: "As few as 10-20 percent of all sexual offences are reported to the police. The Swedish Crime Survey (Nationella trygghetsundersökningen, NTU) provides a better picture of the extent of criminality, with data on both victims as well as perpetrators — which is lacking in the criminal statistics. Of those who are suspected for sexual offences, the majority are men and only about two per cent are women. A majority of the victims are women. In a third of reported rapes, the victim is younger than 15."

Sweden is now second in the world league table of most rapes per country, behind South Africa. In addition to regular shootouts, there is also blatant drug dealing, extortion and internal gang conflicts, with serious violent incidents in public places, the report reads. It means that Swedish people are scared and therefore do not dare contact the police or testify in court.

Malmo, on Sweden's southern tip has a population of 300,000 and of this total 25% are now Muslim. In once peaceful Malmo organised crime now flourishes to such an extent that one in four of its citizens are victims of some sort of crime each year. So many assassinations take place that the Norwegian press call Malmo "Little Chicago" where the police station was blown up after officers tried to investigate a spate of killings.

Anti-Semitism, once unknown in Malmo, has led to an exodus of Jews but there is no protection from elected officials, dependent on the Muslim vote. After a savage attack on a Rabbi in broad daylight the Mayor of Malmo, Llmar Reepalu, stated in response that Jews should "distance themselves from Israel" if they wanted to be safe.

The Swedish government is now a coalition of Social Democrats and Sweden's hard-line Green Party. The housing and city development minister is Mehmet Kaplan, an openly

Islamist Muslim whose stated aim is to "end the occupation of Jerusalem," (he is referring to a "Jewish occupation" of Judaism's holy sites). Kaplan has applauded young Western jihadists who travel to Islamic State controlled territory in Syria and Iraq to commit jihad saying they are no different to the Finnish patriots who once fought against the invading Soviets.

The minister for education Gustav Fridolin, was once deported from Israel after being arrested for violence in support of the militant terror organisation ISM. Minister for the interior is Ardalan Shekarabi of the Social Democratic party. Shekarabi is responsible for Swedish law and order and is a former illegal immigrant who defied a Swedish deportation order by going on the run until a more Muslim-friendly administration gave him amnesty.

Sweden is the first Western nation to politically surrender to Islam with the result that native Swedes are being raped, bankrupted and marginalized in their own country. In the new Islamic Sweden it is a crime to suggest that the rise in rape statistics has anything to do with Islam and the law comes down hard on "Islamophobia", which is treated as a criminal offense. During a Social Democratic Youth League rally in 2007 one man held up a sign that read: "While Swedish girls are being gang raped by immigrant gangs the SSU is fighting racism." He was quickly arrested for "expressing disrespect for a group of people with reference to their national or ethnic background" and sentenced. The court rejected any free speech defence.

In 2013 Swedish prosecutors charged a 22-year-old non-Muslim Swedish man for honking his car horn outside the Fittja mosque near Stockholm because, said the court, of his intention to disturb the Muslim congregation there during prayers. In 2015 a new "nethaters" law came into effect in Sweden allowing the prosecution of those using the internet to criticize immigration or a politician's unwillingness to tackle the immigration issue.

Politicians in Sweden have joined journalists in an abject surrender to Islam. Amun Abdullahi was a Somali refugee who grew up in Rinkeby near Stockholm where she joined Swedish Radio as a reporter. Her report, on one of Sweden's most influential political radio shows, Konflikt, uncovered an Al-Shabab recruitment racket in Sweden and led to Amun getting numerous death threats. Her car was torched on the street one night but she was prepared to defend her professional integrity. What she was not prepared for was betrayal by her own "journalist" colleagues who dismissed Amun's work as "hearsay" and "rumours."

Despite clear evidence of al-Shabab recruitment in Sweden, Randi Mossige-Norheim, one of Sweden's leading liberal journalists, told her it was not her job to judge anyone, even Islamic terrorists. After more death threats Amun's own family disowned her, saying: "You see what the Swedish journalists have done? Why should you want to report (on al-Shabab) when the Swedes don't even want to?" Amun Abdullahi abandoned not only journalism, but also Sweden, moving back to Somalia where she set up a girls' school. She knows that Somalia, where the terrorist organization al-Shabab is based, is dangerous but believes that Sweden is now more dangerous than Somalia. About Swedish journalists she says: 'They hide the truth and silence the people'." (101)

Such is the corruption of the Swedish media by political correctness and hatespeech law that they will no longer run a story about a black or Muslim criminal in an objective manner. When a convicted Muslim rapist is pictured the face is pixelated and stock photos of white men in handcuffs are substituted. When Mulatto rapper David Jassy was arrested for murder in Sweden his face was pixelated to look like a pink blob, giving viewers the false impression that Jassey is white.

This insane perversion of the truth goes hand in hand with the self-loathing dogma successive socialist goverments in Sweden have used to brainwash the electorate into believing mass immigration has been a benefit to native Swedes.

With the Swedish media being essentially an arm of multicultural censorship the last spark of free thought that existed online became the target of more hate speech censorship. Chapter 15, Section 8 of Sweden's criminal code now prohibits the expression of "disrespect" towards Muslims. The law carries a penalty of up to four years imprisonment, requires no evidence of incitement to violence and lacks any objective standard for identifying what "disrespect" actually means. As Sweden goes gently into the long night of Islamized totalitarian decline we need to remember that this kind of law is exactly what the British Labour Party has in store for British voters should they get back into power.

Before the Swedish general election of 2006 the Swedish equivalent to the Muslim

Council of Britain (MCB), the Swedish Muslim League, the largest Islamic organization in the country, published a list of demands. They were similar to the demands made by the MCB a year later on the eve of the British general election.

The Swedish Muslim League wanted state schools to employ imams to teach classes of Muslim only children in Arabic. They wanted a mosque in every town paid for by interest free loans from the local taxpayer; separation between boys and girls in gymnastics and swimming; laws making Islamic holidays public holidays for all Muslims; two hours off from work during Friday prayer; an Islamic burial ground available in every town where only Muslims can be interred and demands that the authorities take even stronger steps to outlaw what they refer to as "Islamophobia" in the public at large.

At that point in time the Muslim population was under 5% of the total population. Today, Stockholm is 25% Muslim and is where five nights of Muslim riots plagued the capital in 2013 and where the following year masked Muslim rioters brought central Stockholm to a standstill as they traded gunfire with police. Today the Swedish city of Malmö has pre-school classes where all teaching is conducted in Arabic. Sweden's cultural suicide is very near complete.

A report from the Swedish National Police Board with accompanying map released on October 24, 2014 showed that control of law and order had been virtually surrendered to Muslim criminal gangs operating in no-go zones where drug dealing backed up with violence is the main economic activity. The police report notes "a wider clientele [in the areas] are increasingly turning to the criminal authorities for justice" with unofficial courts dishing out justice "according to the codes of the home cultures of the dominant gangs". The report also pointed out that these gangs operate check-points in and out of the no-go zones and actively seek confrontation with police to show who's boss and that the number of criminal networks were increasing. Now no longer only in major cities, but in 55 areas spread across 22 cities. The report indicated no-go zones existed especially in areas where new immigrants live in the southern suburbs of Stockholm; for example, Sodertalje (a Muslim-dominated area), also Northeast Gothenburg (a Muslim-dominated area). From these areas the criminal gangs are trying to take control of or affect the citizens in surrounding areas. The Swedish police, hollowed out by race hate laws and political correctness are now increasingly at the mercy of the mafia-like activity of these new Muslim gangs. Two policemen who pursued a suspect into the no-go zone of the southern city of Landskrona found that once inside Muslim turf their police car was rammed and they themselves were surrounded by a baying mob of 50 or more. The officers were forced out into the open where they were cornered and called for backup. A number of nearby patrol cars responded by racing to the scene only to be told by their police commander to stop half a mile away and to not enter the no-go zone. Fearing an escalation of tension and mindful of the Stockholm riots just a year before the officers were left to get out on their own. How is the new Swedish government dealing with the new no-go zones?

From 2015 the Stockholm Policy Academy will be moved out of town to a Left-leaning university where police will be "re-educated" by a new curriculum which will focus on cultural sensitivity, ethical awareness and gender issues.

BELGIUM

In 2013, members of the new Islam Party vowed, in their mission statement, to implement Islamic sharia law in Belgium. Shocked, multiculturalist members of parliament immediately introduced a bill they hoped would limit the power of Muslim extremists (who win elected office at local or national levels) because they were breaking the European Convention on Human Rights (ECHR), which had deemed sharia law incompatible with the ECHR. How long that lasts is anybody's guess but in Brussels it's adherence to the ECHR and the EU dogma of free movement of peoples that has allowed Muslims to become the largest religious group, making up 26% of the capital city's *entire* population.

Brussels, where half of all Muslims in Belgium now live is now the most Islamic city in Europe. In less than 20 years they will be the majority and sharia law will be unstoppable. The Islamist organisation Sharia4Belgium aims to replace democracy with sharia law and has advocated the complete extinction of all Jews. Its leader Fouad Belkacem, alias Abu Imran, told CBN News: "Democracy is the opposite of sharia and Islam." When CBN News asked Imran about "democratic Muslims" he replied: "That's really funny, when I hear someone say I was speaking to a 'democratic Muslim'. It's the same thing as saying I was speaking to a Christian Jew, or a Jewish Muslim or something like that. It's impossible." Research from the Itinera Institute now forecasts that Muslims will be the majority of the population of Brussels by 2030 and 60% of the Belgian population as a whole will be foreign born by 2060, a mini Islamic state at the heart of the European Union. How will that affect the laws handed down by the European parliament?

NORWAY

In Norway crime has reached unprecedented levels in tandem with Islamic immigration, so much so that Norway's jails can't sustain their increasing overcapacity. In 2001, 65% of rapes in Norway were committed by what the police called "non-Western" men - a category consisting overwhelmingly of Muslims. According to official police statistics, in the Norwegian capital, Oslo, 100% of all rapes (2006-2011) were committed by immigrants from "non-Western" countries. In Stavanger, a major Norwegian city, 90% of all rapes were committed by "immigrants." The police report referred to is *Voldtekt i den globale byen* (Rape in the global city – May 2011) which also provides a detailed analysis of the rape statistics in Oslo during 2010. The report highlighted that Muslims who, in 2010, were only 1.5% of the total population in Norway, were responsible for 50% of the country's rape statistics. The solution, according to one of Norway's left-wing academics, is with indigenous Norwegian women. Dr. Unni Wikan, Professor of Social Anthropology at the University of Oslo, recommended that: "Norwegian women must take responsibility for the fact that Muslim men find their manner of dress provocative. And since these men believe women are responsible for rape, the women must adapt to the multicultural society around them."

In 2006, the Confederation of Norwegian Enterprise warned that Norway's petroleum fund, holding NoK billions accumulated over 40 years of North Sea oil production, could be totally drained to pay for unproductive Muslim immigrants

Free of EU imposed political correctness, Norwegian figures were able to show the real cost of their Islamic influx. Based on the 15,400 non-Western immigrants that arrived in 2012 there was a direct outlay of NoK 63 billion, that's more than £6.5 billion… *in one year*. Erlend Holmøy, a senior researcher for SSB, speculated that should non-Western immigration carry on increasing, then: "The cost of it all will have to be covered by the average Norwegian taxpayer, or it will lead to a reduction in capacity and quality of various publicly funded services." Sigrun Vågeng, the director of the Confederation of Norwegian Enterprise found the figures more disturbing.

Vågeng speculated that if non-Western immigration continued on a level equal to 2012 then funding costs would soar to NoK 2,900 billion or approximately £293 billion in the period between 2015-2100 and that the entirety of Norwegian oil-generated wealth would disappear if this influx were not halted.

Norway's response to Islamic immigration has changed since the election of new Prime Minister Erna Solberg in 2015.

She immediately increased deportation of criminal Muslims and those who belong to mosques where jihad is preached back to their countries of origin, with Norway seeing a large reduction in violent crime as a result.

DENMARK

The reason Denmark is not yet at the same point of no return as Islamic Sweden could be that the tide of immigration was temporarily held back by the election of a right of centre government in 2001 which clamped down on welfare benefits for new migrants.

In 2006, the Danish minister for employment, Claus Hjort Frederiksen, spoke publicly of the burden of Muslim immigrants on the Danish welfare system, and the reaction was one of shock: the government's welfare committee had calculated that if immigration from Third World countries were blocked, 75% of the cuts needed to sustain the huge welfare system in the coming decades would be completely unnecessary. In other words, the welfare system as it existed was being exploited by immigrants to the point of eventually bankrupting the government. "We are simply forced to adopt a new policy on immigration. The calculations of the welfare committee are terrifying and show how unsuccessful the integration of immigrants has been up to now," he said.

In 2006 Denmark's Minister of Immigration and Integration, Rikke Hvilshoj, standing up for western values, said: "In my view, Denmark should be a country with room for different cultures and religions. Some values, however, are more important than others. We refuse to question democracy, equal rights, and freedom of speech."

In response to this Denmark's leading radical imam, Ahmed Abdel Rahman Abu Laban, tried an outrageous shakedown on the democratically elected minister by demanding that her government pay blood money to the family of a Muslim murdered in a suburb of Copenhagen. When Hvilshoj correctly told him what stop to get off at the enraged imam argued that in Muslim culture the payment of blood money was the done thing. Hvilshoj replied that what is done in Muslim countries is not what is necessarily done in Denmark. That night, her house was set on fire while she, her husband and children all slept. They managed to escape but were later moved to a secret location. Hvilshoj and the rest of the Danish cabinet were then given bodyguards. The first time that had ever been necessary in modern Danish political history.

St Valentine's Day, 2015 and Omar El-Hussein, a Danish born Muslim charged into a café conference on Art, Blasphemy and Freedom of Expression yelling "Alluha Akbar" then sprayed automatic rifle fire around the room killing Finn Nørgaard, a 55-year-old film director and injuring three others before flagging down a taxi and moving on to a Jewish synagogue where a family and 80 guests were having their child's bat Mitzvah. In an attempt to gain entry and continue his killing spree El-Hussein shot and killed Dan Uzan, 37, an economist at the Danish treasury who had been acting as a volunteer security guard, also shooting two policeman assigned as extra security following the café killing. Danish security released a statement saying El-Hussein was motivated by radical Islam and the Charlie Hebdo massacre in Paris. His intended target was believed to have been the Swedish cartoonist Lars Vilks, who had once depicted the prophet Muhammad as a stray dog. Omar El-Hussein was later shot outside his flat in Copenhagen, after he opened fire on armed officers.

Denmark refuses to detail population statistics based on race or religion but in 2010 Denmark's Jyllands-Posten published independent figures: "Despite making up roughly 5% of the population Danish Muslims account for 40% of welfare expenditures; 50% of convicted rapists; and 70% of all crimes in Copenhagen. A study in Taastrup (city in Denmark) shows that immigrants and their descendants are behind 75 % of all benefit fraud cases — although the proportion of immigrants is only 21%." (102)

The political reaction of Danish prime minister, Helle Thorning-Schmidt (daughter-in-law of former leader of the Labour Party in Britain, Neil Kinnock), was similar to the multicultural guff dished out by Barack Obama after every Islamic atrocity or David Cameron after Drummer Lee Rigby was beheaded in Woolwich or Francois Hollande after the Hebdo massacre in Paris. Must have been some "lone wolf" or random madman, nothing to do with Islam or Thorning-Schmidt's own words, which were: "We don't know the motive for the attacks but we know that there are forces that want to harm

Denmark, that want to crush our freedom of expression, our belief in liberty."
No doubt Thorning-Schmidt will repeat this the next time she addresses the Labour Party conference in Britain, where it will be lapped up by the multi-culti party faithful who have the same pro-immigration belief as all the Stepford Left in Europe and America. A belief that once transplanted from their Islamic hell-holes, lifelong religious and cultural baggage will be left behind and new Muslim migrants will quickly adopt British or French or Danish values. With the Left safely back in power under Thorning-Schmidt the Danish government continues to pay jihad-seekers allowance (unemployment benefit) to "citizens" who have travelled to Syria to join Islamic State. If they return, instead of being arrested, they are given a red carpet welcome home and offered psychiatric counselling. Perhaps such counselling needs to be directed to those in power.

Former FBI trainer and expert on all things Islamic, Robert Spencer exposes the hypocrisy of this: "Thirteen years after 9/11, there is one thing that virtually all our politicians, law enforcement officials, and mainstream media guardians of opinion know: that attack had nothing whatsoever to do with Islam, and neither does any other jihad terror attack, anywhere, no matter how often its perpetrators quote the Qur'an and invoke Muhammad. Islam, we're told again and again, is a good, benign thing – indeed, a positive force for societies, and to be encouraged in the West. Jihad terror is an aberration, an outrage against the Religion of Peace's peaceful teachings. These lessons from our betters are coming more and more often in light of the advent of the Islamic State. These dismissals of the Islamic State's Islam, of course, are designed to assure us that we need not have any concerns about massive rates of Muslim immigration and the Muslims already living among us. One problem with this is that it prevents authorities from calling upon Muslim communities to teach against the doctrines that the Islamic State acts upon, and to work for genuine reform. And so the door remains open to the possibility that the actions of the Islamic State could be repeated in Western countries. Barack Obama, David Cameron and the rest would do far better to confront the Islamic State's Islamic justifications for its actions and call on Muslims in the U.S., the U.K. and elsewhere to teach against these understandings of Islam that they ostensibly reject. But they never do that, and apparently have no interest in doing it. Instead, they foster complacency among the people of the West. For doing so, they may never pay a price, but their people will almost certainly have to pay, and pay dearly." (103)

It's probably too late but at least some of Europe's opposition parties are responding to their civilisation's imminent demise. At the 11th hour Venstre, the largest opposition party in Denmark, has called for the differentiation of its immigration policies based on religion. In other words, a centre-left political party is now calling for rational discrimination against Islamic immigration.

"Venstre's political spokeswoman Inger Støjberg said that it should be more difficult for non-Western immigrants with Muslim backgrounds to come to Denmark. 'It is not necessary to set the same requirements for everyone, because as a general rule there is a big difference in the ability and will to integrate between a Christian American or Swede and a Muslim Somali or Pakistani,' she wrote. Støjberg said it was important to talk frankly about immigration issues. 'To say it directly, it is primarily Muslim immigrants who do not value democracy and freedom. In certain environments, they directly oppose it,' she wrote. 'Too many non-Western immigrants with Muslim backgrounds do not want our freedom-orientated society model.' Støjberg suggested that Denmark should adopt an immigration approach that makes it easier for Westerners and harder for Muslims. 'In the future we should make it easier for those who traditionally can and will integrate to come to Denmark, while we make it more difficult for those who don't have the ability or the will,' she wrote." (104)

With the help of the Danish Peoples Party (DF), constantly denounced by Denmark's broadcast media as "racist", who hold the balance of power in the Danish parliament, certain policies have changed. Denmark now offers non-Western immigrants up to €15,000 to migrate back to their countries of origin. Those immigrants who are not Danish citizens can now be deported for committing crimes of violence and resident permits are denied to those intent on marrying their cousins in Denmark.

Crucially for Denmark there is now the real prospect of a total halt to immigration from mainly Muslim countries or in the opposition's words countries "not oriented towards Western values". Denmark may abide a while longer but Italy is already on the edge of a precipice.

ITALY

October 2014 saw Italy's new Socialist government, led by Matteo Renzi (regarded by the Left as an Italian Tony Blair), become the first EU nation to decriminalise illegal immigration. The Italian navy was then deployed to rescue all illegal migrants crossing the Sicilian channel from Libya. Here's how that worked out.

"The result is an exodus of biblical proportions out of Africa into Italy. So far this year more than 100,000 boat people have arrived in Italy — two thirds of them brought ashore by the Italian navy. That is more than double the number who arrived in 2011, the previous record year. It is estimated that the total by the end of 2014 will surpass 200,000. So far this year Italy has deported only 10,000. Italy's boat people used to originate mostly from sub-Saharan Africa; but — thanks to '*Mare nostrum*', as the new policy is called — they now also come from the Horn of Africa, Syria, Palestine, Afghanistan, Bangladesh and Iraq. The word is out: to get to Europe, get to Italy (via Libya)." (105)

In 2014 more than 170,000 migrants reached Italy by boat from Libya and in 2015 that number is set to double with the EU border agency Frontex estimating that up to one million more migrants are now waiting in Libya to cross the Mediterranean.

Of those who have already made it through doctors report that one in ten are infested with Scabies and one in four are suffering from Hepatitis C. Most of the refugees are single young Muslim men who exactly fit the profile of active jihadi terrorists. When questioned most have said they intend to travel through Europe in order to get to Britain via Calais or to Germany and as long as Britain remains a member of the European Union there is nothing we can do to stop this exodus from arriving at our door.

Italy does not pay unemployment benefits to asylum seekers but the migrants know they will receive generous welfare handouts as soon as they set foot in Britain, Germany or Sweden. Reports that a thousand Italians rioted in Rome in protest against continued Muslim immigration to their country were confirmed in 2015, when a new refugee centre opened up in the Roman suburb of Tor Sapienza. This is just one on the new "welcome centres" now springing up all over Italy to accommodate the thousands of new arrivals. Italian taxpayers are being asked to fork out £10,000 per immigrant to pay for free food and shelter (sometimes in four star hotels when the local welcome centre is full to overflowing), mobile phones, driving lessons and pocket money. This will be needed as most refugees will have each just paid a £2,000 fee to the people smugglers to get across.

Italian police do not insist on fingerprinting new migrants who refuse to have their details recorded in case their human rights are violated. The law states that asylum can only be claimed in the first country of registration so those who refuse to be fingerprinted get what they can from the welcome centres and then move on towards Germany, where the welfare state is more accommodating, and Britain, where asylum law is an open door guarantee of permanent residency.

Islamic State has openly declared that they are smuggling trained fighters across to Europe on these refugee boats yet Italian policy is to allow all comers entry without even cursory identity checks. Renzi's Socialist government is now doing to Europe what his conterpart, Tony Blair, did for Britain, only on a smaller scale so far. Renzi has recently introduced a law preventing the deportation of refugees from Italy to countries where they could have their human rights violated. Will it be any surprise, come the next atrocity on British or French soil to find that the murderers of innocent European citizens had crossed over on a smuggler's boat from Libya?

While David Cameron scuttles round European capitals in a vain attempt to staunch the flow of British taxpayer money going to economic migrants and asylum other European countries take immediate action. France has effectively shut its border with Italy and is sending thousands of illegal immigrants back where they came from. Austria is doing the same thing despite both countries being EU members and part of the Shengen Agreement guaranteeing free movement of people within European borders. Meanwhile the British government allows the Royal Navy to be enlisted in a kind of floating touchy-feely social work mission to ensure that thousands more criminals and jihadists are safely ferried to Britain so they can claim asylum then continue on with their mission to destroy us.

The Islamic tradition of hijra or migration to ever more favourable destinations continuous on a monumental scale in Europe thanks to open borders, welfare payments and political correctness. Why is it the responsibility of Europe to provide a solution to this problem? Most of the refugees are Islamic so why are the immensely rich Islamic Gulf States or Saudi Arabia not providing asylum for those who share the same culture, customs and language?

The biggest lie ever told by the politicians of Britain and Europe is that mass immigration benefits the economy. Even Muslims representing Islamic organisations would be hard pressed to taqiyya out that whopper. The blogger and author Zenster looked at Islamic immigration, and its cost to the Italian economy. He observed: "just how corrosive this process of hijra is, we shall examine with the huge influx of 'refugees' arriving at Italy's tiny island of Lampedusa. To date, more than 50,000 have landed, the vast majority of them being Muslims of North and Central African origin. A little 'cocktail napkin' math will quickly demonstrate the impact of these 'immigrants' and their colonization of Europe. Without including the cost of erecting or furnishing shelters for these 50,000 individuals, just the processing cost per person easily approaches €1,000. This processing cost, multiplied by 50,000 suddenly gyrates into €50 million. Remember, no food costs, utilities, security or health care expenses are factored into maintenance of the refugee centers. This is just the paperwork costs, including the salaries of those bureaucrats who process these 'refugees'. Once released into the Schengen Agreement countries of Europe, these individuals are free to apply for social benefits, subsidized housing and also to receive medical treatment. In some countries such subsidies easily approach €30,000 per year. If 50,000 "immigrants" receive just €30,000 per year in combined benefits that sum represents €1.5 billion in social service outlays annually. This disregards the fact that such newcomers are often chronically unemployable and — as is too often the case with Muslims — voluntarily illiterate, refusing to even learn the host country's language so as to reduce any chance of assimilation or integration. None of this addresses the gigantic outlays related to apprehending, prosecuting and incarcerating the criminal elements amongst these 'refugees'. Throughout Europe, Muslims are disproportionately represented in rape, violent crime and imprisonment statistics. The expense of this criminality reaches into extra billions of Euros per year and does not cover property damage, victim rehabilitation and other ancillary expenses. Nor does this speak to the same criminal practices and consequences resulting from ostensibly legal immigration into Europe by tens of millions of Muslims over the past few decades." (106)

The cultural Marxists who run the European Union continue to press for open door refugee entry via a quota system, described by Hungarian Prime Minister Viktor Orban as "bordering on insanity". In response to said insanity Hungary has now decided to build a four metre high fence along its border to try and stem the tide of illegal immigration. How many of the thousands of refugees who gain entry to Europe are hardline jihadis?

The Socialist government running Italy at the moment doesn't know and doesn't want to know but the families of their victims undoubtedly do.

In May 2015, Italian police released details of a Moroccan man, Abdel Majid Touil, 22, who was arrested at the home where he lives with his mother and brothers in Gaggiano, near Milan. He is suspected of having committed the attack on the Bardo Museum in Tunisia where 21 innocent tourists were slaughtered including British national Sally Adey. Touil had fled Tunisia and arrived in Porto Empedocle in Sicily on a migrant refugee boat on February 17 using the alias Abdullah. The Islamic State claimed responsibility for the massacre.

Like the Australian government, Europe should be processing refugees on North African soil or not at all and instead of ferrying unlimited numbers of migrants onto European soil the Royal Navy should be blockading Libya to stop all migrant boats leaving until it has a government that can control its borders. Of course this will never happen because, as members of the EU, Britain and the Royal Navy have now been cop-opted by the socialist/pro-immigration EU elite onto a joint EU naval task force to ferry armies of illegal and mostly Muslim refugees into the heart of Europe. The same multicultiloons who allowed open door immigration to Britain in 1997 are now in charge of Europe's immigration and free movement laws and no surer way exists to guarantee the continued exodus of African and Middle Eastern populations from their Islamist ravaged societies to our own peaceful and prosperous land, soon to be remade as Islamist ravaged Europe. Islamic State has the conquest of Rome firmly in its sights and their greatest ally in this quest is the unelected Socialist Italian government of Matteo Renzi.

In February 2015 Islamist militants released a video that showed the brutal beheading of 21 Coptic Christians who had been taken hostage in Libya several weeks previously. The brave victims, murmuring Christian prayers in quiet dignity were forced to kneel in the sand on the shore of the Mediterranean Sea before being decapitated by their cowardly executioners. One of their English-speaking killers warns that they are sending a message "from the south of Rome" then, raising his knife to the water, cries out that Islam will "conquer Rome". Somebody needs to have a word with the pope.

HOLLAND

In 2013 there were almost one million Muslims living in the Netherlands, representing

6% of the population. (Britain now has more Muslims living in London that there are in the whole of Holland). Dutch Muslims come mostly from Turkey and Morocco but there are also many Islamic states like Afghanistan, Iraq, Iran, Somalia, and former Dutch colony Surinam. Muslims are concentrated in large urban areas, particularly the four largest cities of Amsterdam, Rotterdam, The Hague and Ulrecht. One in every four (25%) inhabitants of Holland's biggest cities, Amsterdam and Rotterdam, are now Muslim.

In 2011 a report by the Rotterdam Institute for Social Policy Research (Risbo) examining the extent of crime among the Moroccan population in Holland was published at the Erasmus University Rotterdam. The data it used was taken from the Herkenningsdienstsysteem (HKS), a nationwide Dutch police register of criminal suspects. The survey made grim reading for those politicians still keen on Muslim immigration. It was found that 40% of Moroccan immigrants between the ages of 12 and 24 have been arrested, fined, charged or accused of committing a crime during the previous five years. In some Dutch neighbourhoods the Moroccan youth crime rate reached 50% from Moroccan born youth, second generation Islamic youth who have failed to integrate into Dutch society. The report focused on Muslim gangs setting up roadblocks, making non-Muslims pay a toll to continue walking and random robberies, violence and rape involving exclusively non-Muslim victims. The Dutch parliament called for a debate on violent immigrants gangs after evidence that one area of The Hague, known locally as "the sharia triangle", was being run by sharia police.

In Amsterdam, media outlet Het Parool reported that young male Moroccan second-generation immigrants and Dutch citizens are publicly murdering non-immigrant citizens with AK-47s to advance their street credentials.

Meanwhile, the leading critic of Muslim immigration and leader of the Dutch Freedom Party Geert Wilders faces yet another trial for inciting "racial hatred" after pledging in March to ensure there will be "fewer Moroccans" in the Netherlands, prosecutors said. The public prosecutor is to try to get a conviction after the last attempt to convict Wilders on similar charges (Wilders said the Koran was a dangerous book and should be banned from Holland) failed in 2011. Wilders is now under 24-hour guard after being condemned to death by Islamists. Wilders seems genuinely without fear, despite being labeled "far-right" by the Dutch media and the BBC. He is determined to stand up for Dutch freedom against violent intimidation.

In 2014 Wilders addressed the Dutch Parliament with this heartfelt plea: "Recognize that Islam is the problem. Start the de-Islamization of the Netherlands. Less Islam. Close our borders to immigrants from Islamic countries. Immediate border controls. Stop this 'cultural enrichment'. Close every Salafist mosque which receives even a penny from the Gulf countries. Deprive all jihadists of their passports, even if they only have a Dutch passport. Let them take an ISIS passport. Do not prevent jihadists from leaving our country. Let them leave, with as many friends as possible. If it helps, I am even prepared to go to Schiphol [airport] to wave them goodbye. But let them never come back. That is the condition. Good riddance. And, as far as I am concerned, anyone who expresses support for terror as a means to overthrow our constitutional democracy has to leave the country at once. If you are waving an ISIS flag you are waving an exit ticket. Leave! Get out of our country!"

A quarter of Moroccans in Holland live on welfare benefits and in 2014 organizations representing them wrote a letter to the Labour Party threatening to advise Dutch Moroccans to quit supporting Labour unless it stopped a proposal by the minister of social affairs, Lodewijk Asscher, to cut welfare payments to Moroccans who *don't* even live in the Netherlands.

In 2014, Dutch MP Macheil de Graaf, begged his colleagues in the Dutch parliament to begin deporting Muslims before it was too late. De Graaf said Muslims were costing the Dutch $7.2 billion per year in welfare and crime. "The Netherlands must be de-Islamised, all mosques must be closed, jihadists must be expelled and never allowed back, and the borders must be closed to people from Islamic countries. The Dutch government must commit itself to repatriation of Muslims back to Muslim countries so we will not be plagued with honor killings, cousin marriages, anti-Semitism, homophobia, animal abuse, rampant crime. Children at school would not be confronted with halal meat during Christmas dinner, Christmas trees would not be a subject for discussion, and the end of Ramadan would not result in empty classrooms. Islamic immigration, the hijra, has been doing things this way for 1400 years and that will not change. Take a look at the situation in what once was Christian North Africa, and take a look too at Marseilles, at Brussels, or at the Islamic rape hotspot, Rotherham in England. We are in an alarming phase, Madam

President: over the past 40 years no-one has ever seen such a change in the demographics. In cities such as The Hague, Amsterdam and Rotterdam, more than half of the Dutch population has now been replaced by people from other countries, mostly Muslim countries. The birth rate of Muslims is much higher than that of the Dutch, but in France, Belgium and Sweden it is even higher still, and with the open borders, then you know enough. In France, the birth rate among immigrants is 1.3 and for Muslims 3.5, which means that within two generations, within two generations the large majority of the population will be Muslim."

What de Graaf didn't point out was that they wouldn't need to wait two generations because Islamic influence, over what was once the most open society in Europe, was already there for all to see. Where now the Dutch police union says it will not enforce a new burka ban. Where now a court in Rotterdam has bowed to Muslim demands that they remain seated while all others rise when a judge walks into the courtroom, because Islamic sharia law holds that women and non-Muslims are not equal.

In 2008, Bouchra Ismaili, a Rotterdam city councillor, published the following letter: "Listen well, mad degenerates, we are here to stay. It is you who are strangers here, with God on my side I fear nothing, let me give you a tip: Convert to Islam and find peace." Like almost every representative of Islam, Ismaili is an Islamist whose aim is the return of the caliphate and the subjugation of non-Muslims. As the clock ticks down to the long Islamic night the words of Ismaili may have struck home with a senior member of the counter-jihad who just couldn't take it anymore.

In 2013, Dutch politician Arnoud van Doorn, a former member of Geert Wilders's Freedom Party and producer of Wilder's anti-Islam film *Fitna,* announced that he had converted to Islam, tweeting: "There is no god but Allah and Muhammed is his prophet." It wasn't a joke, there are no jokes in Islam. That was it, terrorism works and it's becoming a zero sum game in Europe. Without the help of the state in the fight to preserve liberty those who defy the Islamists in our midst will be gradually killed off, leaving only the Islamists left running things.

On 2 November, 2004 Dutch politician Theo van Gogh was murdered by radical Muslim Mohammed Bouyeri, a Dutch-Moroccan Muslim. The great-grandson of the famous Dutch artist Vincent van Gogh, he took a hard line against Islamic immigration and was tipped to be the next Dutch prime minister. The day before he was killed Van Gough said, in a television interview: "I think the guests are trying to take over the house."

SPAIN

In all of recorded history there are no examples anywhere in the world of Muslim cultures integrating into other cultures. Like all the other Islamic nations, Spain was conquered at the point of a sword, but is unique in that it managed to rid itself of Islamic rule. The "golden age of al-Andalusia" as it is referred to by Islamic scholars and the Western media, was anything but. Children who are now force fed Islam in Europe's primary schools should at least be given access to some historical truth.

During 781 years of Muslim rule in Spain there was constant warfare between Christian and Muslim armies with more than 150 battles fought. Jews and their families had to convert to Islam to avoid being killed or having their children sold into slavery.

As commanded in the Muslim scriptures, Jews and Christians had to pay taxes (jizyah) to their conquerors or be killed and were forced to wear special clothing so they could be easily identified. Islamic State wishes to bring back this Islamic "golden age", all over the world. Many were enslaved and history records that 3000 blonde virgins were demanded by Caliph Al-Walid I of Baghdad while in 1191 the governor of Cordoba took 3,000 Christian slaves from the town of Silves. Also in Cordoba 2000 Jews were massacred by Muslims in 1011, while in 1066 every single Jew, approximately 4000, was massacred. Between 1130 and 1232 Muslims killed approximately 220,000 Jews and Christians in Fez and Marrakesh at a time when every Jewish community in Seville, Cordoba, Jaen and Almeria was being persecuted.

The Spanish finally rid themselves of Muslim rule in 1492 but how soon the lessons learned from history are ignored or forgotten by modern politicians.

Catalonia now has the largest Muslim population in Spain with an estimated 465,000 Muslims, accounting for more than 6% of the total Catalan population of 7.5 million. The Catalan capital, Barcelona, is now the planned site of a mega-mosque. Barcelona's socialist mayor has said the mega-mosque will "increase the visibility of Muslims in Spain." and promote "common values between Islam and Europe". It will be the third largest mosque in the world, behind only Mecca and Medina with space for 120,000 Muslim worshipers, dwarfing the Islamic Cultural Centre in Madrid, already one of the biggest mosques in Europe.

In his book *Jihadism: The Radical Islamic Threat to Catalonia*, Catalan terrorism analyst Jofre Montoto says that at least 10% of all Muslims in Catalonia are radical Islamists, and hardcore jihadists. He describes Catalonia, an important nexus for migrants flowing into Europe as the, "Mediterranean corridor of jihadism".

In Spain, the Socialist Party tried to pass a law that would have allowed more than 500,000 Moroccans resident in Spain to vote in Spanish elections. That measure would have gerrymandered permanent socialist control in all Spanish towns and cities with large Muslim minorities, until the Muslims become the majority. The law was not passed, but only because the socialists lost the general election of November 2011, before they could get it through. Muslim leaders in the Spanish autonomous region of Catalonia admitted they were promised the mega-mosque in Barcelona if they supported independence from Spain in a referendum that was set for November 9. Spanish media reported that officials from Catalonia's ruling Convergence and Union Party (CiU) told all of the approximately 100,000 Muslims in the region eligible to vote that if they supported them in a referendum the mega mosque would be built.

On November 9, 2014 an unofficial vote on independence for Catalonia went ahead after Spain's constitutional court ruled against the holding of a binding referendum. The result of the vote was more than 80% in favour of independence, making a formal vote under a future socialist government inevitable.

In his 2014 article, *Catalonia to Muslims: Support Independence, Get Mega-Mosque*, Soeren Kern points out that: "at least three Muslim proponents of the mega-mosque with close links to the CiU have recently been tied to radical Islam. Spanish counter-terrorism officials say that the individual representing Pakistani immigrants within the CiU, Khalid Shabaz (aka Chuhan), is believed to "hold extreme ideological views." He was arrested in 2011 for fraud and document forgery. During a recent trip to Pakistan, Chuhan was photographed wearing traditional Pakistani dress and holding an assault rifle in his hands. Shabaz's right-hand man, Shaoib Satti, was arrested in January 2013 for heroin trafficking in a major Catalan anti-narcotics sting operation. Noureddine Ziani, a well-known Moroccan proponent of the Barcelona mega-mosque, was deported in May 2013 because the Spanish intelligence agency CNI considered him to pose "a grave danger to the security of Spain." (107)

Kern, a Senior Fellow for European Politics at the Madrid-based Grupo de Estudios, continues with a warning for those separatists who, in dealing with the devil, may end up roasting on a spit, when he concludes: "In an ominous sign for the future of Catalonia, Salafi preachers—who reject democracy because it is a form of government designed by man rather than by Allah—are calling on Muslims who are eligible to vote to support Catalan separatist parties as a means firmly to establish Islamism in Catalonia. Consider Abdelwahab Houzi, a Salafi jihadist preacher in the Catalan city of Lleida who adheres to the radical Wahhabi sect of Islam. He recently declared: "Muslims should vote for pro-independence parties, as they need our votes. But what they do not know is that once they allow us to vote, we will all vote for Islamic parties because we do not believe in left and right. This will make us win local councils and as we begin to accumulate power in the Catalan autonomous region, Islam will begin to be implemented."

A Municipal survey by Spain's local town halls in 2014 revealed that the Muslim population in Spain had increased by 800% since 2001. Illegal immigrants from Syria and Africa continue to storm the fences in Melilla but Spanish police are powerless to deport those who make it over because of European law. Like Britain, Spain's immigration laws are subject to the human rights conventions of the Council of Europe. Spain has been warned by human rights commissioner Nils Muiznieks, that any plan to use Spanish law to legalize deportations was "in clear breach of human rights law". Despite the clear evidence of a generational meltdown in the Middle East requiring the securing of Europe's borders the insanity of the EU's open borders, free movement dogma will continue beyond the point where native Europeans become beleaguered, impoverished and then physically endangered in their own countries.

A five year survey of Muslim immigrant's attitudes to their new host countries published on December 11, 2013 by one of the largest social science research institutes in Europe must have been a kick in the teeth for the multiculturalists who have pinned their hopes on the "liberalisation" of Islam in Europe. It's never going to happen. The survey found that the vast majority of Muslims in Europe believe sharia law should take precedence over the secular constitutions and laws of European democracies. The Six Country

Immigrant Integration Comparative Survey of the attitudes of Muslims in Austria, Belgium, France, Germany, Holland and Sweden came up with telling results. Overall, two thirds (65%) of the Muslims interviewed said Islamic sharia law should be the law of the land in which they live, that's the medieval law allowing stoning of women accused of adultery, death for blasphemy, marriage at 9-years-old for girls and the amputation of limbs for minor thefts (Islamic State are currently cutting off the hands of women caught using mobile phones or smoking).

Worse still, especially for Obama, Cameron and Hollande, who claimed that the Charlie Hebdo murders and the murder of Lee Rigby and Uncle Tom Cobley and all the rest of the beheadings were "nothing to do with Islam", no less than three quarters (75%) of the respondents held the opinion that there is only one legitimate interpretation of the Koran, which should apply to all Muslims. That's bad news for the rapidly diminishing numbers of Jews and following them, the infidels, left in Europe's new Muslim-culture-enriched utopia.

Despite the evidence of a million years of evolutionary programming the Left are unshakable in their insane dogma that only geography divides us and once welcomed into a new Eurotopia radical Islam will vanish like the blue fairy, and if it does not then it's the fault of collective white racism, inherent in all our native populations, who must be re-educated to accommodate the new multicultural norms.

Like the Danes and the Australians conservative thinker Lawrence Auster has concluded that the only way to preserve our civilisation is by ending Muslim immigration into Britain but is highly critical of author Melanie Phillips for her failure to advocate what he sees as common sense. Auster writes: "Religion is about *following God*, and Islam is a religion at the core of which is God-commanded eternal war upon non-Muslims, a fact made numbingly clear on almost every page of the Koran, and confirmed by innumerable jihad warriors and Islamic thinkers over the centuries," he says. "She doesn't see the Muslims' attitudes as *Islamic*. She sees the Muslims' attitudes as *an immoral rejection of morality*. And this is the source of her idea that the Muslim threat to Britain can be removed without removing the Muslims from Britain. If people have immoral attitudes, those attitudes can be changed, and that is Phillips's constant hope. But the hope for moral reform assumes that the people to be reformed share the moral framework according to which their current attitudes are seen as immoral. But Muslims do not share that moral framework. They have an Islamic framework. And the Islamic framework demands the destruction of Israel, the Islamization of Britain, the defeat of Christianity, and the removal of any moral condemnation of Islam, including Islamic terrorism." (108)

There was a candlelight vigil for the dead in Copenhagen in support of freedom, just as there was a vigil in Paris last month and just as there will be vigils in Brussels and Stockholm and London in the very near future. Looking at the faces of those holding up the candles on TV the overwhelming emotion is of their betrayal by the politicians elected to defend them.

As long as Islamic immigration continues into Europe we are importing our own end, an end to free speech, an end to liberal values and an end to our own safety and that of our children. Those who would still protest are shamed by their leaders and how long before those candles go out for good?

CHAPTER TEN

JUST A SHOT AWAY

The Islamic conquest of India is probably the bloodiest story in history. It is a discouraging tale, for its evident moral is that civilization is a precious good, whose delicate complex of order and freedom, culture and peace, can at any moment be overthrown by barbarians invading from without or multiplying within.
William James Durant (1885 – 1981), prolific American writer, historian, and philosopher

The late king of Saudi Arabia, Fahd bin Abdulaziz, was the supreme leader of the world's Sunni Muslims, who account for 85% of all the world's Muslims. King Fahd created and financed the Institute for Muslim Minority Affairs (IMMA) with the purpose of destroying Western governments and replacing their law, man-made law, with sharia law. To this end Fahd gave billions of dollars to fund mosques, madrassas and Islamic schools all around the world.

In his own hand Fahd wrote that the real purpose of a mosque is to: "prevent Muslims from assimilating into Western society so they can act as a fifth column to undermine governments and bring in Sharia Law". From the home of Islam, its leader affirms a completely *political* purpose for mosques, not a religious one. The other 15% of the world's Muslims belong to Shia Islam, with the late Ayatollah Khomeini of Iran being their spiritual leader.

A brief historical note: When the Muslim prophet Muhammad died in 632 AD, there was a disagreement about who would take over the leadership of Islam. Some wanted the prophet's cousin Ali to lead and they became known as the Shi'ites. Those who supported the prophets companion Abu, were from Mecca and became known as the Sunnis. The Shi'ites were defeated in battle and one by one their leaders were assassinated. Islam's forever war to conquer all of the non-Muslim world contains within it a separate war of

Muslim succession between Sunnis and Shi'ites that has also lasted for 1400 years and shows no signs of slackening as they continue to refight that battle, perpetually, wherever they live together.

The day after the 7/7 bombings a widely read London-based magazine, *Muslim Weekly*, published an article by Abid Ullah Jan entitled *Islam, Faith and Power*.

The article boldly stated, without a shred of regret for the London atrocities, that it was the duty of all Muslims to gain political and military power over non-Muslims and that violence and warfare is an obligation for all Muslims so that sharia law and an Islamic state could be established over the whole world.

During the four-day siege in Kenya's Westgate shopping Mall al-Shabaab jihadists raped, tortured, beheaded, dismembered, castrated, gouged out eyes, amputated fingers and hung hostages upon hooks suspended from the mall roof. Using quotes from the *Kenyan Star* newspaper in Nairobi, a London newspaper reported what was said by a forensic medical doctor: "They [the al-Shabaab attackers] removed eyes, ears, noses. Fingers are cut by pliers, noses ripped by pliers... Those are not allegations. Those are f****** truths,... They removed balls, eyes, ears, noses. They get your hand and sharpen it like a pencil then they tell you to write your name with the blood. They drive knives inside a child's body. Actually, if you look at all the bodies, unless those ones that were escaping, fingers are cut by pliers, the noses are ripped by pliers." (109)

These horrifying details of the last moments of many of the hostages at the hands of Islamist terrorists from Somalia's al-Shabaab movement come from a free press, the *Kenyan Star*. The Star reported this against a background of mounting public anger over the deafening silence about the siege from the nation's state owned broadcaster, the Kenyan Broadcasting Corporation, modelled on our own national broadcaster, the BBC.

Dawn Perlmutter, director and founder of Symbol & Ritual Intelligence, is one of the leading experts in ritual murder and religious violence. At the time she commented: "This inexplicable savage violence is typically attributed to psychological warfare, military tactics or individual acts of brutality but for Jihadists they are justifiable sacred acts against the enemies of Islam. They are ritual murders that are consistent with a growing global Jihadist method of operation [MO]. Similar acts of torture, rape, beheading and mutilation regularly occur in Iraq, Afghanistan, Libya, Egypt, Syria and other countries.

The Westgate Mall massacre is comparable to the mass murder of 166 people by members of the Islamist Jihadist group Lashkar-e-Taiba, in ten coordinated shooting and bombing attacks across Mumbai, India on November 26-29, 2008. During their siege operation the LeT Jihadists also took the time to sexually humiliate, torture and mutilate some of the victims before shooting them dead." (110)

In Britain, two and two finally added up to five on the afternoon of May 22nd, 2012. That was the day a British Muslim convert, of Nigerian origin, hacked to death then beheaded a serving British soldier in broad daylight on a street near the Royal Artillery barracks in Woolwich, south-east London…in the name of Islam. Almost instantly the myth of London as a multicultural melting pot, as imagined by the Olympic opening ceremony of 2012 and so cherished by our broadcast media, was instantly replaced by the grimmer reality of London as a Third World killing field where religious murder could take place in broad daylight, just like in Syria.

We know it was in the name of Islam because he went out of his way to have his words recorded on camera. These are the words spoken by Michael Adebolajo on the afternoon of that day; one hand still holding the murder weapons, a machete and large knife, both hands still dripping with the blood of drummer Lee Rigby.

The Daily Telegraph reported on December 18, 2014: "The court at the Old Bailey was replayed a video clip of accused Michael Adebolajo talking to members of the public as he waited for the police to arrive. He said: 'we are forced by the Koran, and Surah, and Tawbah [ninth chapter of Quran]. [There are] many, many ayah [signs] throughout the Quran that says we must fight them as they fight us, an eye for an eye and a tooth for a tooth.'"

Yet the next day the British Prime Minister, David Cameron, stood outside number 10 Downing Street to tell the world that indeed two and two *did* now add up to five and that the motivation for the killing, as described by the killer himself, was incorrect.

Cameron's statement began: "there is nothing in Islam that justifies this truly dreadful act." His words were relayed by the BBC, but the words of the killer and any reference to Islam were completely censored. Since then Cameron has repeated the "Islam is a religion of Peace" mantra after every subsequent Islamist atrocity, most recently after the Taliban murdered 132 schoolchildren in Pakistan in December 2015. Why?

Those watching the national news that night might have felt somewhat short-changed or at the very least plagued by an uneasy confusion about just what, exactly, was really going on? Was Cameron saying that the killer was confused about his own motivations, or that his motivations were wrong, or was Cameron possibly positioning himself as an expert on the meaning of the verses in the Koran quoted by the killer?

The question even the most laid-back layman felt the need to ask his elected leader after such savagery followed by such flummery is to what extent have the basic facts about Islam and its relationship to violence and terrorism across the world been concealed from the British public? Not long after the Rigby murder it was revealed that Michael Adebolajo, had not only been known to the British police for years but he had been arrested in Kenya in 2010 for joining an Islamic terrorist group... then freed to return to Britain on the recommendation of no less than the British High Commissioner.

After Lee Rigby's murder the British police swung into action... but not in the direction that logic would seem to have dictated. There was no investigation and arrest of Adebolaja's known associates or those of his Muslim accomplice in murder Michael Adebowale or searches of the mosque where they may well have been radicalised. No, the police swung into action against eleven members of the British public, who they detained for alleged "anti-Muslim speech crimes". Among them two Bristol men, aged 22 and 23, who had posted tweets "of an allegedly racist or anti-religious nature." (111)

Detective Inspector Ed Yaxley, of Avon and Somerset Police, gave the following statement soon after the horrific murder of Lee Rigby.... *about the tweets*: "These comments were directed against a section of our community. Comments such as these are completely unacceptable and only cause more harm to our community in Bristol. People should stop and think about what they say on social media before making statements as the consequences could be serious." Nothing said about the murder, nothing to see here, move along. It seemed that despite a heinous, perhaps treasonous crime being committed, that required a sophisticated police response, the immediate targeting of police resources was to be the investigation and arrest of members of the public who may have committed what can only be described as "thought crime". Against Islam!

Here, on display, was the politically correct mindset of our police authorities and politicians in the home of parliamentary democracy, and their response to the murder made them look like rabbits caught in the headlights of radical Islam… or was this strange and unsettling response symptomatic of a wider dysfunction? Could it be that this "moderate" Islam is not what most Muslims believe but instead is what the multiculturalists like Cameron and the Labour Party and the BBC and the Liberals *believe* that Muslims believe. A *real* expert on Islam, Daniel Greenfield, a Shillman Journalism Fellow at the Freedom Centre, explains: "When American and European leaders insist that Islam has nothing to do with the latest Islamic atrocity, they are not referencing a religion practiced by Muslims, but an imaginary religion that they imagine Muslims must practice because the alternative is the end of everything that they believe in. Their moderate Islam is light on the details, beyond standing for social justice, fighting Global Warming and supporting gay rights, because it is really multiculturalism wearing a fake beard. When a Western leader claims that Islamic terrorists don't speak for Islam, he isn't defending Muslims, he's defending multiculturalism. He assumes that Muslims believe in multiculturalism because he does. Moderate Islam is just multiculturalism misspelled. Its existence is a firm article of faith for those who believe in multiculturalism. Dissuading a believer in moderate Muslims from his invented faith by citing the long trail of corpses or the hateful Hadiths that call for mass murder is futile because these are not the roots of his religion. He doesn't know what a Hadith is nor does he care. As a social justice man in good standing, he attributes the violent track record of Islam to European colonialism and oppression. He has never read the Koran. He has read a thousand articles about how Muslims are oppressed at the airport, in Gaza, in Burma and in Bugs Bunny cartoons. They are his new noble savages and he will not hear a word against them. Having colonized their identities in his imagination (despite the marked up copy of Edward Said's Orientalism that he keeps by his bedside) he treats them as reflections of his ego. When you say that moderate Muslims don't exist, you are calling him a bad person. When you challenge Islam, you are attacking multiculturalism and he will call you a racist, regardless of the fact that Islam is as much of a race as Communism, Nazism or the Mickey Mouse Fan Club were races. The moderate Muslim is an invention of the liberal academic, the secular theologian, the vapid politician and his shrill idiot cousin, the political activist." (112)

On Tuesday, 4th February, 2015 Islamic State released a video online showing Flight

Lieutenant Muath al-Kasasbeh of the Royal Jordanian Air Force being doused in petrol and burned to death. It is hard to imagine a more horrific way to die yet Flt Lt al-Kasasbeh showed incredible bravery and dignity, almost standing to attention as he was consumed in flames, finally toppling over in what must have been excruciating agony. The reaction of President Barack Obama was in keeping with his refusal even to mention Islam in connection with any of this or any other Islamic state atrocities. Despite the fact that the brave Jordanian pilot was a Muslim, Obama later monotoned about the evils of *Christianity* and its connection to slavery: "Unless we get on our high horse and think this is unique to some other place, remember that during the Crusades and the Inquisition, people committed terrible deeds in the name of Christ. In our home country, slavery and Jim Crow all too often was justified in the name of Christ," said the leader of the free world. Jihadi John must surely now be quaking in his boots. What the free world cried out for was the kind of leadership offered by Jordan's King Abdullah, who, quoting Clint Eastwood's revenge speech in *Unforgiven* was heard to swear revenge. His first action was to execute two convicted Islamist terrorists then to intensify Jordan's bombing campaign against Islamic State.

Those who burned alive Flt Lt al-Kasasbeh would have been aware that the president of the United States of America had promised the Islamic-dominated United Nations in 2012, that: "The future must not belong to those who slander the prophet of Islam." This at a time when Jews, closely followed by Christians, were being ethnically cleansed from the Middle East and free speech was being ethnically cleansed from Europe. At such a time this president was saying freedom of speech was expendable and those who killed the last free journalists in Europe at the offices of Charlie Hebdo would have noted it well.

The mindset of multiculturalists like Obama, Cameron and Hollande are on display, tragically, throughout the Western world. The celebrated author of *Clash of Civilisations* (a book now banned by the European Commission) Samuel P. Huntington, wrote about multiculturalism in his final work, saying: "Multiculturalism is in its essence anti-European civilisation . . . It is basically an anti-Western ideology." (113)

Let's go back in time just a little bit. In July 2005, Shezad Tanweer one of the four Muslim suicide bombers who killed 52 and injured 770 London commuters on July 7, had his funeral in the family's village near Lahore in Pakistan. Of the four bombers, three were British born sons of Pakistani immigrants. At the funeral there was no body but there were thousands of people who hailed Tanweer as a "a hero of Islam."

Just after the bombings the deputy assistant commissioner of the Metropolitan Police, Brian Paddick, issued a statement, saying that: "Islam and terrorists are two words that do not go together." Paddick's response showed just how much the Left's state multiculturalism had reduced a once proud and respected service into a mouthpiece for political dogma. What major terrorist atrocity since 9/11 *has not* been committed by Islamic terrorists? This was George Orwell's warning about two plus two making five brought vividly to fruition.

If it looks like a duck and quacks like a duck, it's a camel, according to our PC police but the trouble is the public don't believe them. In 2006 a YouGov poll found that 73% of Britons agreed that: "the West is in a global war against Islamic terrorists who threaten our way of life". (114) The Left's response to this is not to change policy but to change the public. More race hate/Islamophobia law, more re-education through our schools with the prospect of the Left's boot on the faces of our children, forever.

In case any senior police spokesperson might step away from Paddick's proscribed mantra there was a warning at the time from the leader of the Muslim Council of Britain (MCB) Dr Muhammad Abdul Bari, who said: "Some police officers and sections of the media are demonising Muslims, treating them as if they are all terrorists, and that encourages other people to do the same. If that demonisation continues, then Britain will have to deal with two million Muslim terrorists, 700,000 of them in London." (115)

Not even a veiled threat and that was in 2006 and now in 2015 there are more than one million Muslims living in London and according to most surveys most of them sympathise with the actions of Islamic State. An alien army of potential jihadists encamped in our capital. Even those on the "right", if it exists anymore in modern Britain, have been lazily suckered by the narrative of a "moderate Islam". Paddick should, at least, have been aware that because Muslims view Islamic attacks on the infidel as "jihad", and not terrorism, their spokesmen, like those from the Muslim Brotherhood, can deny their support for terrorism to our gullible authorities. According to one Islamic expert: "This, in fact, is the idea long spearheaded by Mideast academics and talking heads—that there are 'nonviolent' Islamists and 'violent' Islamists, and that the best way to weaken the appeal of the latter is to cooperate with the former, which, after all, shouldn't be too hard, since the 'good cop moderates' come in suits, smile, and shake hands over cups of coffee. And yet, just as the 'good cop/bad cop' is a false dichotomy in that both 'cops' are working together and for the same goal, so too is the 'nonviolent Islamist/violent Islamist' a false dichotomy in that both Islamists are working together and for the same goal—the resurrection of a Sharia-enforcing caliphate, which the Islamic State ('violent Islamist'), led by Abu Bakr al-Baghdadi, a former Muslim Brotherhood member ('nonviolent Islamist'), recently accomplished." (116)

Wole Soyinka, 76, first African winner of the Nobel Prize for literature who was born in Nigeria and studied at Leeds University in the 1950s, said: "England is a cesspit. England is the breeding ground of fundamentalist Muslims." He added: "Its social logic is to allow all religions to preach openly. But this is illogic, because none of the other religions preach apocalyptic violence. And yet England allows it."

One of the most prolific and respected academics on the subject of Islam is Robert Spencer, who has led training seminars on Islam and jihad for the United States Army Command, the FBI and the Joint Terrorism Task Force. His detailed study of Koranic text leaves him in no doubt as to the motivation for Islamist violence.

He states that: "There are over a hundred verses in the Qur'an that exhort believers to wage jihad against unbelievers." (117)

Spencer then goes on to explain the most notorious verse in the Koran the Verse of the Sword. For those Muslim Islamists who take the literal word of the Koran as a call to action what Spencer says would confirm Islam's intolerance for non-Muslims. Spencer certainly believes all notions of Islam being a religion of peace are a cruel deception, and that real Islam is a violent, repressive faith whose real representatives are Osama bin Laden, the Muslim Brotherhood, Islamic State and the Taliban.

IS or ISIS or ISIL or Daesh

The IS jihadis are killing all the Christian men they capture. In one recent incident 1500 men were executed in front of their wives and families. In another incident, 13 Yazidi men who refused to convert to Islam had their eyes plucked out, were doused with gasoline and burned alive. When the men are killed, captured women and children are enslaved to be used for sex, deployed as human shields in battle zones, or sold to be used and abused as their new owners see fit. In response, the United States has ironically called for "greater cooperation". UN Ambassador, Samantha Power, urged all parties to come together and "prevent ISIL from obliterating Iraq's vibrant diversity".

For Sunni Muslims, who make up most of British Muslims, what happened when the Muslim prophet Muhammad died in 632 is still just as relevant today, in the 21st century. Sunnis and Shi'ites are endlessly refighting an endless battle which took place 1400 years ago in their forever war which, thanks to EU asylum and human rights legislation coupled with mass refugee migration from Libya and the Middle East, will soon be endlessly fought in the streets of our once peaceful and civilised European cities, as the Muslim population grows. Where does it end? It doesn't, because there can be no end to this slaughter unless there is an end to this religion. Once they have killed all of the Jews then killed or enslaved all the infidels they will start to kill each other for generation after generation to come.

Islamic expert Ibn Warraq comments that: "It is extraordinary the amount of people who have written about the 11th of September without once mentioning Islam. We must take seriously what the Islamists say to understand their motivation, [that] it is the divinely ordained duty of all Muslims to fight in the literal sense until man-made law has been replaced by God's law, the Sharia, and Islamic law has conquered the entire world. The Koran does not support, he added, assertions by liberal Muslims that feminism, human rights, egalitarianism and religious tolerance are compatible with their religion." (118)

Right now the IS atrocities happening in the Middle East are beginning to be replayed on a smaller scale with Kurds and Sunni Muslims clashing on the streets of Copenhagen and in Malmo, unreported by state media, cowed by fear of being labelled "Islamophobic". This is the reason why we need to know the number of Muslims as a percentage of the larger British population, because the evidence shows that Muslim behaviour in Western societies like ours changes in accordance with their increasing numbers.

Whenever any courageous member of the press, like Douglas Murray, or any government official, or non-Islamic religious body asks what Islam is really up to organisations claiming to represent Muslims (and all such organisations are run by Islamists who follow the same general ideology as Islamic State) like the Muslim Council of Britain

(MCB), will immediately use their tried and tested defence of victimhood to protest that they are being unfairly targeted, are the victims of a conspiracy, Islamophobia, racism.... but the facts tell us otherwise.

The "Islam has been hijacked" myth is now all pervasive in Western broadcast media and is used by Islamic apologists like Mehdi Hasan to deflect attention from the historical fact that Islamic goalposts have not moved in 1400 years.

When placed under oath, even when there is overwhelming evidence of guilt, an accused Muslim will use taqiyya (lying to the infidel) to counter the allegation by reverse accusing and claiming that Muslims are always "victims of Islamophobia, racism, or religious intolerance". The former leader of the PLO, Yasser Arafat, is on record condemning the 9/11 attacks to the Western media in English while at the same time praising them in Arabic. He is not the only Muslim leader to dupe the West. Turkey is a member of NATO and its president Recep Tayyip Erdogan is, apparently, our ally.

In 1997, Turkey's prime minister, Recep Tayyip Erdogan, stated: "the mosques are our barracks, the domes are our helmets, the minarets are our bayonets and the faithful are our soldiers".

Even for an elected Islamic leader, mosques perform one function only ... as military bases for jihad. The Ayatollah Khomeini handed down many fatwa's, or religious rulings, during his time but what he said about the purpose of mosques needs restating: "Friday prayers are the means of mobilizing the people, of inspiring them to battle. The man who goes to war straight from the mosque is afraid of only one thing - Allah". For the leader of the Shia Muslims the mosque is there to urge those at Friday prayers to jihad against the infidel, it's as simple as that. Backing up the mosques are sharia courts.

Dr Denis MacEoin holds degrees from Trinity College, Dublin, Edinburgh University and Cambridge (King's College). From 1979-80, he taught at Mohammed V University in Fez, Morocco, before taking up a post as lecturer in Arabic and Islamic Studies at Newcastle. In a 2009 report for the think-tank Civitas, Dr MacEoin found there were more than 85 sharia courts already operating in Britain. In an article for a London newspaper MacEoin warned against sharia law coming to Britain, with the helping hand of the Labour Party.

He said: "sharia has already entered the UK through a back door". The report warned of "creeping sharia" and the tacit acceptance of sharia principles in British law, and proved that these unofficial courts are already busy applying Islamic law to resolve various disputes from inside mosques." (119)

The report, *The Hijacking of British Islam*, written by MacEoin, revealed that hardline Islamist/jihadi material was found at more than a quarter of the 100 mosques he visited across Britain during the year long project. One book, *Fatawa Islamiyah*, which urges the execution of apostates, was found at Regent's Park mosque and at the East London mosque in Whitechapel. Muhammad Abdul Bari, the secretary-general of the Muslim Council of Britain (MCB), is the chairman of the East London mosque. The researchers said that they found further controversial works during visits to mosques in Manchester, Birmingham, Edinburgh, Oxford and High Wycombe.

The rise of sharia law will mean the end of English law and this growing rejection of British justice and the rule of law was pinpointed by the chief inspector of constabulary, Tom Winsor, in January 2014. He said that some ethnic minority communities were now turning their backs on police and rarely, if ever, call them to deal with crimes as serious as honour killings and sexual assaults against children. Winsor went on to say: "There are cities in the Midlands where the police never go because they are never called. They never hear of any trouble because the community deals with that on its own ... They just have their own form of community justice." (120)

CHAPTER ELEVEN

JUST SHUT UP!

"First they came for the Socialists, and I did not speak out — because I was not a Socialist. Then they came for the Trade Unionists, and I did not speak out — because I was not a Trade Unionist. Then they came for the Jews, and I did not speak out — because I was not a Jew. Then they came for me — and there was no one left to speak for me."

Pastor Martin Niemöller, poem conceived in a Nazi concentration camp

Professor George Steiner is a Fellow of Churchill College, University of Cambridge. He has held professorships at Yale, Geneva, New York and Oxford and was elected Fellow of the British Academy in 1998. He is a renowned literary critic, essayist, novelist, scholar and teacher and undoubtedly one of the cleverest men in Britain. Steiner's Jewish family fled the Nazi's from France in 1940.

Professor Steiner made headlines in 2008 with remarks to a Spanish newspaper *El Pais*, when discussing his new novel. Racism, he said, is inherent in everyone. Racial tolerance is only skin-deep. "It is very easy to sit here in this room and say racism is horrible. But ask me the same thing if a Jamaican family moved next door with six children and they play reggae and rock music all day. If they had adopted civilised values - which have nothing to do with class or race, everything to do with decency."

Steiner was expressing what he felt is a universal truth about human behaviour, that we still have a small group or tribal identity, most at ease in the company of others like ourselves. This fits well with the Out-of-Africa theory of human origins that reveals that modern Homo Sapiens had their beginnings in Africa about 250,000 years ago and then moved northwards.

The harsh, prolonged winters they endured gave rise to evolutionary selection for higher IQ to deal with the problems of raising children, building shelters and gathering food during an ice age. Without a sophisticated language, group mores placed value on greater intellect married to a killer instinct that dominated and remained until the development of agriculture around 10,000 years ago.

Despite the Left's touching belief in multiculturalism we cannot unprogramme a quarter of a million years of genetically embedded killer instinct in the blink of an historical eye. Steiner recognises that too much competition among alien cultural groups could be problematical. The group will tolerate new arrivals who share similar values and behavioural norms and will live peacefully together no matter what the colour of their skin or their religion. However, by being forced to accept those who behave in an intolerable manner, who reject similar values, who hate the established order and all it stands for, the host group is forced into a rapid escalation towards conflict and violence. Condemnation from the Left for being "racist" ignores the facts. All of the Left's assumptions about the viability of multiculturalism and the compatibility of wildly differing cultures are 250,000 years out of date. Steiner is in conflict with this new cultural fascism and so is science.

Any scientist who pursues a line of research in conflict with the cultural Marxist doctrine of universal equality will now find themselves under attack from the universities that employ them and all the institutions of thought control will line up to vilify them as "racists".

Scientists like James Watson, who prefers a quiet life, will shy away from confrontation and academics with the courage to stand up to the totalitarian Left are few.

One was J. Phillipe Rushton, a British expert on intelligence. Rushton argued in *Race, Evolution, and Behaviour* (1995) that different races show consistent patterns that reflect different reproductive strategies. East Asian behaviour was related to the fact that they had smaller families but took extremely good care of them. White Caucasians were in the middle of this grouping and at the other extreme were black Africans. Their behaviour was shown to be consistent with having larger numbers of children, but not spending as much time looking after them. His book was meticulously researched and documented showing that at one extreme were East Asians who were the most intelligent, showed most sexual restraint, had fewer children and were most law-abiding. Rushton proved that East Asians averaged higher on IQ tests than Whites in the U. S. and in Asia with the worldwide average IQ for East Asians being about 106; for Whites, about 100; and for

Blacks about 85 in the U.S. and 70 in sub-Saharan Africa.

"Race differences show up by 3 years of age, even after matching on maternal education and other variables. Therefore they cannot be due to poor education since this has not yet begun to exert an effect. That's why Jensen and I looked at the genetic hypothesis in detail. We examined 10 categories of evidence," said Rushton.

For publishing this work Rushton was pursued by the politically correct for the rest of his life. The *Toronto Star* campaigned to have him removed from his job at the University of Western Ontario by openly accusing him of racism. The premier of Ontario, David Peterson, personally telephoned the president of the University of Western Ontario demanding he be dismissed.

Later, the attorney general of Ontario began a police investigation to see if Rushton could be prosecuted under laws banning promotion of "hatred against any identifiable group." His lessons were continually disrupted by activists chanting "racist" and he was openly assaulted while walking on campus. Rushton was eventually barred from the classroom and made to record lectures on video tape for students to watch in private. Would America's custodians of liberty, the Founding Fathers have fared any better had they been alive today?

Thomas Jefferson wrote the American Declaration of Independence in 1776. All of his life he opposed slavery calling it a "moral depravity" and contrary to the laws of nature, which decreed that everyone had a right to personal liberty. At a time when slave labour was the norm all over the world Jefferson drafted a Virginia law (1778) that banned the importation of African slaves into America. Today he would have been condemned as a racist and his right of free speech removed because of his observations on what he believed was black intellectual inferiority in comparison to other races.

He wrote: "Some have been liberally educated, and all have lived in countries where the arts and sciences are cultivated to a considerable degree, and have had before their eyes samples of the best works from abroad. The Indians, with no advantages of this kind, will often carve figures on their pipes not destitute of design and merit. They will crayon out an animal, a plant, or a country, so as to prove the existence of a germ in their minds which only wants cultivation. They astonish you with strokes of the most sublime oratory; such as prove their reason and sentiment strong, their imagination glowing and elevated. But never yet could I find that a black had uttered a thought above the level of plain narration; never see even an elementary trait of painting or sculpture. In music they are more generally gifted than the whites with accurate ears for tune and time . . .Whether they will be equal to the composition of a more extensive run of melody, or of complicated harmony, is yet to be proved. Misery is often the parent of the most affecting touches in poetry. Among the blacks is misery enough, God knows, but no poetry." (121) What John Stuart Mill wrote in *On Liberty* and what the Enlightenment proved was that no opinion should be suppressed that may contain a grain of truth. The state cannot be the final arbiter of truth because no one can. Only by rational argument and free discourse can truth be arrived at.

The American Left were jubilant when Dinesh D'Souza was convicted of making illegal campaign donations. D'Sousa is the Indian-American author of *The End of Racism: Principles for a Multiracial Society* (1995). His book argued that racism in America, which was once systematic, was now just episodic. D'Souza wrote: "In other words, racism existed, but it no longer controlled the lives of blacks and other minorities. Indeed racial discrimination could not explain why some groups succeeded in America and why other groups did not. The old civil rights model held that groups at the top of society got there through discrimination. Yet the empirical evidence showed that the two most successful groups in America were Asian Americans and Jews. Certainly these two groups didn't succeed by keeping everyone else down; rather, they succeeded by out-competing everyone else. Moreover, these were minority groups that had not allowed discrimination to keep them down. As for African Americans, their position near the bottom rung of the ladder could be better explained by cultural factors than by racial victimization."

The author became the number one hate figure of the Left when he released *2016: Obama's America*, a documentary critical of the president. In his bestselling non-fiction D'Sousa argued that if groups provoke hostility on account of their behavior then it is rational to discriminate against them thus implying that it is not racist to be wary of African Americans who commit crime, as long as you do not discriminate against African Americans who behave well. Again, D'Souza's ideas were controversial and many would disagree with them but does that mean he has no right to voice them?

The Enlightenment or Age of Reason which began in 1650 allowed Europe and America to cast off the superstition, repression and fear that had dominated the medieval world. Enlightenment thinkers were able to question the rational basis of all beliefs and oppose the authority of the church and state. This led to all of the great scientific, political and social advances that we in the West now take for granted.

Because open scientific enquiry was permitted we learned that the Sun did not revolve around the Earth because the church said so, modern medicine began to replace spells and incantations and there was the beginning of equality between the sexes and race and religious toleration.

This never happened in the Arab states of the former Ottoman Empire where foreign science was forbidden by the clerics and printed books were banned for centuries. Once, Muslim mathematicians, building on the foundations left for them by the Greeks, were able to invent algebra. After the clerics established sharia law the free exchange of ideas vital to scientific progress was banned.

Religious calligraphy was all that Islam allowed and so the Muslim world was cut off from scientific advance and left marooned in the 7th century. A survey by the UN in 2003 revealed that only 330 books are translated into Arabic every year. In the last 1,400 years of Islam less than 100,000 books from the outside world have been translated into Arabic. This is about the same number translated into Spanish from English in a single year. This cultural and scientific backwardness is reflected in the fact that if you exclude the peace prize only 11 Muslims have ever won the Nobel Prize out of a total number of 800 and if we look at those 11 Muslim winners, seven (including Yasser Arafat) were awarded peace prizes. That leaves four Muslim Nobel winners.

On April 26, 2014, on the steps of Winchester Guildhall in Hampshire, Paul Weston, chairman of Liberty GB and a candidate in the European elections, was arrested then charged with Racially Aggravated Crime under section 4 of the Public Order Act. His alleged crime (which could land those convicted in prison for two years) was quoting what Winston Churchill wrote about Islam.

"How dreadful are the curses which Mohammedanism lays on its votaries! Besides the fanatical frenzy, which is as dangerous in a man as hydrophobia in a dog, there is this fearful fatalistic apathy. The effects are apparent in many countries. Improvident habits, slovenly systems of agriculture, sluggish methods of commerce, and insecurity of property exist wherever the followers of the Prophet rule or live. A degraded sensualism deprives this life of its grace and refinement; the next of its dignity and sanctity. The fact that in Mohammedan law every woman must belong to some man as his absolute property – either as a child, a wife, or a concubine – must delay the final extinction of slavery until the faith of Islam has ceased to be a great power among men. Thousands become the brave and loyal soldiers of the faith: all know how to die but the influence of the religion paralyses the social development of those who follow it. No stronger retrograde force exists in the world. Far from being moribund, Mohammedanism is a militant and proselytizing faith." (122)

This had prompted a member of the public, who had taken offence at the quote, to call the police. Winston Churchill was, like Thomas Jefferson, one of the greatest historical champions of freedom, the man who saved Britain from conquest by Nazi Germany. Compare the arrest of a democratic politician standing in a democratic election to the (in)action of the police in Luton town centre, 2009, when The Royal Anglian Regiment were having a homecoming parade after returning from a tour of duty in Helmand province, Afghanistan.

As they paraded through the town they were barracked by Islamic radicals openly chanting; "murderers" and "baby killers" and "British soldiers burn in hell". This open incitement to violence, contrary to the law of incitement and racial hatred, resulted in no arrests at all. The only threats of arrest from the police that day were made to outraged locals who shouted "scum" at the Islamists. Today, British soldiers and policemen are advised not to wear their uniforms in public when off duty in case they attract the attention of these Islamists who would murder them.

I have little doubt that were Sir Winston Churchill alive today he would, like Jefferson, be prosecuted for inciting racist hatred under Labour's 2006 Race and Religious Hatred Act or similar legislation. The greatest political figure of any era would certainly have been arrested by the same modern day appeasers and collaborators who would have doomed Britain in 1940.

We can put an actual date on the beginning of the end of free speech in Britain and the end of free speech in Europe. On January 14, 1989, more than 1,000 British Muslims marched through Bradford and symbolically burned a copy of Salman Rushdie's novel *The Satanic Verses*. There were open calls to murder Rushdie from the massed gathering. Abdul Quddus, the secretary of the Bradford Council of Mosques, called for Rushdie to hang because he had "tortured Islam." No one was arrested for incitement to violence. In Leicester the Labour MP Keith Vaz marched at the front of a 3,000-strong mob whose intention was to burn an effigy of Rushdie (he certainly wasn't out there marching in defence of Rushdie's right to free speech).

After such a display of intolerance should Vaz have been allowed near any position of power and influence again in our tolerant liberal democratic state? This is what the novelist Anthony Burgess wrote about the incident: "I gain the impression that few of the protesting Muslims in Britain know directly what they are protesting against. Their Imams have told them that Mr Rushdie has published a blasphemous book and must be punished. They respond with sheeplike docility and wolflike aggression. They forgot what Nazis did to books … they shame a free country by denying free expression through the vindictive agency of bonfires….If they do not like secular society, they must fly to the arms of the Ayatollah or some other self-righteous guardian of strict Islamic morality." (123) Vaz is now (2014) chairman of the home affairs select committee which examines and influences the policy of the Home Office (that's the great office of state in charge of policing and immigration).

Who will stand up for the freedoms our politicians now take for granted? How far can they crawl on their knees in fear of offending before being overrun by the pitiless beheaders? On September 30, 2005, the Danish newspaper Jyllands-Posten published 12 cartoons; some of the prophet Muhammad, in an attempt to foster a free discussion about Islam. Almost immediately Muslim organizations in Denmark began holding public demonstrations. A Muslim Danish delegation visited Pakistan and Saudi Arabia to create awareness (stir up trouble) about the cartoons. There was little real violence until a dossier of the cartoons was handed to the Organization for Islamic Cooperation (OIC) in December who complained that the Danish prime minister, Lars Rasmussen was "under par" in defending his country's right of freedom of speech and expression. That was the blue touch-paper lit and trouble soon began in earnest, resulting in more than 100 deaths. Thousands of violent protesters set fire to the Danish Embassies in Syria, Lebanon and

Iran. In Gaza protesters burned the flags of Denmark, France, Norway, Holland and Germany. A Pakistani imam offered $1 million reward for anyone who would kill the Danish cartoonists who drew the offending skits. A Muslim minister in the Indian government offered a $10 million reward for the head of the cartoonists or their publishers, a proposal that won the support of India's Islamic court. Muslims living in the West, most on the welfare state largesse of the European Union, began a full boycott of all Danish goods.

Not one British newspaper or TV channel had the courage to defend free speech by printing the cartoons. Many in Europe, Australia and New Zealand had done, in a show of solidarity with Denmark, knowing they were defending *their* rights to freedom of expression. In London there was a demonstration of thousands of British Muslims in front of the Danish embassy where on open display were placards that read: "Behead those who insult Islam," "Freedom Go to Hell" and "Massacre those who slander Islam." While the demonstrators chanted: "Nuke Denmark," "May they bomb Denmark so that we may invade that country and take their wives as war booty", "Khaibar Khaibar, O Jew, the army of Muhammad is coming for you".

These numerous incitements to violence, right under the nose of the British constabulary, resulted in only two arrests… now here's the punch-line. The only protesters arrested were two secular Muslims who, showing great courage, had the offending cartoons on placards to show solidarity with the West's hard won right to free speech, rights that do not exist in any Islamic nations. As they were carted off by the British plod they could have been forgiven for thinking they were part of some Monty Python sketch. The Labour Government had surrendered completely to the most flagrant incitements to violence seen on the streets of the British capital since the end of the Second World War, and no one was laughing.

On January 7, 2015 came the massacre of cartoonists at the offices of *Charlie Hebdo*, a satirical magazine located in Central Paris near Bastille Circle. Two men in their early thirties, the brothers Said and Cherif Kouachi — French citizens of the Muslim persuasion and of Algerian descent — murdered eight journalists and cartoonists who happened to be there, as well as two menial workers and two policemen. The terrorists claimed they were "avenging Prophet Muhammad." In 2006, out of defiance against

Islamist intimidation, *Charlie Hebdo* had reprinted the caricatures about Muhammad previously published by the Danish magazine *Jyllands-Posten*. In 2011 and 2012, the French magazine published further sets of anti-Islamist caricatures with Muhammad as a main character. The Kouachi brothers were able to flee Paris in spite of an enormous manhunt that involved thousands of policemen and gendarmes all over northeast France. Eventually, they were trapped and shot on January 9 by special anti-terrorist units at a printing office in Dammartin-en-Goële, some 30 kilometers east of Paris. In the meantime, on January 8, another terrorist, Amedy Coulibaly, 33, a French Muslim of Senegalese descent, shot a policewoman at Montrouge in southern Paris and fled. He was apparently looking for a Jewish school located nearby. On January 9, Coulibaly attacked Hyper Casher, a kosher supermarket in eastern Paris. He killed four customers and wounded several others. About fifteen customers, including a mother with a baby, were able to hide underground in the shop's refrigerated rooms. Coulibaly was shot by the anti-terrorist units later in the evening.

It was suggested by many commentators that every free newspaper in the world should have simultaneously published the Mohammad cartoons to show that they were not cowed by this attack on our most basic freedoms. The suggestion was ignored, the moment lost, forever. I became a journalist because I wanted to be part of the most noble vocation on earth employing its most precious commodity, free speech. In his 1859 essay *On Liberty* John Stuart Mill wrote that "there ought to exist the fullest liberty of professing and discussing, as a matter of ethical conviction, any doctrine, however immoral it may be considered" and that the limits of such liberty should be defined by the "harm principle", only, not by social offence. This great concept of free speech links our Judeo-Christian heritage with all that was best of the Enlightenment and the struggle of the disenfranchised over centuries, it is a unique creation of Western civilisation.

What we have now is another unique phenomenon; journalists who oppose free speech and either don't know or could care less about how it came to be. British TV's "just shut up" moment came on 14th January 2014 when Dharshini David, the SkyNews presenter on call, was interviewing *Charlie Hebdo* staff writer Caroline Fourest live on air. "I'm very sad, very sad that journalists in U.K. do not support us," said Fourest who had survived the attack at the magazine's Paris office. She continued: "That journalists in the

U.K. betray what journalism is about by thinking that people cannot be grown enough to decide if a drawing is offending or not because you are not even showing it." Fourest then, without warning, reached down for a copy of the current edition of *Charlie Hebdo* with Mohammad on the cover and brought roughly one third of the picture into frame, at which point former BBC employee Dharshini David, herself an Asian, went into some kind of meltdown, saying: "We at SkyNews have chosen not to show that cover, so we'd appreciate it, Caroline, for not showing that. I do apologize for any of our viewers who may have been offended by that." The TV feed was cut as those "offended" viewers she had aimed her remarks at, presumably Muslims, breathed a sigh of relief and another nail in the coffin of free speech was banged home.

A whole new cabal of "islamojournalists", that presumably do not believe in free speech or only when it excludes criticism of Islam, are appearing daily on our TV screens. Later that day, on another programme, BBC's *This Week*, French-Algerian Nabila Ramdani defiantly told presenter Andrew Neil that the *Charlie Hebdo* cartoons were "incitement to racial hatred" and had "caused the violence". Ramdani continues to make regular appearances on BBC current affairs programmes like *Dateline London* at taxpayers' expense but rarely mentions that there is no free press in Islam. What we have allowed, with mass immigration from Islamic countries, is the importation of a theocratic culture incompatible with our own, now accompanied by Islamic journalists in favour of hate speech law. Do the Islamists accept hate speech law because they wish to defend the "offended" or do they believe it is a means to an altogether different end?

Modern hate speech legislation was born after World War II. There was a feeling then that hatred needed to be curbed to prevent another outburst of fascist hysteria. But it wasn't Western governments calling for laws against hate speech - it was the authoritarians in the Soviet Union.

In 1948, world leaders gathered to construct a Universal Declaration of Human Rights, and the Soviet representatives argued that the section on free speech should be qualified by strictures against hate speech. They proposed an amendment making it a crime to advocate "national, racial or religious hostility". Such efforts to water down freedom of speech in the name of combating hate were opposed by Western delegates. From the US, Eleanor Roosevelt said a hate speech qualification would be "extremely dangerous" since "any criticism of public or religious authorities might all too easily be described as incitement to hatred" (how prescient she was). In later discussions, British representative Lady Gaitskell, wife of Labour politician Hugh Gaitskell, said a hate speech amendment would "infringe the fundamental right of freedom of speech".

The Soviets lost on the hate speech front in 1948. But they kept pushing. They were finally successful in 1965 with the creation of the UN's International Convention on the Elimination of All Forms of Racial Discrimination.

The story of hate speech law is the story of the West's slow but sure ditching of freedom of speech. Where once Western leaders opposed the criminalisation of words — "whatever their nature" — more recently they've come to see certain speech as dangerous after all, and something that must be punished. We're witnessing the victory of the Soviet view of speech as bad and censorship as good, with various members of the modern West's chattering classes unwittingly aping yesteryear's communist tyrants as they call for the banning of the "advocacy of hatred", and a corresponding demise of the older enlightened belief that ideas and words should never be curtailed.

This offence-phobia is not only a contradiction of reality it is also a contradiction of human nature. About the one thing Marxist's have in common is that they are *always* wrong, about everything - and the thing they have been proved most wrong about is the nature/nurture debate. The Left have never been too keen on science because of its inconvenient insistence on provable facts, peer reviewed and testable evidence. The Left's dogma was always dead set that nurture would come out the winner in the nature/nurture debate. If it could be shown that what happens after you are born is more important an influence than the genetic congress that takes place before it would mean that capitalist society (nature) was to blame for the failure of children to reach the academic standards needed to achieve success. Cue more state intervention, state control and more taxation to pay for it (better nurture). In other words, Venezuela.

This is how political correctness, the totalitarian language of the 21st century destroyed the world's greatest living scientist.

In December 2014 James Watson announced he had become a "non-person" and was selling his Nobel Prize: "James Watson, the world-famous biologist who was shunned by the scientific community after linking intelligence to race, said he is selling his Nobel

Prize because he is short of money after being made a pariah. Mr Watson said he is auctioning the Nobel Prize medal he won in 1962 for discovering the structure of DNA, because 'no-one really wants to admit I exist'."

He said his income had plummeted following his controversial remarks in 2007, which forced him to retire from the Cold Spring Harbor Laboratory on Long Island, New York. "Because I was an 'unperson' I was fired from the boards of companies, so I have no income, apart from my academic income," he said. In 2007, *The Sunday Times* ran an interview with Dr Watson in which he said he was "inherently gloomy about the prospect of Africa" because "all our social policies are based on the fact that their intelligence is the same as ours – whereas all the testing says, not really". He told the newspaper that people wanted to believe that everyone was born with equal intelligence but that those "who have to deal with black employees find this not true". (124)

Nothing non-PC is safe anymore as Trevor Phillips, a former chair of the Equality and Human Rights Commission, so eloquently pointed out in his Channel Four documentary *Things We Won't Say About Race That Are True*. The Ayatollah Khomeni once famously said that there were no jokes in Islam and if you live in Britain today you must come to terms that the same now applies to all of us. A joke at the expense of Islam could see you end up in jail, whichever way you slice it. Or dead, as Rory Bremner feared, as reported in *The Daily Telegraph*: "Well-known political impressionist, Rory Bremner, during an interview with Sir David Frost on the BBC documentary, Frost on Satire, admitted he feared joking about Islam. When [I'm] writing a sketch about Islam, I'm writing a line and I think, 'If this goes down badly, I'm writing my own death warrant there.' Because there are people who will say, 'Not only do I not think that's funny but I'm going to kill you' – and that's chilling...If you're a Danish cartoonist and you work in a Western tradition, people don't take that too seriously. Suddenly you're confronted by a group of people who are fundamentalist and extreme and they say, 'We're going to kill you because of what you have said or drawn.' Where does satire go from there, because we like to be brave but not foolish'." (125) Are there any jokes allowed about Islam in Britain now?

The BBC reported (online): "A teenage girl and 39-year old man who desecrated an Edinburgh mosque by attacking it with strips of bacon have both been jailed. Chelsea

Lambie, 18, from Paisley, was sentenced to 12 months and Douglas Cruikshank, from Galashiels, to nine months. They attached bacon to door handles and threw strips inside Edinburgh's Central Mosque on 31 January 2013. Cruikshank pled guilty. Lambie was found guilty after denying the charges. Sheriff Alistair Noble, at Edinburgh Sheriff Court, said: 'It does not seem to me there is any way to deal with this case other than by custody.' During an earlier trial, the court heard a Blackberry mobile phone was found in Lambie's clothing when she was arrested at her boyfriend's house. Messages sent on January, 31 included: 'What you do last night?' The reply was: 'Went to the mosque in Edinburgh and wrapped bacon round the door handles, opened the door and threw it in ha ha ha'." (126)

Although there are increasing numbers of prosecutions being brought before the courts for racially-aggravated offences there is a reluctance to convict those who can use Islam as a get-out-of jail-free card. In December 2011 four Somali Muslim girls were convicted of viciously attacking a white care worker Rhea Page while screaming "white slag" and other obviously racist terms at her. Page was minding her own business after a night out in Leicester city centre when the unprovoked attack occurred that left her unconscious on the ground as she was repeatedly kicked in the head.

However, despite the evidence to the contrary, the judge decided that the attack was not racially motivated and none of the girls were given jail time. Judge Brown accepted the mitigation that as Muslims, the girls were not used to being drunk. None of the girls subsequently apologised to their victim who maintained she was attacked simply because she was white.

Yet this is what happens if you are white and British and seen to be pranking Islam, as reported in a national daily: "Four men were jailed for throwing a pig's head into a mosque just two days after the murder of soldier Lee Rigby. The friends dumped a carrier bag containing the severed pork head in the car park of Blackpool Central Mosque in Lancashire, in front of shocked women and children. Preston Crown Court was told the pals had organised the crime as a prank, knowing it would be seen as an insult in a Muslim place of worship. Thomas Ashton, 21, Andrew Warner, 31, Travis Crabtree, 25, and Steven White, 28, all from Blackpool or Lytham-St-Annes, were locked up today for a total of just over three years." (127) It subsequently turned out that the pig's head was actually dumped in the car park of the mosque not the mosque itself. A stupid prank indeed, but deserving of three years jail time? Correct me if I'm wrong but this incident happened in England and not Saudi Arabia, didn't it?

This is sharia law in action being divvied up by sharia-compliant judges who will fall over themselves to be even more sharia compliant as the increasing Muslim population of Britain demands more sharia law.

The death knell of freedom in Britain is being sounded loud and clear now. When time is called on our time honoured right to speak our mind without fear of state prosecution we will have our newest fear of offending Islam to thank for it; and it will only be the beginning of the draconian measures necessary to ensure Britain's transition to a sharia-compliant state. If Labour doesn't come back with more laws to make certain there is no mention of anything that could be construed critical of Islam then the multiculturalists in the Conservative Party look likely to do their work for them.

At the annual Conservative Party conference in September, 2014 the Home Secretary, Theresa May, announced plans for what she called Extremism Disruption Orders (EDOs), which would allow judges to ban people who are deemed to be "extremists" from broadcasting, protesting or posting messages on the internet without the permission of the state. These orders, panic measures to combat the spread of Islamic ideology, would also have the side-effect of labelling "extremist" then criminalizing anyone who dared to oppose the spread of sharia law in Britain or who holds politically incorrect views. The fear that these EDOs could all but eliminate any criticism of Islam, (as Labour's original Race and Religious Hatred Act tried to do in 2006) was confirmed on October 31, 2014 when a national daily newspaper published details of a letter written by chancellor George Osborne, telling his constituents that the EDOs would not be limited to fighting Islamic extremism: "The ultimate objective of the EDOs, Osborne wrote, would be to 'eliminate extremism in all its forms' and they would be used to curtail the activities of all those who 'spread hate but do not break laws'."

Osborne added that the new orders—which will be included in the Conservative Party's election manifesto—would extend to any activities that "justify hatred" against people on the grounds of religion, sexual orientation, gender or disability. Osborne also revealed that anyone seeking to challenge an EDO would have to go to the High Court and file an appeal based on a question of law rather than a question of fact. (Meaning that no jury could decide on the matter, it would be left to the judges alone.)

In an interview with the *The Daily Telegraph*, the director of the National Secular Society, Keith Porteous Wood, warned that individuals who criticize the spread of Islamic sharia law in Britain could be deemed racist, and silenced through an EDO. He said: "The Government should have every tool possible to tackle extremism and terrorism, but there is a huge arsenal of laws already in place and a much better case needs to be made for introducing draconian measures such as Extremism Disruption Orders, which are almost unchallengeable and deprive individuals of their liberties. Without precise legislative definitions, deciding what are the 'harmful activities of extremist individuals who spread hate' is subjective and therefore open to abuse now or by any future authoritarian government."

On November 2014, Teresa May gave parliament details of a new anti-terror bill giving more power to the police allowing government agencies to force telecommunications firms to hand over data on the identity of specific computer or mobile phone users. With each and every new power our freedoms are reduced on the road to a totalitarian society, and all of it avoidable because the authorities fear upsetting our rapidly growing Muslim population.

New laws *are* actually needed to stop the dissemination and advocacy of sharia law including the abolition of sharia courts where they exist in Britain. There must also be regular inspections of mosques to look for pro-violence materials and any mosques advocating jihad, or any aspects of sharia law, should be closed.

The Muslim Council of Britain and all other Muslim advocacy groups should also be surveilled by the security services and those who are found to have Islamist connections removed from the country. Any teaching of Islam in British schools must come with a health warning about its 1400-year war against unbelievers and ultimate aim of a global caliphate. All foreign aid to Islamic nations with sharia-based constitutions would be given only in return for the granting of basic human rights and freedom of speech in Islamic countries. Wouldn't this be a better way of preventing "extremist" violence? Naturally the vocal Islamist element within the Islamic community will claim victimisation, racism or Islamophobia but that smokescreen has already been rumbled in

Australia, whose anti-terror laws are likely to preserve their freedoms and peace longer than our head-in-the-sand half-measures.

On October 9, 2014 the *Sydney Morning Herald* reported on their own anti-trerror legislation and Muslim clerics immediately and predictably played the victim card. "Grand Mufti of Australia Ibrahim Abu Mohammad and the Australian National Imams Council have called for the offence of "advocating terrorism" to be removed from the so-called Foreign Fighters Bill, currently before Parliament.

They went public with their opposition on the same day Prime Minister Tony Abbott backed the draft legislation as essential to reining in "preachers of hate", including the radical Islamic group Hizb ut-Tahrir. "Muslims warn anti-terror laws could prevent teaching from the Koran. In its submission, the Islamic Council of Victoria said the new law would incriminate Muslims who support, 'legitimate forms of armed struggle', including resistance to the Assad regime in Syria and the Palestinian conflict with Israel." (128)

Islamophobia, racism, and The Crusades are constantly invoked as cause and justification of Muslim victimhood. Yet, if an objective look at Islamic history was allowed in schools would the mask of victimology be torn off? This is the Islamic history you will never found taught in schools because we fear to tell the truth.

A History of Victimology

The Islamic mantra of victimlogy, that it's the West to blame for all their troubles, that Islam loves peace and that The Crusades prove all this to be true cannot be sustained by even a cursory glance at the history books. It should be taught in all our schools but politically correct history is taught instead. The Muslim narrative that "Crusaders" unjustly invaded their lands may have *some* element of truth but ignores the events leading up to them as the forces of Islam expanded west out of Arabia. Here is the history of the Muslim Crusades.

673-678 Muslims besiege Constantinople, capital of Byzantine Empire.

710-713 Muslim Crusaders conquer the lower Indus Valley.

711-713 Muslim Crusaders conquer Spain and impose their new Islamic kingdom of Andalus.

732 Muslim Crusaders stopped at the Battle of Poitiers by the Franks of France who, at the last gasp, halt Arab advance into Europe.

785 Foundation of the Great Mosque of Cordoba

789 Muslim Crusaders take Morocco. Christoforos, a Muslim who converted to Christianity, is executed.

807 Caliph Harun al-Rashid orders the destruction of non-Muslim prayer houses and of the church of Mary Magdalene in Jerusalem.

809 Muslim Crusaders conquer Sardinia, Italy.

813 Christians in Palestine are attacked and forced to leave.

831 Muslim Crusaders capture Palermo, Italy.

855 Revolt of Christians in Hims (Syria).

837-901 Aghlabids (Muslim Crusaders) conquer Sicily.

869-883 Revolt of black slaves owned by Muslims in what is now known as Iraq.

937 The Church of the Resurrection, known as the Church of the Holy Sepulchre is burned down by Muslims.

At this point a pause, to take in just what was decreed by Muslim caliph Al-Hakim. Christianity began in 33 AD when Jesus of Nazareth was crucified on Mount Golgotha and buried in a tomb that had been cut out of a rock located in a nearby garden. After three days he rose from the dead and from that moment the Tomb of the Resurrection became the holiest place for all Christians. The original Church of the Holy Sepulchre was created by the Roman Emperor Constantine in 335 to provide a single place of worship, enclosing all these most sacred Christian sites under one magnificent church, that was actually two connected churches. One built around the excavated hill of the Crucifixion and near the cross found by St Helena (Constantine's mother) and another, a magnificent rotunda over the Rock of Calvary, the tomb of Jesus. This was the greatest wonder of the biblical world and it was destroyed by Al-Hakim in an act of vandalism unmatched in religious history. Imagine the pope authorising the simultaneous destruction of the Kaaba stone at Mecca and the city of Medina and you will have some idea of what was destroyed by Al-Hakim.

In **846** Rome was sacked and the Vatican desecrated by Muslim Arab invaders and in **1453**, Christianity's second greatest church the Hagia Sophia in Constantinople, now Istanbul, was conquered by Muslim Turks and remains in Muslim hands to this day and is about to be turned into a mosque in order that Turkey be rid of its despised Christian heritage. Only after all of the Islamic invasions of Western Christendom and the destruction of its holiest site did Pope Urban II, in **1095**, launched the first Crusade leading to the capture of Jerusalem in **1099**. Muslims continued their aggressive expansion until they were finally stopped at the gates of Vienna in **1683**, having already conquered all of the formerly Christian countries of the Middle East. There is not one nation on earth that has voluntarily adopted Islamic culture or rule.

Just 10 years after the birth of Islam the jihad came out of Arabia. What we today refer to as the "Islamic world" was once Christian and only became Islamic at the point of a sword. A mere decade after the birth of Islam in the 7th century, land conquered by Islam included Syria, Algeria, Egypt, Morocco, Tunisia, Libya, Iraq, Iran, parts of India and China as well as much of Europe including Portugal, Spain, Austria, France, Greece, Italy, Sicily, Switzerland, Hungary, Russia, Poland, Bulgaria, Ukraine, Lithuania, Romania, Albania, Serbia, Armenia, Georgia, Crete, Cyprus, Croatia, Bosnia-Herzegovina, Macedonia, Belarus, Malta, Sardinia, Moldova, Slovakia, and Montenegro. The beginning of what we call the Dark Ages are usually dated to the deposition of the last Roman Emperor, Romulus Augustulus, in 476 AD and the fall of Byzantium. It is widely held that following this Europe was plunged into endless misery by a combination of Germanic invasions and the spread of Christianity. Many documentaries and books depict barbaric hordes of German Goths, Vandals and other tribes descending on the Roman provinces in the 400 and 500's AD and destroying the Roman high culture of the Mediterranean basin. This disaster was supposedly supplemented by the spread of a backward, superstition ridden Christianity. These cultural calamities were blamed for plunging Europe into ten centuries of chaos which destroyed classical learning and economic prosperity. This is the anti-Christian picture that was popularized by Edward Gibbon in 1776 with his publication of the widely read *Decline and fall of the Roman Empire*. It was a theme picked up by many academics who followed and is still prominent today. If you believe this scenario you should also read *Mohammed and Charlemagne* by Henri Pirenne for an alternative perspective. Pirenne was the leading medieval scholar of the early Twentieth Century. He published *Mohammed and Charlemagne* in 1937, long before the current chaos in the Middle East. His ideas were widely accepted among the academics of his time but unfortunately have been largely forgotten or ignored of late as they do not fit in with politically correct ideas about Islamic history. The basic argument of the book is simple; the fall of the Roman Empire is normally dated to 476 AD when the last Western Roman Emperor was deposed by Odoacer the leader of a Germanic tribe. In the aftermath of this defeat German Tribes moved into Italy and other Roman provinces and established a series of Gothic Kingdoms.

The current view is that Europe then plunged directly into the Dark Ages. However, when Pirenne examined everyday life inside the provinces of the former Roman Empire following the Germanic invasions he found that little had changed. The aqueducts and sanitation systems continued to work, the schools remained open, taxes were collected, the road system was maintained, foreign trade was abundant, money was coined and the standard of living remained high. His detailed examination of the period's records shows very clearly that life continued virtually unchanged for the next 250 years.

This is no surprise, as it must be remembered that the German invaders had no desire to destroy the Roman Empire, their objective was to live in it and enjoy the fruits of its higher standard of living. While the Germans did initially engage in taking of booty and pillage they nevertheless soon settled down and adopted the Roman way of life. They adopted Roman agricultural practices, Roman law, Christianity and in most areas, Romance languages.

Whose Dark Ages?

However when we get to the early 700s AD life begins to change drastically: coinage disappears, artisans are forced to give up their trades and go back to living on the land, books disappear, schools close, the roads and aqueducts and other infrastructure are no longer maintained and the standard of living throughout the Roman world begins to decline sharply.

What happened? The answer is simple. This was when Islamic armies began their war of conquest against the West. Starting in the late 600s AD Arab forces invaded Egypt, North Africa and the old Fertile Crescent area. With them they brought not only Islam but primitive practices which resulted in economic collapse for the entire region from which it has never recovered, even to this day.

Ancient Roman, Egyptian and Persian agricultural practices were destroyed in most of the conquered territories and as a result food production plummeted as ancient agribusiness was replaced by subsistence farming. Cities were abandoned as their inhabitants were forced back on to the land in order to avoid starvation. The Fertile Crescent area of Iraq and Iran suffered particularly harshly as the loss of the old farming technology, especially its well planned irrigation works, resulted in the contamination of the Tigris-Euphrates Basin due to salt percolation, turning it into the barren desert seen today.

The other economic killer was the Islamic destruction of the old overland trading system. In the ancient world there had been large scale foreign trade extending from China to Britain. The Islamic refusal to deal with the "Infidels" led to the decline of this trade and the destruction of the second most important component of the ancient economy: trade with India, China, Persia, Egypt and the other advanced economic centres of the ancient world. This trade did not recover until the Age of Exploration when Europeans discovered how to sail around the Islamic barrier to foreign trade.

Why is this Important? The Dark Ages were an enormous setback for European civilization. Today, most of the world believes that Christianity shares a great deal of the blame for causing this disaster, even going so far as to compare it unfavourably, in a revisionist version of history, which depicts Islam as the saviour of ancient Western knowledge.

Islamic scholar and expert on Islamic affairs, Professor Daniel Pipes offers an explanation: "Summarizing these statements, which come straight out of the Islamist playbook: Islam is purely a religion of peace, so violence and barbarism categorically have nothing to do with it; indeed, these 'masquerade' and 'pervert' Islam. By implication, more Islam is needed to solve these 'monstrous' and 'barbaric' problems. But, of course, this interpretation neglects the scriptures of Islam and the history of Muslims, seeped in the assumption of superiority toward non-Muslims and the righteous violence of *jihad*. Ironically, ignoring the Islamic impulse means foregoing the best tool to defeat jihadism: for, if the problem results not from an interpretation of Islam, but from random evil and irrational impulses, how can one possibly counter it?" (129)

Because there has been no united rejection of the literal interpretation of Islam the loudest voices in Islam, the ones calling the shots, are those who can quote the 7th Century scriptures best. Do we think that if radical Islam gained power in France the great treasures of the past would be safe from destruction? Do we think the Mona Lisa would be saved from having an Islamist boot put through it? I wouldn't bet on it.

In Egypt under the Muslim Brotherhood rule of Muhammad Morsi, Muslim clerics called for the demolition of Egypt's Great Pyramids as "symbols of paganism," which Egypt's Salafi party had previously planned to cover with wax. Under what Islamists call Jahiliyyah, the age of ignorance before Islam, any art or culture predating the time of Mohammad is said to be idolatry and worthy only of destruction. When Arabian Muslim tribesmen invaded and conquered Egypt in 641 many Egyptian antiquities were destroyed as "relics of infidelity". In 832 the Caliph of Baghdad visited conquered Egypt and ordered his troops to demolish the Great Pyramid of Giza. Luckily, months of destructive effort did only minimal damage (they didn't have high explosives then). How many of us have heard the story of the Sphinx losing its nose due to Napoleon's army when there is historical evidence that those responsible were the Muslim Mamluk slaves, who used it for target practice. According to early Muslim writers, the great Library of Alexandria, which contained a complete history of the ancient world, was denounced as a repository of pagan knowledge, then destroyed under bin al-As's reign in compliance with Caliph Omar's order.

The Muslim narrative of historical victimhood reached its zenith in the campaign of the Palestinians for statehood. American presidential candidate and former leader of the US Congress, Newt Gingrich, got into hot water with the liberal press by calling the Palestinian's an "invented people". Yet what of the following historical facts about the Palestinians can be disputed?

"They are indistinguishable from those Arabs who live in the surrounding artificial states such as Iraq, Jordan, Saudi Arabia or the other entities throughout the Middle East created by the colonial powers, France and Britain. Both powers were victorious after the Ottoman Turkish Empire lay defeated at the end of World War I. Both of these European powers carved artificial borders across the corpse of what had been Turkey's empire in the Middle East, and both France and Britain have left a resulting legacy of war and violence ever since. One such territory, previously occupied by Ottoman Turkey for 400 years, was the geographical entity known sometimes as Palestine. But there is no such thing as a Palestinian people; no such thing as a Palestinian history; and no Palestinian language exists. There has never been any independent, sovereign Palestinian state in all of recorded history – let alone an Arab independent state of Palestine. You will search in vain for Palestinian Arab coinage or Palestinian Arab archaeological artifacts specifically related to any Palestinian Arab king or ancient leader. But what you will find are coins, pottery, ancient scrolls, all providing conclusive, empirical and millennial evidence of Jewish civilization dotting the land known correctly as Israel – not Palestine. The present-day so-called 'Palestinians' are an Arab people sharing an overwhelmingly Muslim Arab culture, ethnicity and language identical to their fellow Arabs in the Middle East and North Africa, with few if any distinctions." (130)

That is the bald truth of history and it is never taught in schools for fear of causing offence to Muslims. What our children are taught is that we should be ashamed of our past, our culture and our civilisation and embrace the fiction of the Left that British history is all about oppression and genocide. Thus white working class children in England are robbed of their own past, of their own national identity and of a cultural identity that should be taught with justified national pride.

Thus cultural Marxism paves the way for cultural jihad and the destruction of our civilisation from within by its lethal combination. As Gingrich points out: "There has been a desperate desire among our elites to focus on the act of terrorism rather than the motivation behind those acts. There has been a deep desire to avoid the cultural and religious motivations behind the jihadists' actions. There is an amazing hostility to any effort to study or teach the history of these patterns going back to the seventh century. Because our elites refuse to look at the religious and historic motivations and patterns which drive our opponents, we are responding the same way to attack after attack on our way of life without any regard for learning about what really motivates our attackers. Only once we learn what drives and informs our opponents will we not repeat the same wrong response tactics, Groundhog Day–like, and finally start to win this long war. Currently each new event, each new group, each new pattern is treated as though it's an isolated phenomenon — as if it's not part of a larger struggle with a long history and deep roots in patterns that are 1,400 years old. There is a passion for narrowing and localizing actions. The early focus was al-Qaeda. Then it was the Taliban. Now it is the Islamic

State. It is beginning to be Boko Haram. As long as the elites can keep treating each new eruption as a freestanding phenomenon, they can avoid having to recognize that this is a global, worldwide movement that is decentralized but not disordered. There are ties between Minneapolis and Mogadishu. There are ties between London, Paris, and the Islamic State." (131)

Today we are at a point where history and facts must be "erased" and rewritten, because truth is racist-Islamophobic-anti-Muslim bigotry. Historical revisionism has taken on a new life, as history is scrubbed and manufactured Muslim myths are presented as fact. Pioneering historian Bat Ye'or recently visited the British Museum and found that "Palestinian propaganda and its cohorts of EU bowdlerizing troops have also visited the Museum – which is why all the information notes pertaining to the artefacts that mention the history of the Kingdoms of Judea and Israel now also mention the word 'Palestine' – even 3,000 years B.C. – while the name was only given to the land in 135 A.D. by Roman Emperor Hadrian when he incorporated it into the Roman Empire." (132)

If Islamists want an everlasting armed struggle, as they have for 1,400 years and are likely to do so for another 1,400 years, then they should be allowed to do so from their countries of origin in the Middle East.

In November, 2014, a statement by Prime Minister David Cameron on the killing of Fusilier Drummer Lee Rigby was read out in the House of Lords. Cameron opined that the murder was a betrayal of Islam and Britain's Muslim communities but in the "debate" that followed, Lord Pearson said to his fellow peers: "My Lords, are the government aware that Fusilier Rigby's murderers quoted 22 verses of the Koran to justify their atrocity? Therefore, is the Prime Minister accurate or helpful when he describes it as a betrayal of Islam? Since the vast majority of Muslims are our peace-loving friends, should we not encourage them to address the violence in the Koran – and indeed in the life and the example of Muhammad?"

The response from Muslim Labour MP Khalid Mahmood was a furious reaction to an invite to open debate, "This [intervention by Pearson] is just complete nonsense. Obviously he hasn't read the Koran. Islam is about submission to the Almighty. It is not about war against anybody else. I find it absolutely offensive that this guy is still able to say this. I will actually tomorrow make a complaint formally to the Lords speaker on this issue. This is not tolerable and it should not be tolerated at all." It's clear that Muslims, even in the House of Lords will not allow any debate on the Koran.

Despite being a Muslim, Khalid Mahmood is clearly not an authority on Islam, someone who is an authority and who *has* read The Koran is leading academic Raymond Ilbrahim, who points out Osama bin Laden's understanding of "moderate Islam".

"Our talks with the infidel West and our conflict with them ultimately revolve around one issue — one that demands our total support, with power and determination, with one voice — and it is: does Islam, or does it not, force people by the power of the sword to submit to its authority corporeally if not spiritually? He then answers his own question: Yes. There are only three choices in Islam: [1] either willing submission [conversion]; [2] or payment of the jizya, through physical, though not spiritual, submission to the authority of Islam; [3] or the sword — for it is not right to let him [an infidel] live. The matter is summed up for every person alive: either submit, or live under the suzerainty of Islam, or die." (133)

Fight the Future

By 2020 things begin to change rapidly as the continued need to borrow more than £100 billion each year to pay for the ever expanding welfare bill tears gaping holes in successive budget forecasts.

Constant violence among London's unemployed migrants now spilling out from Muslim no go zones goes viral, copycat fashion, to Britain's other major cities. Police in Manchester, Birmingham, Liverpool, Sheffield and Leeds struggle to quell the nightly eruptions of mayhem sparked by social media alerts. The London murder rate spirals out of control yet Islamic violence or black on white violence gets no front page headlines despite the fact that entire communities are now effectively at war with the police and the rest of Britain. The Labour Party, firmly back in control of the "super-diverse" state created by Blair/Brown's open door immigration policies now decide to abolish the Independent Police Complaints Commission and replace it with a Police Standards Authority. This new authority becomes a statutory body allowing racial thought crime to become law, a path laid out by the Macpherson report of 1999 which stated that the police were institutionally racist, and the establishment of the notion that even if a crime is *perceived* to be racist, despite there being no proof, then it must be racist.

The new police authority has this doctrine as its guiding ethos. Witnesses are called and compelled to give evidence against those who they suspect of having muttered racist language under their breath. Investigations about alleged racist behaviour at football matches from passers-by are launched as a priority over crimes of murder, robbery or rape committed by Muslims or ethnic minorities.

It is the end of individual freedom in Britain as the police pursue those alleged to have uttered "Islamophobic" remarks in their own homes. The politically correct chief constables now take their policing cues from the new authority in ways that the Stasi would have approved of while ignoring the growing chaos and violence on the streets that is leading Britain into civil war. Elsewhere Labour's relentless focus on diversity goes on with the passing of Labour's Education and Diversity Act 2021 that ensures a return to "child based" education with extra marks for diversity-based learning, unravelling the short term gains made by the Conservative government of 2015. Science, RE, English literature, Geography and History are reviewed and found wanting by the new Cultural and Religious Awareness studies review board, chaired by a member of the Muslim Council of Britain. These subjects are made more "diverse" in an attempt to appease offended Muslims who want the teaching of Christianity removed from the curriculum. Muslim leaders, representing communities who have little to show in tax contributions since their arrival in Britain 25 years earlier, blame their idleness on the requirement to learn English and demand that the languages of Urdu, Bengali and Arabic become part of the national curriculum replacing German, Spanish and French. The economy and its dwindling band of industrialists, already split into ever smaller groups of patriots determined to stick it out, watch in horror as the living standards of one major city after another…London, Manchester, Birmingham, Leeds, Luton, Bradford fall off a cliff as state taxes are funnelled into Muslim community projects. Journalists in Britain are now licensed by BBCweb, the state media controller which successfully prevents any of this bad news from seeping into the wider public's consciousness. The Education and Diversity Act is followed by the Blasphemy Act of 2022. This is basically a return to the Labour Race and Religious Hatred Act which had been amended by the House of Lords in 2006 limiting the scope of the Act to: "A person who uses threatening words or behaviour, or displays any written material which is threatening… if he intends thereby to stir up religious hatred." This required that there was the *intention* of stirring up religious hatred.

The Labour government tried to block this amendment but lost the House of Commons vote on 31 January 2006 when their leader, Tony Blair, accidentally failed to vote for the Act in the second division. Thus, by one vote, was some semblance of free speech preserved for another 16 rears.

The new Act of 2022 was once again applied to threatening abusive or insulting words or behaviour, all written material in print or on the internet and any recordings or programmes intended to or likely to stir up religious hatred. This time, just like before, these serious offences required *no criminal intent* and applied not only to words spoken in public but *also in private*, encompassing plays, films, works of fiction, political argument, TV, the sermons given by priests and the jokes told by comedians. Thought crime was now on the statute book and Britain had surrendered its freedom to religious thuggery. This was the big law that the Islamists, working from within Britain's institutions, had been waiting for. A law preventing all criticism of Islam.

Radical Islam, aided and abetted by the Left's useful idiots, had used Labour's obsession with racism to allow Islam to be legally reclassified as a separate *race* so that now any criticism of Muslims would be seen as racist, despite the glaring fact that Islam was open to believers of different ethnicities and races. Labour brought this law because of pressure from their now 100 plus constituencies with majority Muslim constituents, who themselves were egged on by their imams at Friday prayers in one of the 100 new mosques built in the previous decade. Labour's appeasers argued the law was necessary because Jews and Sikhs were already protected by existing law, but Muslims were not. Those who dared argue that Jews and Sikhs were protected as *ethnic or racial groups*, not because of their religion and that Muslims do not constitute a single race were shouted down and outvoted. It was now illegal to criticize Islam in any way, or the Koran or the actions of any individual Muslim in Britain.

Walking through any of the 33 Arab boroughs of London we can now see only women dressed from head to foot in the Niqab, ethnic Arab foods shops and Islamic restaurants. The shopping centres are the same only with the accompaniment of Arabic music blaring out onto the street. Signs written in Arabic are everywhere with many pointing towards

Mecca. Islamic flags are draped over churches now converted to mosques. Almost overnight young men with long beards and black flowing robes backed up by thuggish supporters patrol the towns and cities of Britain. They are the British Mutaween, the Islamic religious police and they are on the lookout for anyone breaking sharia law. Girls not dressed in full niqab are told to cover up or go home, those who do not attend Friday prayers or have not converted to Islam are made to pay the jizyah, the Islamic tax. Those who refuse are sentenced to death at the Islamic courts that have multiplied across the country like topsy. Where did these people come from, how have they the right to do this to us? wonder the indigenous British people, now reduced to second class status within their own country. Who allowed this to happen? But by now it is too late. Within months of the passage of the blasphemy act ethnic hate has became institutionalised in Britain and white flight has gathered pace from a trot to a gallop. Those Jews who had not already emigrated, and could do so, did. It was 1933 all over again. Desperate parents without the price of a flight or a black market visa moved like refugees to areas in the south-west and the East of England, a flight for safety moving in ever decreasing circles. Property prices in Cornwall, Cumbria and Norfolk double almost overnight. The Labour politicians who had sold out their own people now crowed at their demise and cheered the disintegration of the hated capitalist system in Britain. Behind closed doors their cowardice is openly despised not only by the disenfranchised white electorate but also by their new Muslim overlords. A new atmosphere of perceived ultra-racism becomes all pervasive. Bill posters blame the collapse of public hygiene, the filth littering the streets, random violence, kidnapping and murder on the infidel white minorities of Britain's Muslim majority cities. Muslim holidays like Ramadan became more prominent than Easter or Christmas, both now outlawed as haram (forbidden) under sharia law.

The soft Left's naïve efforts to find common ground only serve to isolate the already cowed and fearful group once referred to as "moderate Muslims" and speed the transition to a hard-line Islamic rule demanding British institutions adapt to sharia law with banks, schools, social workers, the army and the police all becoming more and more Islamic. The police, neutered as a peace keeping organisation by the Blasphemy Act, could only just stay out of trouble themselves. They stay clear of Muslim no-go areas and confine their duties to processing the victims of gang violence without seeking out the criminals responsible. Fear pervades their every action with any accusation of racism being enough to make the BBC nightly news and end their slim hopes of a police pension. More and more Muslim councillors are elected and the Muslim minister for religion in the Labour government makes clear his intention of challenging the prime minister for the leadership at the next party conference.

The BBC, now the only broadcaster, makes nightly exposes of new racial crimes committed against Muslims, wheeling on a variety of academics and social work experts whose exhorted advice is for the police to deal severely with those who promote negative stereotypes of Muslims while ignoring the hate crimes being perpetrated against whites in every major city in England.

On every BBC crime drama whites are portrayed as criminals or degenerates, news reports use white British citizens to stand in for Muslims accused of rape, police spokesman openly lie about crime figures so as not to include Muslim gang rape crime. As the flight to the remaining majority white towns continues the BBC now turns to its investigative "reporters" to uncover the "truth" about these enclaves as the newest, most violent and racist threat to society and to Muslims. A typical episode of EastEnders shows a white barman making a joke about Islam and then being hounded out of the bar by non-racist whites before being arrested by police. Another episode focuses on white children teaching their dogs to hate Muslims or employers who are blamed for Muslim dependency on welfare benefits while simultaneously discriminating against them, refusing to give hard working Muslims a job.

Meanwhile, out in the real world, non-Muslim schoolchildren and old age pensioners find it hard to even walk past hostile Muslim gangs, who hang out all day long near playgrounds and town centre mosques. Taunts, hostile stares and violence are a constant threat. In state schools Muslim children are now in the majority, white children in the way of Muslim school gangs are pushed and punched then forced to apologize. Thanks to continuous pressure from the MCB all schools must now have a prayer room with a poster of Mecca and a copy of the Koran, where Muslim students can pray five times a day, with facilities for ritual washing before prayers.

Old "infidels" legally deprived of the state pension, are made to step on the road to avoid

Muslim groups walking the pavements. A statue of murdered politician Nigel Farage is regularly vandalised but the vandals are never prosecuted.

If attacked, any non-Muslim who fights back would later find his home suddenly besieged by his attacker and his attackers' extended family of brothers, sisters, uncles and friends. These new criminals, imported from the Third World and with their Third World values intact, know they will never face any criminal profiling or any accusations of racism as English Common Law has been effectively wiped from the statute book.

Drugs begin to flood into the country from a network of jihadi sources based outside Britain to the network of jihadi sources based inside Britain. A tsunami wave of rape, murder and child abuse goes unreported in the media, acknowledged only by the guarded whispers of a minority of white Brits marooned in the disintegrating cities. Islamic riots, constantly sparked by media reports of blasphemy, become Islamic demands for a separate state in Muslim majority areas.

In 2030 a Labour/Islam Party coalition government agrees to small independent Muslim "committees" ruling Birmingham, Leicester, Luton, Sheffield, Bradford, Manchester and most of London and the Act of Islamic succession is rubber stamped by parliament. Almost immediately contraband rockets and grenades pour into Britain's newly autonomous Muslim majority cities as internecine warfare between Sh'ite and Sunni explodes locally in a continuation of a conflict that has lasted 1,400 years in the Middle East. The forever war has come to Britain, just as it came to France five years earlier. Now the non-Muslim refugees who fled after the Muslim takeover of France find that the safe haven they assumed Britain to be has gone the way of their own land. In Europe now only Switzerland, Serbia and Poland stand against Islamic expansion and aggression but the EU condemns their resistance as racist and Islamophobic and imposes economic sanctions. Amid the wreckage and devastation of what used to be the free world destitute Christian refugees set their sights on emigration to the United States, Canada or Australia, as do a new wave of Islamic hopefuls tired of all the violence and the knowledge that Britain's welfare state is finally out of funds.

CHAPTER TWELVE

SEPARATION

Though there are many trouble spots around the world, as a general rule it's easy to make an educated guess at one of the participants: Muslims vs Jews in "Palestine", Muslims vs Hindus in Kashmir, Muslims vs Christians in Africa, Muslims vs Buddhists in Thailand, Muslims vs Russians in the Caucasus, Muslims vs backpacking tourists in Bali, Muslims vs Danish cartoonists in Scandinavia. The environmentalists may claim to think globally but act locally, but these guys live it.
Mark Steyn, America Alone (2006)

We've been up against this threat before. A monoculture with reverence for a messianic leader: hatred of Jews and homosexuals, women as second-class citizens, contempt for a free press and freedom of conscience, the aim of global domination by the use of violence and terror. The above describes the Nazi Party but how exactly does radical Islam differ from that template? Islamism is by far the most frightening of the three totalitarian spectres Western civilisation has had to face so far.

Had the Nazis won the Second World War those not enslaved or liquidated would at least have been allowed to eat and drink what they liked, to wear what they liked, to fall in love and marry who they wanted. Had Communism triumphed there would still have been equality of races and of the sexes. Sharia law would outlaw even those small mercies.

If sharia ever becomes the law of the land here in Britain non-Muslims face a bleak future as subhuman outlaws within their own ancestral borders. Had we lost the Second World War or the Cold War and ended up under the yoke of Nazism or Communism most would have suspected that these ideologies would not last forever and would be likely to perish in time, along with their deranged leaders.

If we were ever to completely submit to sharia law there would be no such hope.

Islamism is the true heir of the virulent fascism the Western democracies vanquished in the Second World War and the violent revolutionary Communism it *thought* it had defeated in the Cold War. These are the new totalitarians; time travelled from the 7th Century and now here to conquer, convert or kill us all.

At the moment I don't include the majority of British Muslims from outside London who are not yet committed to jihad. Unfortunately with the advent of mass immigration from Islamic countries and the spread of the true word on the Internet these "moderates" are rapidly being eclipsed by radicalised Muslims, who now rule the Islamic roost in London and in our prisons. Radicalised Muslims are Islamists who want to live in parallel, segregated societies funded by the jizyah (welfare state) and who support the introduction of sharia law *for now* but who seek the imposition of an Islamic state by force *when they have the numbers.*

Most *secular* Muslims living in Britain were willing to abide by our laws, enjoy our freedoms but not assimilate…unless encouraged to do so by a requirement to at least learn the English language. Without any such encouragement what we have allowed the post-1997 wave of immigrant Muslims to do is create in our cities the backward Islamic societies they, presumably, took leave of in order to come to Britain for a better life.

Cut off from the moderating influences of traditional civic society, unable or unwilling to learn English and radicalised by Arab speaking imams in British mosques up and down the country and on the internet, more and more are becoming willing converts to an Islamist revolution. What else can they do when they are told that it is the duty of *all* Muslims to wage jihad against the unbeliever until sharia law prevails?

At this point secular Muslims, fearful of their own apostasy law will fall into line believing that a nation of soft multiculti degenerates will lack the guts to rise up and defend their own birthright. The prospect of leaving our children the legacy of a life lived in a brutal post-Christian country is now very real if we don't do something to stop Islamic immigration into Britain.

There can be no peace for any of us long term while the numbers of Islamists continue to grow along with the rapid growth of Islamic immigrants and while they can say they have their holy book on-side as a written constitution to prove to peaceful Muslims that they are *not real Muslims* at all. Islamists can point to the scriptures, chapter and verse, to prove it. Those who say Islam will reform itself are ignoring the fact that it already has, into the distilled version we see practiced by the savages of Islamic State, a stone's throw away across the Mediterranean.

After the beheading of Lee Rigby, "moderate" Muslims took to social media in force in order to air the alleged grievances they "suffered" in their adopted home rather than make any effort to condemn the violence perpetrated in their name. When Michael Adebolajo was given a whole life prison term his brother, rather than accept the verdict, claimed that the convicted killer was instead the victim of "Islamophobia."

While the lessons of history should have taught us to keep a wide berth from all things Islam the shocking ignorance and naivety of the Blair/Brown government has locked us in an embrace with an ideology/religion that has consumed every society it has ever settled over.

In 2006 an extensive poll conducted by *The Sunday Telegraph* showed that 40% of British Muslims *wanted* sharia law in Britain. That 40% figure seems to be a baseline constant and it crops up in almost every poll taken on the issue. It means that, almost a decade ago, 40% of British Muslims *wanted* to end British freedom and replace it with sharia law. They *may* want to do it peacefully but when they become the majority, they *will* act and they *will* become the majority in Britain, after 2050.

For now, our imperative is to ensure that sharia law gains no foothold in any free society. That means no leniency from British judges for any Islamist who calls for jihad, who seeks to impose Islamic rule, promote suicide terrorism, second class citizenship for non-Muslims, the death penalty for adultery or apostasy and honour killings of women.

This conduct has no place in any civilised society and those who advocate it must be stripped of their citizenship and removed from British soil. The security services estimate that the 2,000 "British citizens" who have already travelled to Syria to join the war on the West are being joined by at least one more a day with more than 700 fighters having recently *returned* to Britain, allowed "home" to plot more atrocities against innocent civilians. Why are we allowing these people back in? Once out of the country the passports of those who are intent on murder should be cancelled and those who try to return should have the door shut firmly in their faces. But that will make them "stateless" complain the taxpayer funded activist lawyers, and is against international law.

So, Britain needs to declare war on IS, as IS has declared war on Britain and legislate that anyone travelling there is guilty of treason and then legally confiscate their passports, under international law.

Islam is rapidly gaining ground in the West where, by a combination of thuggish intimidation and political pressure on what they see as our weak PC elites it aims to introduce laws which will curtail our freedom to speak out against those aspects of Islam that offend our common decency. If offending someone and inciting hatred is a crime then anyone and any Muslim can claim to be offended by any speech they want to suppress.

How many Islamic states have free speech? The criminalization of speech or thought is the first act of a totalitarian state and too many of our freedoms have already been sacrificed on the altar of mass immigration.

We need to stop Islamic immigration into Britain now or it will soon be too late. I say this not out of any anger or prejudice towards British Muslims but because I fear the consequences of not doing so and by doing nothing condemning future generations, our own sons, daughters and grandchildren, to the endless darkness of Islamic theocratic rule in Britain.

Islamic State say that they practice the real Islam as found in their holy book and it will be that version that conquers the world if we allow it. Islam cannot win in a direct confrontation with the West but it will win by being allowed in through the back door of immigration and then multiplication. Without being able to control our own borders there is nothing we can do to stem the inexorable tide of refugees heading to Britain from the Middle East and Africa. The only way to save our children from a brutish future of intolerance and hatred is to demand of our politicians a complete halt to immigration from countries not oriented towards Western values, and that means immigration from Islamic nations.

Even if all of the experts mentioned in this book are wrong about the supremacist aims of Islam, even if all of the conquests and atrocities documented throughout Islamic history prove nothing, even if three thousand dead after 9/11 or those killed in London on 7/7 or the Mumbai killings or the Westgate Mall Massacre or the Charlie Hebdo murders or the butchered body of Lee Rigby don't convince us, should we not at least be buying ourselves and our children a little insurance, just in case?

Shouldn't we be saying that, just in case the evidence really does stack up in favour of an Islamic Britain after 2030, we owe it to those who will come after us to put a brake on the mass importation of a culture that might regard us, at best, as an irritant host, or at worst, as infidels to be subdued and then enslaved or killed?

When your children or grandchildren ask you why you betrayed them so badly by your inaction, what will you say?

BIBLIOGRAPHY

CHAPTER ONE

(1) *Gatestone Institute 21/7/2011.*

(2) *BBC online news 6/1/2008.*

(3) *Mary Jackson, New English Review (July 2008).*

(4) *Dominic Kennedy, The Times, January 10, 2014*

(5) *The Black Book of Communism.*

CHAPTER TWO

(6) *BBC news, 12/2/15.*

(7) *Mark Steyn, America Alone, page 89.*

(8) *Dr Peter Hammond Slavery, Terrorism and Islam - the Historical Roots and Contemporary Threat.*

(9) *Julie Birchill, The Spectator, 22/11/14.*

CHAPTER THREE

(10) *Macer Hall, Daily Express 15/9/11.*

(11) *The Brussels Journal, 12/7/2005*

(12) *Passed to The Daily Telegraph by WikiLeaks, 4 Feb 2011*

(13) *BBC Panorama, 10/4/14.*

(14) *Sue Reid, Daily Mail, 14/2/2014.*

(15) *The Sunday Times, 8/2/15.*

(16) *The Daily Mail. 7/10/14.*

(17) *ukpublicspending.co.uk .*

(18) *The Daily Telegraph, 13/10/13.*

(19) *The Sunday Times, 12/9/14.*

(20) *Douglas Murray, Standpoint, March 2013.*

(21) *Free riding foreigners: the next NHS scandal. We heal the world – and you pay for it. The Spectator, 23/2/2013.*

(22) *Recent Immigration to the UK: New Evidence of the Fiscal costs and Benefits by Professor Christian Dustmann and Dr Tommaso Frattini (November 13, 2013)*

(23) *Ed West , The Spectator, 6/11/14.*

(24) *Rod Liddle, The Spectator, 6/12/14.*

(25) *MigrationWatch News, May 4, 2009.*

CHAPTER FOUR

(26) *David Walker, The Guardian, September 5, 2000.*

(27) *Sharia for Dummies by Nonie Darwish, FrontPage, 27 August 2010.*

(28) *The Daily Mail 30 January, 2013.*

(29) *Robert Tait, The Daily Telegraph, 2/3/15.*

(30) *Larisa Brown, The Daily Mail, 26 June 2014.*

(31) *Nicholas Hellen, The Sunday Times, 21 April 2013.*

(32) *Harriet Arkell, The Daily Mail, 22/11/13.*

(33) *Cyril Dixon, The Daily Express, September 13, 2013.*

(34) *Sara Malm, The Daily Mail, 20/2/2013.*

(35) *The Daily Mail, 30/4/14.*

(36) *The Daily Telegraph, 7/5/14.*

(37) *Joe Curtis, Waltham Forest Guardian, 4th October 2013.*

(38) *The Daily Mail, 26 October 2014.*

(39) *The Daily Mail 16/8/14.*

(40) *The Daily Mail, 15 August 2014.*

(41) *Adam Taylor, The Washington Post, 12/6/14.*

CHAPTER FIVE

(42) *The Independent, 2/9/2003.*

(43) *Nick Cohen, The Spectator, 21/1/15.*

(44) *Where's the Lead in the Pencil? by Mark Steyn, Steyn on the World, January 14, 2015.*

(45) *The Daily Mail, 1/1/15.*

(46) *Lawrence Auster, A View from the Right.*

(47) *Melanie Phillips, The Daily Mail, 18/3/2013.*

(48) *The Daily Mail, 22/12/14.*

(49) *Littlejohn, The Daily Mail, 'These human rights parasites should be tried for treason'.*

(50) *Rod Liddle, Sunday Times, 1/2/15.*

CHAPTER SIX

(51) *BBC news, 6/9/2006.*

(52) *Tom Rawstrone, The Daily Mail, 13/5/2011.*

(53) *Andrew Gilligan, The Sunday Telegraph, 27/2/2010.*

(54) *Rachel Kerbaj and Sian Griffiths, The Sunday Times, 2/3/2014- 9/3/2014-and 16/3/14.*

(55) *Tim Shipman, The Sunday Times, 8/6/14.*

(56) *The Daily Telegraph, 12/ 6/2014.*

(57) *Dispatches, Channel Four, 1/3/2010.*

(58) *Andrew Gilligan, The Daily Telegraph, 18/1/2014.*

(59) *Sian Griffiths and Richard Kerbaj, The Sunday Times, 28 September 2014.*

(60) *The Guardian 7/2/15.*

(61) *Nonie Darwish , article for the The Gatestone institute Feb5, 2013.*

(62) *FoxNews.com 23/12/14.*

(63) *Al-Monitor 5/3/15.*

(64) *Translated by Nicolai Sennels, via 10News.dk:*

(65) *James Delingpole, Breibart, 27/8/14.*

(66) *Arab. Islamic Law: Girls Can Be Married "Even If They Are In The Cradle" By Raymond Ibrahim on December 30, 2014 in 'From The Arab World, Islam'.*

(67) *Islington Tribune, January 27, 2012.*

(68) *BBC online, 16/5/12.*

(69) *Becky Evans, The Daily Mail, 4/2/13.*

(70) *Hayley Dixon, The Daily Telegraph, 16 May 2013.*

(71) *James Delingpole, Breitbart, September 18, 2014.*

(72) *'60 Year Old Legendary Rock Star Converts to Islam to marry 16 Year Old Child Bride' freepatriot.org, 23/11/13.*

CHAPTER SEVEN

((73) The Daily Mail, 28/6/14.

(74) *The Daily Telegraph, 28/12/12.*

(75) *The Daily Telegraph, 14/6/13.*

(76) *Paul Austen Murphy, American Thinker, 10/9/14.*

(77) *Melanie Phillips, Londonistan, page 6 intro.*

(78) *Andrew Gilligan, The Daily Telegraph, 25/12/10.*

(79) *Arthur Martin and Ian Drury, The Daily Mail, 27/3/15.*

(80) *The London Evening Standard, 23/10/2009*

(81) *British Future, an independent, non-partisan think-tank.*

(82) *Runnymede Trust: February 2012 Ethnic Minority British Election Study – Key Findings by Professor Anthony Heath, University of Oxford and Dr Omar Khan.*

(83) *Melanie Phillips, Londonistan, p163.*

CHAPTER EIGHT

(84) *Can We Trust the BBC? by Robin Aitken.*

(85) *Ed West, The Spectator, 28/10/14 'Border controls are a basic human right – is it un-Christian to oppose mass immigration?*

(86) *The Daily Mail, 22/1/11.*

(87) *The New Statesman, 2/9/10.*

(88) *Josh Halliday, The Guardian.com, 3/7/13.*

(89) *The Sun, 3/10/2005.*

(90) *Can We Trust The BBC? by Robin Aitken.*

(91) *Raymond Ibrahim, The Commentator, 16/12/14.*

(92) *Rajeev Syal, The Guardian, Thursday 7 August, 2014.*

(93) Douglas *Murray, The Spectator, 19/7/14.*

(94) *Douglas Murray, the Spectator 8/8/14.*

(95) *The DailyTelegraph, 11/8/14.*

(96) *John Howard Kuntsler, Klusterfuck Nation, 28/7/14.*

(97) *Efraim Karsh, Middle East Quarterly, summer 2014. 'Palestinian Leaders Don't Want an Independent State'.*

(98) *'Austerity for Europe, Increased aid for the Palestinians', The Commentator, 27/11/2011.*

(99) *Ruthfully Yours, 16/10/13.*

CHAPTER NINE

(100) *BBC news online, 22/2/12.*

(101) *nationell.nu 25/5/13.*

(102) *Jyllands-Posten, August 31st, 2010.*

(103) Robert Spencer, Frontpagemag.com 11/9/14.

(104) The Local, 28/7/14.

(105) Nicholas Farrell, The Spectator, 6/9/14.

(106) Why will it End? by Zenster, September 16, 2011.

(107) Gatestone Institute, 7/8/14.

(108) Lawrence Auster, A View from the Right.

CHAPTER TEN

(109) Cartrina Stewart, The Independent, 26/9/13.

(110) Dawn Perlmutter, FrontPage Magazine, October 1, 2013.

(111) The Daily Mail, 25/5/12.

(112) 'Moderate Islam Is Multiculturalism Misspelled', FrontPage Magazine, September 2, 2014.

(113) Samual .P. Huntington, Who Are We?

(114) The Daily Telegraph, 25/8/06.

(115) Steve Doughty, The Daily Mail, 11/9/06.

(116) Islam's Good Cop/Bad Cop routine, October 25, 2014, (from the Arab World, Islam) by Raymond Ibrahim.

(117) Robert Spencer, The Politically Incorrect Guide to Islam, P33.

(118) Ibn Warraq, The Washington Times, One Nation under God? April 13, 2003.

(119) Denis MacEoin, The Guardian, 29 June 2009.

(120) The Times, 18/1/2014.

CHAPTER ELEVEN

(121) Thomas Jefferson, Notes on the State of Virginia, 1781.

(122) Sir Winston Churchill; The River War, first edition (1899) Vol. II, pages 248-50.

(123) Anthony Burgess, 'Islam's Gangster Tactics', the Independent newspaper, 1989.

(124) The Daily Telegraph, 10/12/14.

(125) Rory Bremner 'afraid' to joke about Islam, Nick Collins, Telegraph, June 15, 2010.

(126) BBC online, 20/6/14.

(127) The Daily Mirror, 17/11/14.

(128) Heath Aston, Sydney Morning Herald.

(129) Daniel Pipes, The Washington Times, March 9, 2015.

(130) israelnationalnews.com 20/11/13.

(131) Newt Gingrich, National Review, 26/3/15.

(132) A Day at the Museum by Bat Ye'or Translated from the French by Jean Szlamowicz.

(133) The Al Qaeda Reader, Raymond Ibrahim, p42.

APPENDIX ONE
A Chronicle of the Demise of Free Speech in Britain

In **1984** a British headmaster, Ray Honeyford, wrote an article for *The Salisbury Review* where he questioned the values of multiculturalism, and was hounded out of his job by accusations of racism from an orchestrated political alliance of the hard left with ethnic-minority groupings.

In **1986** new legislation was passed to counter the rhetoric of such men as Ray Honeyford in the form of the Public Order Act 1986, Section 17 of which clarified racial hatred as being: *"..hatred against a group of persons in Great Britain defined by reference to colour, race, nationality or ethnic or national origins."*

Section 18 clarified racist behaviour as: *"The use of words or behaviour or display of written material intended or likely to stir up racial hatred."*

The maximum penalty for any individual found guilty of contravening this act was two years imprisonment.

In **1993** a young black male called Stephen Lawrence was stabbed to death by a gang of five white youths in Eltham, south London.

The case was mishandled by the police which led to media hysteria and an investigation by Sir William Macpherson who subsequently published a study in **1999** known as the Macpherson Report which labelled the police as "institutionally racist" and introduced the eighteen words which effectively ended real free speech in Britain.

"A racial incident is one that is perceived to be racist by the victim or any other person."

The door was now wide open for a whole raft of anti-libertarian legislation which was itself a response to the growing numbers of migrants settling in Britain without limit.

In **1998** the Crime and Disorder Act 1998 extended a maximum jail sentence over and above a normal sentence if racial aggravation was used in crimes up to and including murder.

In **2003** the Criminal Justice Act, made flesh the warnings of George Orwell by defining a "hate crime" as: *"Any incident . . . which is perceived by the victim or any other person (my italics) as being motivated by prejudice or hate."* This meant that for the first time in English jurisprudence it didn't matter whether a crime had been committed before an arrest could take place so long as someone could claim to have been "offended" or the victim of a "hate crime".

Along with this law grew, like topsy, a huge new bureaucracy of taxpayer funded (through legal aid) race hate activists to police the free use of language, defending those who declared themselves to have been offended. This turned all notions of just law on its head as those prosecuted became the victims of someone else's opinion, often a bigot with an axe to grind.

In **2006** the Racial and Religious Hatred Act was passed which classified religious hatred along the same lines as racial hatred and extended the jail sentence for transgression to seven years.

In **2007** the Criminal Justice and Immigration Bill was passed, with an amendment that bought homophobic hate crime in line with the definition of racial or religious hatred, including a maximum jail sentence of seven years. It is those 18 words from the Macpherson report have been used by the Labour Party's new thought police to effectively snuff out free speech. It all happened so fast that before we knew it we were already well on our way to a full blown police state.

In 2002, Robin Page, a television presenter, was arrested for inciting racial hatred when he stated that people living in the countryside, and who supported fox hunting, should be granted the same rights as blacks, gays and lesbians. The police claimed they had received reports from distressed persons unknown.

Fourteen-year-old schoolgirl Codie Stott was arrested over a "racial incident" in 2006, after she asked to be moved to a different discussion group where her fellow pupils actually spoke English. She was released without charge but only after spending several hours in the cells where her DNA was taken.

Much to the chagrin of the Muslim Council of Britain, Robert Kilroy-Silk was not prosecuted for inciting racial hatred after he described Muslims as suicide bombers and limb amputators in a 2004 *Independent* newspaper article. The police wanted to prosecute but were advised by the Crown Prosecution Service there was insufficient evidence. Despite this, Kilroy-Silk still lost his job.

In 2006, Nick Griffin, Chairman of The British National Party was acquitted (at the second time of asking) for inciting racial hatred, after he publicly accused Islam of being a wicked and vicious faith. His acquittal, after Muslims were lawfully deemed a religion rather than a race, was the prime motivation for the religious aspect introduced into The Racial and Religious Hatred Act 2006.

Author Lynette Burrows was cautioned by the Metropolitan Police in 2006, for suggesting that male homosexuals did not make ideal adoptive parents. This was during the "debate" over the introduction of new rights for homosexual males to adopt children built into The Equality Act 2006, which was passed without asking whether homosexual males were more likely to commit child abuse than heterosexual couples (which, according to the Family Research Council, they overwhelmingly are. Note: this report has now been censored).

In 2005 Maya Ann Evans was arrested for reading out the names of British soldiers killed in the Iraq war whilst standing next to the Cenotaph, a memorial to the war dead close to the House of Commons. In so doing, she contravened section 132 of The Serious Organised Crime and Police Act 2005 which had purportedly been enacted to prevent terrorist attacks at the seat of British government.

APPENDIX TWO
Venezuela

The Left in Britain adore this country more than any other. This is because from 1999 to 2014 it completely did away with private enterprise in order to implement an undiluted socialist economy financed by the greatest crude oil reserves on the planet. What could go wrong? Everything, and by 2014 even the BBC was reporting on massive unrest there. "Venezuela's president Nicolas Maduro has said the number of deaths which can be connected to two weeks of anti-government protests has risen above 50. Official estimates put the number killed in clashes at 13. Mr Maduro has blamed the violence on fascist groups. He was speaking ahead of a meeting intended to put an end to the unrest, sparked by anger at high inflation, rampant crime and food shortages." (1)

Maduro was widely suspected of having fraudulently achieved his narrow victory over the opposition in the 2013 election with the help of state control of the media and the brutal suppression of opposition voices. At this moment in time I'm watching internet footage of cities and towns across Venezuela filling with outraged citizens, students and old people demanding that Maduro quit because inflation is running at more than 50%. On top of that it has the highest murder rate in South America to go with food shortages and repression of political rivals by para-military police. With the state being the only employer of any note in Venezuela, Maduro has ordered all state employees onto the streets (or be sacked, presumably) to counter-demonstrate while security forces have saturated Venezuelan suburbs.

Due to 13 years of relentless persecution of honest or independent journalists almost every non-governmental press outlet has been "democratised", meaning shut down. Despite the monumental oil reserves there are shortages of electricity, medicine, even toilet paper as inflation spirals away. In a country awash with oil, power cuts black out 70% of the capital Caracas on a daily basis and water is severely rationed. Here's a conundrum. How could it be possible to wreck an economy that has more oil than Saudi Arabia in less than a decade? The answer, it seems, is to elect socialists to run it. That's what happened in Venezuela, and the economy has been run into the ground with the estimated loss of nearly two *trillion* dollars over the last 13 years.

Hugo Chávez's was Venezuela's president from 1999 to 2013, about as long as the British Labour's Party's last stint in office, with similar disastrous results.

After surviving a short-lived coup in 2002 Chavez moved to concentrate the power he had initially gained through the ballot box. He abolished 95% of all private industry and nationalised the oil companies so that basically the state ran everything, a true socialist vision. By his second full term in office this concentration of power had been made possible by the complete intimidation of the independent judiciary, allowing Chavez to censor or liquidate anyone who criticized him or who opposed his socialist agenda.

They still had all that oil wealth though, how bad could it get? At that time a British Petroleum report concluded: "The South American country's (crude oil) deposits were at 296.5 billion barrels at the end of last year, data from BP show. Saudi Arabia held 265.4 billion barrels, The 2010 estimate for Venezuela increased from 211.2 billion in the previous report." (2)

A Human Rights Watch report catalogued how easy it was for the judiciary to be hijacked. It reported: "In 2004, Chávez and his followers in the National Assembly carried out a political takeover of Venezuela's Supreme Court, adding 12 seats to what had been a 20-seat tribunal, and filling them with government supporters. The packed Supreme Court ceased to function as a check on presidential power. Its justices have openly rejected the principle of separation of powers and pledged their commitment to advancing Chávez's political agenda. This commitment has been reflected in the court's rulings, which repeatedly validated the government's disregard for human rights." (3)

The independent media were his next target: "Under Chávez, the government dramatically expanded its ability to control the content of the country's broadcast and news media. It passed laws extending and toughening penalties for speech that "offends" government officials, prohibiting the broadcast of messages that "foment anxiety in the public," and allowing for the arbitrary suspension of TV channels, radio stations, and websites."

The radicals who seized power in Venezuela offered the same simple solutions the radical left has always offered; seizure and control of the Supreme Court, the intimidation of journalists and defenders of human rights and the suppression of the fundamental rights of ordinary Venezuelan citizens.

Then, as the basic facts of economic life manifested themselves, the economy tanked and inflation went into orbit with Chavez eventually having to rule by decree over a citizenry in open rebellion, despite the greatest oil legacy of any nation on earth. We don't have Venezuela's oil wealth, but what we do have is an opposition who want to follow in the footsteps of those who bankrupted it. Here's how Chavez did it. By nationalizing firms in the agri-business (also known as stealing), as in the case of the Vesty Group who had 200,000 hectares of land and a herd of 120,000 cattle used to produce beef for the British market. This was "liberated" under Chavez's agrarian revolution.

Also nationalised were the financial and construction sectors and the entire oil industry which then became 95% of the entire export economy. This outstanding example of Marxism in action had its first fallout in 2010 when Venezuela suffered nationwide blackouts as its main hydroelectric power plant shut down. After killing the private sector stone dead then force feeding the state like a *foie gras* duck Venezuela's economy began to frack and its leaders began a desperate search for people to tax. By 2012 public debt as a percentage of GDP had climbed to 49%, despite record world oil prices.

So it was the "millionaires and billionaires" they started squeezing with punitive taxes until, to their shock/surprise, the rich all left the country taking their financial, entrepreneurial and intellectual skills with them. With the despised "fatcats" gone Chavez needed to look elsewhere for loot. The only squeezable productive group left were the middle classes who didn't earn enough to emigrate, and when *they* had been tax-soaked into oblivion the whole system began to wobble like a Nepalese village. Water wasn't being pumped because the electricity supply system, nationalised in 2007, was no longer working. Chavez blamed the water shortages on capitalism and demanded that everyone cut their shower time to three minutes.

But wait a minute, Chavez was a *socialist* wasn't he? So when his apologists looked to shore up support for their failed state from overseas who lined up to help keep the red flag flying? The British Labour Party, of course. This eulogy comes from one of Chavez's most useful apologists, Owen Jones: "He represented a break from years of corrupt regimes with often dire human rights records. His achievements were won in the face of an attempted military coup, an aggressively hostile media, and bitter foreign critics. He demonstrated that it is possible to resist the neo-liberal dogma that holds sway over much of humanity. He will be mourned by millions of Venezuelans – and understandably so." (4)

Perhaps if Jones could have put down his Marxist reader long enough to look at Amnesty International's annual report of 2013 he would have had an inkling of what real courage in the face of state tyranny required: "Judge María Lourdes Afiuni remained under house arrest throughout 2012. In September, unidentified gunmen drove past the building where she lives and opened fire, aiming towards her apartment. In November, she disclosed publicly that she had been raped while in jail. Judge Afiuni was detained in December 2009 and remained imprisoned for over a year. She was charged with offences including corruption, abuse of authority and association to commit a crime. She had ordered the conditional release of a banker who had been held in custody awaiting trial for more than two years, a decision within her remit and in line with Venezuelan law."

Jones's student union rants are an insult to those whose brave defence of freedom of speech his newspaper column ignores. Jones's misty-eyed view of Venezuela is shared by these Labour MPs who signed a House of Commons motion welcoming the "social development model" provided by Chavez's Venezuela.

Those who put their name to this included; Emily Thornberry, Helen Goodman, Jon Cruddas, Clive Efford, Mary Creagh and David Hamilton. Normally this kind of sub-Militant Tendency grandstanding would provoke hoots of derisive laughter, as it did under Neil Kinnock's Labour leadership. Not this time though, because these Labour MPs are all part of Ed Miliband's shadow ministerial team and, should Red Ed get elected, likely to be promoting a similar agenda to the one that brought Venezuela to its knees.

Then there is the Venezuela Solidarity Campaign which organised a rally on May 10, 2014 to defend Chavez's "legacy" by condemning the Venezuelan opposition's "right-wing violence", by that they mean the students who must really be, well.. fascists, racists, Islamophobes and stooges of the US government? Just like Maduro says they are. The patrons of this group include the usual suspects of the hard left including Labour MP Diane Abbott, Ken Livingstone, John Pilger and Trade Union supremo Bob Crow supported by a cast of 18 national trade unions affiliated to it, including the Communist Party of Britain. No doubt in solidarity with all the journalists arrested in Venezuela, *The*

Guardian published a full page manifesto/statement affirming that: "There is no justification for violent opposition to the elected government in Venezuela" signed by all of the above and a veritable who's who of the hard left in Britain including university lecturers, academics, Black Activists Rising Against Cuts, CND, Stop the War Coalition and the editorial staff of the Communist *Morning Star*.

The Left is consistent in two respects: It never learns from the past (that Socialism doesn't work, anywhere, ever) and it's wrong about everything, always. This demonstration of wilful ignorance means that apologists for the kind of economic insanity that's just ruined Venezuela are back in the mainstream of Labour Party thinking. Despite the catastrophic failure of their 13-year mismanagement of the British economy the Labour Left think they are coming back to finish the job.

The collapse of Venezuela's oil industry may well be a harbinger for a Labour-run British economy post 2015. Maybe the dim radicals who run Labour believe that, like some rag week prank, you can continue to cram students into a red telephone box indefinitely.

Population

The Optimum Population Trust (OPT), whose patron is Sir David Attenborough, published The Overpopulation Index to mark World Population Day in 2010. This was the first international table to rank countries according to how sustainable their populations were. In other words, if the British economy ever went tits up due to some unimaginable calamity like say, an energy shortage, how many of the masses now crammed onto our little island would be able to survive.

The higher the index number means the more resources a country is consuming and the more dependent they are on other nations, and the most overpopulated.

Being in the top 20 is bad and *nine* Middle East nations make it into the top 20, despite their oil wealth. Where is Britain? At 17th, a worse position than China at 29 and India at 33, the nations with the biggest populations on earth.

The report stated that: "UK population grew by a staggering 394,000 in the year to mid-2009, an increase equivalent to a city larger than Cardiff. The British population was officially projected in 2009 to rise by about 0.7 per cent a year to reach 71.6 million in 2033 – adding the population of another London to our already overcrowded island. Growth at the 2008-09 rate of 0.7 per cent a year, if continued, would take our numbers to 115 million before the end of this century. England alone is home to 52 million people, making it the fifth most densely populated country in the world - if small city and island-states are excluded - with its inhabitants packed in at 398 per square kilometre. That's even more crowded than Japan." (5)

Per size of population, Britain is the most indebted nation on earth. Official government figures show public sector net debt was **more than 1.2 trillion** at the end of November 2013. That's just what we owe in **total** but adding to that mountain every year is (in 2012/13) net borrowing of **£116.5 billion.** That's the money we use (all of it) to pay for welfare benefits NOT including the NHS or education budgets. The last time we saw borrowing on that scale was in 1976 when we were the "Greece" of Europe and the IMF had to bail out the Labour government of Jim Callaghan. But even then borrowing was nowhere near £116 billion a year. Borrowing had *never* been more than £100 billion a year until Gordon Brown managed to explode the economy by borrowing £157billion! And we've borrowed more than £100 billion every year since. As I write this bankrupt Greece is about to crash out of the Eurozone because of its inability to service the debt which has led to its national downfall. How much is that debt? On current rates of exchange it amounts to £229 billion, yet Britain continues to accumulate that level of debt every two years! This annual car crash economy we are living through will see our national debt rise to more than £1.5 trillion in 2016 and is Labour's double whammy legacy to old England.

The country is broke and before long the cracks will get wider and the whole edifice will come apart where the glue once held. If the public were to be made aware of just how imperilled we are there would undoubtedly be panic, but even with the best efforts of the BBC/EU, The Human Rights Act and Labour's hate legislation this state of blissful ignorance will be popped by the next financial crisis; a black swan in the shape of interest rate rises, the continuing Middle East crisis or the Greek economic meltdown …like the song says, something's gotta give.

(1) BBC online 27/2/14
(2) *BP annual Statistical Review of World Energy 2010.*
(3) *Human Rights Watch 5/3/2013.*
(4) *Owen Jones The Independent, 6/3/2013*

(5) Rosamund McDougall Co-chair of the Optimum Population Trust 2002-2005 and joint Policy Director 2006-2009.

APPENDIX THREE
The Industrialisation of Space: (what might have been?)

The banking crisis of 2008 was the last warning to humanity that the party, started in 1945, really was now over. Overpopulation relative to available raw materials means that we cannot continue to consume our ecological resources at the same rate without facing disaster. The financialization of the world economy that led to the collapse of industrial growth across the developed world was only the manifestation of a deeper crisis. It's crunch time because the real wealth creating economy, the one that runs on fossil fuels and produces things of physical value that can be traded and sold, is literally running out of gas. That's why the virtual economy stepped in and made a fiscal bubble that gave us the illusion of growth for a while, but even that bubble has now burst. What we are left with is the parasite virtual financial economy, now also rapidly running out of scams to cover up the fact that the real economy no longer works the way it used to. In order to continue to deliver real rewards, the real economy must ultimately see real development. His rivals tittered when Newt Gingrich said his policy would be to build a base on the Moon by 2020 if he won the presidential election; doubtless they would have laughed at Christopher Columbus when he said the world was round had they been running against him in 1492. Instead America elected Barack Obama to the presidency in 2008, a race activist who doubled the nation's debt while cutting NASA's budget.

A 2011 report *Costs of War* by researchers with the Eisenhower Research Project at Brown University tried to put a tag on the fiscal cost of the Iraq and "AfPak" wars and found that: "The US federal price tag for the Iraq war - including an estimate for veterans' medical and disability costs into the future is about $2.2 trillion dollars. The cost for both Iraq and Afghanistan/Pakistan is going to be close to $4.4 trillion, not including future interest costs on borrowing for the wars. Many of the wars' costs are invisible to Americans, buried in a variety of budgets, and so have not been counted or assessed. For example, while most people think the Pentagon war appropriations are equivalent to the wars' budgetary costs, the true numbers are twice that, and the full economic cost of the wars much larger yet."

Official NASA documents have shown that a base on the Moon, including three Lunar hotels, could have been built over a 10 year period for a cost of between $25 -$50 billion. Included in this figure would have been a three-stage shuttle system, a space taxi system linking the industrial base and new tourist hotels and a shuttle service from the lunar surface to lunar orbit. Even if the estimated cost had doubled or increased tenfold (unlikely) it would have still been peanuts compared to the ruinous Middle Eastern wars fought by George W. Bush and the reckless economic profligacy of Barack Obama. Use Virgin Galactic's amateurish efforts as a starting point and imagine the rush for seats on the next shuttle to the Lunar Hilton as part of an adventure overseen by the professionals at NASA or ESA. Imagine unlimited amounts of clean energy at rock bottom prices from nuclear fusion reactors using helium-3, found abundantly only on the lunar surface. Compare the money Bush spent on deposing Saddam Hussein with all the money NASA has ever spent (1958-2011) in all of its history, a comparatively tiny sum of $790 billion dollars. According to Nobel Prize-winning economist Joseph Stiglitz the wars in Afghan and Iraq cost more than three *trillion* dollars.

Imagine a space elevator built from a port on Earth to the Moon's first industrial city of Shackleton, incorporating a cable made of graphene, a new shipping lane down to Earth for a new industrial revolution being shaped on the Moon. For less than *one* trillion dollars all of this could have become real and our planet's green spaces and fragile ecosphere, now in the throes of terminal soil degradation and water depletion, could have remained untouched by industrialisation. The demand for jobless engineers, scientists and technical specialists would have literally become astronomical. Entrepreneurs from all over the world would have flocked first to the new space construction sites in America, Russia, India, Europe and China and then to the cutting edge lunar base to employ their talents creating new industries and revolutionising old ones.

Such an ambitious enterprise could have utilised all of mankind's ingenuity and ambition in establishing industry for peaceful progress. Mining the lunar regolith then developing networks of Moon-based power plants would have created a real economy in space that would have made Earth rich again, without destroying its ecosystem. What a waste.

Printed in Great Britain
by Amazon